ON CONTEMPORARY
LITERATURE

ON CONTEMPORARY LITERATURE

BY

STUART PRATT SHERMAN

"Man must begin, know this, where nature ends,"
MATTHEW ARNOLD.

Essay Index Reprint Series

 BOOKS FOR LIBRARIES PRESS
FREEPORT, NEW YORK

First Published 1917
Reprinted 1970

STANDARD BOOK NUMBER:
8369-1480-5

LIBRARY OF CONGRESS CATALOG CARD NUMBER:
75-105037

TO
PAUL ELMER MORE

For permission to reprint the essays in this volume, I am indebted to the Editor of *The Nation*. Since their original appearance they have been revised and in several instances greatly enlarged.

I have been accused of being a besotted " Victorian " —a kind of creature which ought to be extinct, very obnoxious to the younger critics, yet still so numerous as to constitute a not negligible element in the procession of our days. To give a certain color to the charge I have included an essay on Alfred Austin, whom I regard as the most amusing of the Victorian poets.

Mr. Henry Holt asks me to allay, if possible, the resentment of those who may inquire why Shakespeare has been smuggled, like a Joseph's cup, into the corn of a volume on contemporary literature. Shakespeare is here because I find him the most interesting and suggestive of living writers. His presence helps one to distinguish the values of his competitors. His humanism serves as a measure of the degrees of their naturalism. Reflective readers will perceive, I hope, that the object, if not the ostensible subject, of the essay on Shakespeare is also the object of the essays on Mr. Wells, for example, and Mr. Dreiser and Mr. George Moore.

CONTENTS

ON CONTEMPORARY LITERATURE

INTRODUCTION

THERE was perhaps a time when the literary critic was expected to tell the public the truth about books and authors. Current philosophy bids us relinquish that vain expectation. The critic may indicate the position of an author, and he may, if he chooses, compare that position with his own. But as for truth, it is a personal and private matter not to be measured by any common standard. Candid novelists like Mr. H. G. Wells admit that they make their " truth " as they need it. Courageous philosophers like Professor Dewey boldly proclaim that they abandon their " goodness " when it stands in the way of those who manipulate events. The modern sage in danger of martyrdom swiftly cuts loose from the forlorn hope and reattaches his conscience to a " going concern." " For what is truth, after all," asks the relativist, " but some definite person's impression at some definite point of view? Name the person and indicate the point of view, and I shall know how to value his truth." " And what is goodness," asks the cheerful pragmatist, " but the thing that goes? "—in an autocracy, presumably, the will of the autocrat, in a democracy the vote of the majority. The notion that one person is better qualified than another to fix values in literature has recently been designated by one of literature's professors as the favorite and most persistent fallacy of criticism. " Holding the critic's opinions to be obligatory upon other readers," says one of Professor Dewey's followers in an interestingly anarchical treatise on " The Social Criticism of Literature," " is very like ' fiat money '—easy to issue but sometimes harder to realize upon. No power on earth can make a book really valuable to me if it is not so."

I admit the force of the relativist argument—with a certain reservation. Though contemporary history may appear to be overwhelmingly against me, I cannot bring myself absolutely to abandon the ancient notion of human *progress*. Sages whom I revere assure me that we do not advance, that we merely pass through recurrent cycles of change. I cling fondly to the hope that they are mistaken. Iconoclasts declare that the critic's " childish estimate of *The Swiss Family Robinson* probably differs widely from his grown-up verdict upon it. But his second judgment is not necessarily a truer judgment than the first, nor the first than the second." If we must relinquish the general presumption that the judgment of maturity is better—that is to say, truer— than the judgment of childhood, we should hasten, in the interest of democratic fair play, to extend the political, as we have already extended the educational, franchise to the kindergarten. We may come to that point; but common sense is not yet ready for the abdication involved in our reaching it. Common sense still clings to the antique notions of growth toward power, ripening toward wisdom, progress toward truth. The moment that one admits the reality of progress, one has immediately to admit the reality of the object toward

which progress is made; and the way is open for the
establishment of standards and measures for marking
the advances in our course and also those aberrations
and retrogressions which occasionally justify the " martyrs " in standing fast against the main movement of
their time.

A critic who deals with his contemporaries should not,
however, show himself utterly out of sympathy with the
spirit of his age. In the essays here assembled, I hope
it will be found that I have exhibited a certain respect
for the " relativity of knowledge." Yet what is sauce
for the critic is sauce for the criticized. If the critic
can give us no absolute truth, neither can the creative
artist. I feel this so strongly that in examining the
work of poet or novelist it appears to me above all
interesting and important to go behind the work and to
discover the workman and his point of view. He gives
me a " criticism of life " seductively and imposingly
disguised as a representation of life, designed to capti-
vate my emotions and intelligence, and in some degree
to alter my conception of truth. It is thoroughly pertinent to the business of criticism to inquire searchingly
what manner of man is offering his eyes for mine. When
an author hands me a book entitled " The Way of All
Flesh " or " The Way of the World " my sympathies
with the relativist are roused at once; the first leap of
my curiosity is to know how much of the world, what
aspects of the flesh, can be seen on the level and at the
point of observation where the author habitually takes
his stand.

The reader of many books discovers that at a certain

level and at a certain point of view all the observers are impressed with the infamous nature of man; on another level and at another point of view all the observers sing the praises of our aspiring humanity; at still another level and at a third point of view all the observers are smitten with the glory of God. Naming these levels and these points of view is an elementary step toward more difficult sub-classifications. Now and then one meets a man who violently objects to being placed and classified. He takes pride in saying "I am not an 'ist' nor an 'ite' and I subscribe to no 'ism.'" In all probability he is not an author; for the beginning of effective authorship is usually the adoption or the acceptance of a definite point of view. It may be that he is an author with shifting and inconsistent points of view—Goldsmith, for example, of whom Johnson exclaimed: "Sir, he knows nothing; he has made up his mind about nothing." It may be that he is, like Montaigne, a man who has made up his mind not to make up his mind: in which case he has subscribed to the most catholic of all " isms "—skepticism. In general we may predict that the man who imagines himself *sui generis* will discover some day, after the fashion of M. Jourdain, that he has been an " ist " all his life without knowing it. May the classifications in this book help him toward that useful bit of self-knowledge. Knowing one's class is knowing one's " place in the world," and knowing one's place in the world is knowing one's *relative* value. To assist authors and readers in the process of self-recognition and self-appreciation is one of the pleasures of criticism.

Some years ago an English writer, impressed by the

relativity of our knowledge and by the vast power of imposition lodged in the hands of the literary critic, proposed a means to prevent the guileless public from thinking more reverently of critical " authority " than it ought to think. He urged all honest practitioners to preface each of their articles with a brief confession of faith in some such fashion as this: " I am a member of the Church of England (or an Atheist, Dissenter, or what not) ; a Conservative (or a Liberal, Radical, or what not) ; a Classicist (or a Romanticist, Realist, or what not) ; belong to the *Spectator* set (or the *Saturday Review*, or the *Daily Mail*, or what not). This sensitively honorable proposal, it will be remembered, was anticipated in its essential feature by the device of Bottom—" Tell them that I, Pyramus, am not Pyramus, but Bottom the weaver: this will put them out of fear." Superfluous Bottom's device may have been; it was inspired by a tender humanity worthy of all emulation. It is in his spirit that I write this " prologue " to indicate the point of view from which I have been studying the tendencies in contemporary literature.

I write this " prologue " under the impression—no doubt temporary, yet for the moment almost overwhelming—that we are living to-day in the worst of all possible worlds. It is, at any rate, a world of which every intelligent man must feel ashamed. It is an absurd world. By the more or less immutable nature of things it is so constituted that the path of life for the ordinary man in the ordinary course of events is beset from the cradle to the grave with pitfalls of mental and physical pain. On this precarious pathway men with but a trifle less than the average sureness of footing and indulgence of fortune are so constantly in misery that pain appears to them the one steadfast reality. Revising the Greek poet quoted by Saint Paul, they are ready to say: " In pain I live and move and have my being." Philosophers even in the halcyon days of peace have opined that fortitude is the supreme virtue and freedom from pain the supreme felicity of our decaying nature. For in this world of birth pangs and death pangs, insensate and involuntary forces of nature are in unintermitting conspiracy against the happiness of man. Yet he, at the present moment, with the utmost deliberateness, with all the energy of his will, with all the resources of his intellect is seeking, in all quarters of the globe, to multiply pain beyond all recorded precedent—pain to the body and pain to the heart—disease, dismemberment, and death, to body, mind, and spirit. For the moment I speak not of the ulterior purposes of the men who, in Professor Dewey's admirable phrase, "manipulate events." The ulterior purposes of those who triumph will undoubtedly have to be pronounced benign and beautiful. But I speak now of man's immediate acts and facts, his means and not his ends; and those are of an absurdity beyond tragedy—colossal, stupefying. So that the present stage of human "progress" calls to remembrance the regions which Dante visited, places "mute of all light," where souls blaspheming the Divine Power are whirled in an infernal hurricane, or writhe in fire, or sunk to the lips in ice devour one another.

No man, Socrates assures us, knowingly chooses what is not for his own good. Then what " sweet thoughts,

what longing " have led men to this *doloroso passo?*
Carlyle described the French Revolution as " truth
dancing in hell-fire." To my vision, at least, the truth
that dances in the hell-fire of the war of the German
Invasions—in which we live, move, and have our being—
is the old truth declared by the grim seer of Florence:

> Intesi che a così fatto tormento
> enno dannati i peccator' carnali,
> che la ragion sommettono al talento.—

" I learnt that to such torment are doomed the carnal
sinners who subject reason to lust. . . . ' The first
of these concerning whom thou seekest to know,' he then
replied, ' was Empress of many tongues. With the vice
of luxury she was so broken, that she made lust and law
alike in her decree, to take away the blame she had
incurred.' "

This last phrase, " that she made lust and law alike
in her decree, to take away the blame she had incurred,"
sums up for me a deep, many-branched ruinous tendency
of contemporary thought. This is the logical conclusion
of the naturalistic philosophy which has been for many
years subtly extending its influence in all countries and
in every field of human activity. It is the logical conclusion of repudiating all standards, teaching one's
conscience to trot in the rut of events, and making one's
truth as one needs it. The primitive savage is taught to
believe that his happiness depends upon the observance
of tabus. The modern savage is taught by a thousand
sophists to believe that tabus are the only obstacles
between him and his happiness. He " blasphemes the

divine power " by identifying its dictates with his appetites, so that no check of religious superstition or of reasoned reverence remains in his consciousness to oppose the indefinite expansion of his " self-love." The devil, as Goethe represents him, is the spirit that denies. Mr. Paul Elmer More, certainly one of the most penetrating moralists of our times, says that this is clean kam. The spirit that denies, he declares, is God. I do not recall any single utterance from living lips that has impressed me as more profoundly illuminating. I should not like to think that denial is the only aspect of God, but I am sure that it is the aspect of God most ignored by those who flatter themselves that because they have forgotten him he has forgotten them. And I am as certain as I can be of anything that God is a spirit who denies the validity of adopting the laws of the physical universe for the moral regiment of man.

The great revolutionary task of nineteenth-century thinkers, to speak it briefly, was to put man into nature. The great task of twentieth-century thinkers is to get him out again—somehow to break the spell of those magically seductive cries, " Follow Nature," " Trust your instincts," " Back to Nature." We have trusted our instincts long enough to sound the depths of their treacherousness. We have followed nature to the last ditch and ditch water. In these days when the educator, returning from observation of the dog kennel with a treatise on animal behavior, thinks he has a real clue to the education of children; when the criminologist with a handful of cranial measurements imagines that he has

solved the problem of evil; when the clergyman discovers
the ethics of the spirit by meditating on the phagocytes
in the blood; when the novelist returning from the
zoölogical gardens wishes to revise the relations of the
sexes so as to satisfy the average man's natural craving
for three wives; when the statesman after due reflection
on " the survival of the fittest " feels justified in devour-
ing his neighbors—in the presence of all these appeals
to nature, we may wisely welcome any indication of a
counter-revolution.

Literary criticism has been an accomplice in the usurpations of the naturalistic philosophy. Disillusioned,
it should be an ally in the revolt against it. There are
signs of insurrection in many quarters. For the valor
and high spirits of his revolt one welcomes the critical
writings of Mr. G. K. Chesterton. Fighting with intellectual mountebanks, he has stolen some of their
weapons; he has taken his stand in what his adversaries
will assail as a " mediæval " citadel; yet in his *Orthodoxy*, despite its archaic elements, he has produced the
most brilliantly sensible book that has come in recent
years from the embattled journalists of London. In
France assailants of naturalism ordinarily wear the
antique armor of the Catholic faith, and appeal to traditions which are of comparatively little potency in
English-speaking lands. Professor Guérard, a Frenchman, writing in this country on French thought in the
nineteenth century, attacks the same foe without a
return to Rome, and on grounds open to the young
people who modestly call themselves the " intelligentsia."
I have found much anti-naturalistic virtue in a little

book by Sigurd Ibsen, the son of the dramatist, which was translated into English in 1913 with the title, *Human Quintessence*—persuasive by reason of its large concessions to the enemy and the author's unwillingness to take refuge in a metaphysical or theological thicket. Professor Shorey has just made a spirited sally against the naturalistic educators in *The Assault on Humanism.* Mr. W. C. Brownell, whose criticism is invariably distinguished by its high and fine civility, has in his recently published *Standards* discharged among the Barbarians a quiverful of arrowy and exquisitely pointed satire. But Mr. Paul Elmer More and Professor Babbitt, in more or less obvious cooperation, are, I think, the critics in America who have most consistently striven to make the movement against naturalism conscious of itself and agressive and formidable. They have defined its objects, illustrated its principles, contrived its strategy, and richly provided it with munitions of war—Professor Babbitt in *The New Laocoon* and elsewhere, Mr. More in the impressive series of his Shelburne Essays.

There are at least three ways of discrediting the current naturalism or " scientific monism." The most difficult, perhaps, is to attack it upon purely metaphysical grounds. The most unanswerable is to oppose it with religious intuitions. The simplest and possibly not the least effective is to meet it with Johnsonian common sense, appealing to the general reason and experience of mankind against the conclusions of the ratiocinative faculty of the individual. In America the critical movement which opposes naturalism is not, if I understand it, distinctively religious but distinctively humanistic. It seeks not primarily to reclaim man for God but to reclaim him for civil society; not so much to fit him with wings as to persuade him to shed the horns and hoofs which he has been wearing in his long *après-midi d'un faune.* The humanist therefore requires no complex philosophical apparatus. He may keep the peace with scientific monism as a theory of great logical cogency, and yet assert that the really consistent monist is " a phenomenon we have never seen and never shall see." In effect he dismisses the theory as irrelevant to human needs and, indeed, contradictory to human experience. Though he shun the metaphysical abyss and profess his inability to climb the steeps of mystical insight, he is at one with the saints in his clear perception of the eternal conflict between " the law for things " and " the law for man." This is the rock upon which the humanist builds his house.

In the natural world he discerns no genuine law of progress, no conservation of values, no unity of purpose, but brutal cross purposes, blind chance, and everlasting change. The notion that the Darwinian " survival of the fittest " indicates an aristocratic tendency in nature, he deems a vulgar error based upon a confusion of adaptation to environment with conformity to ideal ends. In human society, on the other hand, Mr. Ibsen, for example, detects an " impetus," unique in character, which " urges us to bring our existences and the conditions about us into agreement with an ideal picture we bear in our hearts." In the human consciousness Mr. More detects an " inner check " which, in the interest of character, opposes the push of instinct, the expansive

impulse of the *élan vital.* " All the experience of the
past," says Professor Babbitt, " cries, as though with a
thousand tongues, through the manifold creeds and systems in which it has been very imperfectly formulated,
that the highest human law is the law of concentration."
To call this unique " impetus," this " inner check," this
" law of concentration " human or to call it divine—is
not this in the present state of our ideas a tolerably
insignificant matter of nomenclature?   Certainly the
matter of quintessential importance is to recognize this
impulse and to exalt it.   For it cleaves the universe in
twain as decisively as the fiat that divided the waters
which were under the firmament from the waters which
were above the firmament.

The line of progress for human society must therefore
be in the direction of this human impetus.   It cannot
possibly lead " back to nature," but must steadily show
a wider divergence from the path of natural evolution.
Society is in great part an organized opposition to
nature, and it justifies itself only when it maintains its
ground.   It is irrelevant to approve or condemn this or
that possible line of conduct on the basis that it is or is
not in conformity with nature.   It is pertinent only to
inquire whether it is in harmony with the constitution
and aim of the human organization.   It is not according to the tendency of clay to become a pot or of wood
to become a table, but it is of the very essence of the
artisan and the artist to overcome the tendency of wood
and clay.   It is according to the nature of an animal to
preserve its own life and to reproduce its species, but it
is of the essence of a man to lay down his life out of

reverence for his great-grandfather and to check the impulse to indiscriminate reproduction out of consideration for his great-grandson. The impulse to refrain thus indicated we can find nowhere in nature. It is part of the pattern or design of human society that lies in the heart of man.

The application, then, of biological terminology to human institutions—now common among German and other political philosophers—is fraught with confusion and illegitimate inferences. Society is not, after all, an organism but an " organization." It is not determined wholly, like organisms, by environment and previously existing forms of society, but partly by a vision of forms that have never existed and by a passion for approximating them. It is not unfolded naturally and spontaneously, but artificially and by contrivance. Its laws are not statements of observed relationships among forces; they are the forces themselves—the shaping, creative energy of the special human impetus, stemming the tide of natural impulse, and saying, " Here and there thou shalt go, and no farther." Yet we speak of the evolution of society and the evolution of animals as if polar bears and political constitutions ran on all fours, had begun to trouble the womb of chaos at much the same epoch, and had been delivered to a passively expectant world by a similar spasm of vital energy. Hypnotized by the passes of a facile monism, the consciousness of man sees itself playing but a cognitive and spectatorial part in history, accepts the universe as it would accept an avalanche, and lies down in a deep paralysis of the will to await what the morrow may bring forth.

To the humanist not the least interesting consequence
of the present war will be its effect upon the philosophy
of naturalism and its expression in literature; for the
conflict presents itself to his eyes as essentially a
struggle between the masters of the " law for things "
and the servants of the " law for man." When in the
summer of 1914 the German army went roaring and
singing and destroying over the borders of Belgium into
France, sweeping all the painfully constructed works of
man before it, it struck the imagination, in spite of its
mechanical organization, like a river in flood, seeking
the sea, like a ruthless natural force, following nature's
laws; and so its own apologists have described it.
When Belgium checked it, when France and England
dammed it, when one ally after another hemmed it in,
the counterstroke was quite uniformly described in terms
equivalent to far-off Asiatic Siam's declaration of war
(which comes as I write) as an effort to " uphold the
sanctity of international rights against nations showing
a contempt for the principles of humanity." Here for
German and other naturalistic thinkers is the grand disillusion. Here for the humanist is the hope amid the
horror. Humanity does after all recognize certain
rights and principles as fixed and established; in hours
of ease speaks of them like a wanton; but when need
arises, dies for them as for the possession that is dearer
than life. The victory of the Allies should logically be
reflected in a literature exalting the vindicated " law for
man." Haunted by memories of the fiery ruin wrought
by those who made lust and law alike in their decree, it
should not seek in nature for the order, stability, justice,

gentleness, and wisdom that only man has ever desired
or sought to create. It should mirror a society more
regardful of its ascertained values, more reverent of its
fine traditions, more reluctant to take up with the
notions of windy innovators. It should, in short, suggest in its own subtle way the desirability of continuing
to work out in the world that ideal pattern which lies
in the instructed and disciplined heart.

I

THE DEMOCRACY OF MARK TWAIN

Any one who has thought of Mark Twain merely as
the author of many books may well be recommended to
make his acquaintance as a puissant American personality through the three thick volumes of Mr. Paine's
biography. As an inducement to that considerable
undertaking I record here the experience of a reader
who approached the enterprise with a distinct apprehension that he would be overtaken by fatigue before he
emerged from the two-hundred-and-ninety-sixth chapter
and plunged into the twenty-four appendices. He was
thinking of Mark Twain as a humorous writer; and his
mind was still irritated by memories of the extravagant
admirers who in recent years have saluted the veteran
of a thousand ovations as a superlative artist, a profound moralist, and a grave philosopher. He reflected
on the fact that the biographer was something of an
idolater and that his biography was the fruit of six
years' labor, during four of which the subject had
offered himself for study, and had dictated volumes of
recollections. He suspected that these 1,719 pages
would constitute a last disproportionate monument
under which the old humorist would be buried. Then
he opened the book and began to read.

When he left off reading, two or three days later, he

found it difficult to escape from the interesting illusion
that he himself was Mark Twain.   He felt as if he had
just returned from a prolonged exploration of the
world, and were rounding out in tranquility a restless
life that had extended over three-quarters of a century.
He looked back over a stream of experience of historical
breadth and national significance.   He had been carried
back to the days of Andrew Jackson, and, with the hope
and hunger of the westward migration, had drifted as
the slave-holding John Clemens out of Kentucky into
Tennessee and on to Missouri, and there had died,
dreaming in poverty of his 75,000 acres of Tennessee
land unsalable at twenty-five cents an acre.   In 1835 he
had been born again in the son, Samuel Leghorne
Clemens.   Half-educated, mischievous, and clever he
had set type for a struggling little journal in Hannibal,
Missouri, ten years before the Civil War, and had made
his first " sensation " by printing in his brother's paper
a poem very faintly reminiscent of Robert Burns, inscribed " To Mary in H—l " (Hannibal).   He had
taken one end of a Testament, his mother holding the
other, and had promised not to " throw a card or drink
a drop of liquor," and had set out to see the world, still
as a printer, in St. Louis, New York, Philadelphia,
Keokuk, and Cincinnati.   But then he heard the call of
the Father of Waters, and for four years was pilot,
and studied the intricate mysteries of the Mississippi,
and laughed and jested with rivermen from St. Louis
to New Orleans, till a shell from the Union batteries
exploded in front of his pilot-house and ended that
chapter.   Then for a few days as second lieutenant of

an extemporized militia company, he rode a small yellow
mule to the aid of the Confederacy. Next the golden
flare in the far West caught his eye, and couched among
the mail-bags behind six galloping horses, he swapped
yarns across seventeen hundred miles of plains till he
reached Carson City, and became a miner, and suffered
the quotidian fever of the prospector, and filled his
trunk with " wild-cat " stock, and knew the fierce
life of frontier saloons and gambling hells. From the
unremunerative pick and shovel he turned to the bois-
terous, bowie-knife journalism of the *Enterprise*, and
thence to vitriolic humor on the *Morning Call* in San
Francisco, and he sent his name to the Atlantic coast
with *The Jumping Frog of Calaveras County*, and
lined his pockets with gold by a great news " scoop " in
the Sandwich Islands.

It was 1866, he was thirty-one years old, and his
" career " had just begun. He now entered a forty-
year engagement as a public lecturer, and competed
successfully with Fanny Kemble and P. T. Barnum,
and made himself know to hundreds of thousands whom
he convulsed with laughter. At the same time he became
a great traveler, perlustrated the cities of his native
land, plundered the vineyards of Greece, presented an
address to the Czar, visited Jerusalem with the Innocents, sojourned in England and gossiped with the
Prince of Wales, in Germany and dined with the
Emperor, in India and was entertained by a native
prince in Bombay, interceded with President Krueger
for the prisoners of the Jameson Raid, captured the
cities of Australia and New Zealand, and exacted trib-

ute from the whole world. Three or four years after
the Civil War he had begun to throw off books as a
comet throws off meteors. Then he took up the burdens
of a publisher, bargained with General Grant for his
memoirs, and sold a quarter of a million copies where
the other bidder had planned for a sale of five or ten
thousand. His imagination took fire at a dream of
magnificent wealth, and he became a great speculator,
and in one year invested $100,000 in projects, and
sank a fortune in an unperfected type-setting machine,
and went into bankruptcy. Then, at the age of sixty
he girded himself anew and made another fortune in
three years and repaid his creditors to the last dollar,
and in a few years more had accumulated a third fortune for himself, and drew annual royalties equal to the
salary of the President of the United States, and built
himself splendid mansions, and rested from his labors
on an Italian mahogany bed, clad in a dressing-gown of
Persian silk. Then the University of Oxford summoned
the printer, pilot, miner, reporter, traveler, lecturer,
author, publisher, capitalist across the sea, and robed
him in scarlet, and made him a Doctor of Letters, and
he retired into unofficial public life till, in 1910, the call
came to set his course toward the sinking sun.

This is not the biography of an author; it is a part of
the prose Odyssey of the American people; and it will
continue to be read when many of Mark Twain's writings are forgotten. It will continue to be read because
it conveys in relatively brief compass the total effect
which he spent his lifetime in producing—with American
recklessness and prodigality, with floods of garrulous

improvisation.   Mr. Paine loiters a little, it is true,
through the years of Mark Twain's final prosperity,
but that was the period of his personal relations with
his hero, and we must forgive him if, like an artist
infatuated with his subject, he paints us several portraits differing only slightly in attitude and shading.
His first two volumes are really marvels of compression;
he disposes, for example, of the trip to Palestine in
twenty-odd pages, and of the voyage around the world
in less; yet very likely he tells about as much of those
famous expeditions as after the lapse of a hundred years
a more sophisticated posterity will stay to hear. From
first to last he rejects tempting opportunities to digress
into history and overflow into description; he supplies
only so much setting as serves to bring the actor into
higher relief. He is under an illusion, I believe, as to
the value of Mark Twain's theology and philosophy and
literature; but his sense of what we may call biographical value is admirable. His book is full of animated and
characteristic phrase, gesture, and attitude. He has
extenuated nothing of his hero's weakness or his
strength, and has set forth with all possible veracity
the processes through which the man of the frontier
became, without losing his essence and his tang, quite
literally the man of the world.

No one recognized more frankly than Mark Twain
himself that in a sense he was a raider from the Border.
He never pretended to be the thing that he was not, and,
on the other hand, he was never ashamed of the thing
that he was. He planted himself, according to the
Emersonian injunction, squarely upon his instincts,

accepted " the society of his contemporaries, the connection of events," and, with a happy faculty for turning everything to account, capitalized his very limitations. It was one of the secrets of his immense personal effect that he never felt nor looked like a scholar or a thought-worn literary person, but rather like a man of affairs—erect, handsome, healthy, debonair—in his earlier years like a prosperous ranchman, later like a financier, a retired field-marshal, an ambassador, or, as his friends would have it, like a king. It was an iron constitution, tempered in the Mississippi and tested in the mining camps of the West, that enabled him to endure the stupendous fatigues of his great lecturing tours, to throw off 100,000 words of a novel in six weeks, to toil—without exercise and smoking heavily—all day and half the night, and, when he was past seventy, to talk copyright for hours with a hundred and fifty different Congressmen and radiate superfluous energy at a dinner in the evening, or to play billiards with his biographer till four o'clock in the morning.

If a kind of unconscious frontier impudence persuaded him of his competency as a Biblical critic, and carried him into the realm of abstract ethics, and led him late in life to add the weight of his authority to the followers of Delia Bacon, it was a kindred and valuable mental innocence that made the first fifty years of his life a perpetual voyage of discovery, sharpened his observation and his appetite for experience, and preserved the vernacular vigor of his speech. Had he undergone in his formative period the discipline of an older and firmly stratified society, he would have been

saved from some lapses in taste, but he would have
lacked that splendid self-confidence which is born of
living among a relatively homogeneous folk, and which
in the long run explained his unrivaled power, on the
platform and in print, of getting in touch with his
public. As pilot, miner, and Nevada journalist he
found his most profitable associates among men rather
than among women, and formed the habit of addressing himself to a robust masculine audience—a habit
which gives him an almost unique distinction in American literature, and marks him clearly as belonging
to the heroic age. He was " a man's man." It is a significant fact that he was introduced to his future wife
by her brother, who had become a great friend of his on
the voyage of the Innocents. It is an equally significant
fact that the friendship terminated and the brother
departed on a journey when he learned that the humorist
intended to marry his sister. If Mark Twain ever became a lion among the ladies, it was because they liked
lions, not because he made any special concessions to
the ladies. He detested Jane Austen, her works, and
her world; and unabashed he accounted for his antipathy: " When I take up one of Jane Austen's books,
such as *Pride and Prejudice,* I feel like a barkeeper
entering the kingdom of heaven." What he thought of
the " kingdom of heaven " he has set forth in another
place.

No American writer has ever enjoyed a more purely
democratic reputation than Mark Twain. From village
celebrity to international renown, he has been advanced
stage after stage by popular suffrage. The plain, un-

bookish citizen holding both his sides at a public lecture has helped roar him into eminence. The freckled, brown-legged pirate who finds Tom Sawyer nearer to his business and his bosom than Robinson Crusoe has played no negligible part in the campaign. The vote of the retired merchant reading *A Tramp Abroad* in preparation for a European holiday told decisively in his favor before the tardy voice of the professional critic assented. Only when an overwhelming majority of his fellow country-men had established his position, did the universities formally recognize the fact. And one suspects that for him as he strolled into the Sheldonian Theatre clad in scarlet to receive his degree from Oxford the pleasantest note of the occasion was the " very satisfactory hurrah " from the audience.

In the last few years of his life he received a higher honor than a degree from any university however vener-able; he received the highest honor within the gift of the Republic. Let us distinguish here, not his three " manners " but the three aspects of his reputation. Like a political orator making his maiden speech or invading hostile territory, Mark Twain had broken the reserve of his first audience with a string of irresistible " funny stories " and a comic recital of his travels. Handicapped by uproarious laughter, he produced a number of books which demanded serious consideration, but his leonine head had grown gray before he lived down his reputation as a " platform humorist." At about the time of his seventieth birthday, however, he obtained a reconsideration of his case, and the gravest tribunals decided that he indubitably belonged in the history of literature, if, indeed, he was not the " foremost American man of letters." After that, national feeling about him crystallized rapidly into its final state. He appeared in white flannels in midwinter, declaring that white was the only wear for a man with seventy clean years behind him; we were significantly pleased. When our newspapers had made one of their occasional " little breaks " in reporting the result of his serious illness, he cabled from the Bermudas that the reports of his death were " greatly exaggerated." It was a phrase that we all envied, from our Presidential phrase-maker down; we recognized that he was no longer a mere literary man—he was a national character. When he died we abandoned the last reservation. We said with one voice: *He was an American.*

To the foreign critic this ultimate tribute may seem perplexingly cheap and anticlimactic. That is, of course, due to the mistaken notion that we number some five score millions of Americans. As a matter of fact, we number our Americans on our ten fingers; the rest of us are merely citizens of the United States. Any one who will take the trouble to be born may become a citizen. To become an American requires other talents. We are more than doubtful about the status of Washington: he was the Father of his Country, but he lacked a certain indispensable tang. Lowell— forgetting Franklin, who had the tang—said that Lincoln was the first American. From certain indications it looks as if Mr. Roosevelt might turn out to be an American. Only the other day [1] he sent us a message to

[1] Written in 1910.

this effect: " I know that the America.. people will agree
that I could have acted in no other way than I did act."
The American is a man of destiny. His word and deed
flow inevitably out of the American character. On the
one hand, he does a thing because it is right; on the other
hand, the thing is right because he does it. Revising
the thought of Henry V we may say, Nice customs
curtsy to great Americans.

This point is strikingly illustrated by a story which
Mark Twain tells on himself in one of the chapters of
his autobiography. It was in 1877, before a company
including all the leading " geniuses " of New England,
banqueting in honor of Whittier's birthday. When
Mark Twain's turn came, he rose and entered upon a
fictitious " reminiscence." Out in southern California
he had knocked at a miner's cabin, and announced himself as a literary man. The miner replied with marked
ill-humor that he had just got rid of three of them,
" Mr. Longfellow, Mr. Emerson, Mr. Oliver Wendell
Holmes—consound the lot. . . . Mr. Emerson was a
seedy little bit of a chap, red headed; Mr. Holmes was
as fat as a balloon; he weighed as much as three hundred, and had double chins all the way down to his
stomach. Mr. Longfellow was built like a prizefighter.
. . . They had been drinking, I could see that." And
so on.

At the words " consound the lot," Twain had expected
a peal of laughter, but to his amazement " the expression of interest in the faces turned to a sort of black
frost." The whole story was a dismal failure; it was
years before the author recovered from the shame of it.

Speaking for the moment as a pious reader of O. W. Holmes, James Russell Lowell, and *The Atlantic Monthly*, I am not in the least surprised at the New England frost. And I know very well that Jane Austen or Thackeray or George Meredith would have agreed with the New England geniuses that Mark Twain's reminiscence was a piece of crude, heavy, intellectual horse-play—an impudent affront offered to Puritan aristocracy by a rough-handed plebian jester from Missouri. But hear Mark Twain thirty years after the event:

I have read it twice, and unless I am an idiot, it hasn't a single defect in it from the first word to the last. It is just as good as can be. It is smart; it is saturated with humor. There isn't a suggestion of coarseness or vulgarity in it anywhere. What could have been the matter with that house? . . . If I had those beloved and revered old literary immortals back here . . . I would melt them till they'd run all over that stage!

In his mellow Indian summer Mark Twain himself grew conscious that he had become an American. He knew, therefore, that the speech was right, *because he had made it.* I confess to a doubt whether those " old literary immortals " would, if they were among us, laugh at it even now; for the man who laughs with Mark Twain must be capable of feeling himself, for the moment, neither better nor worse than " the overwhelming majority " of his fellow citizens; and the New England " immortals " were incapable of feeling themselves in that mean position, even for a moment.

Mr. Paine, like some other recent critics, dwells with

a kind of retaliatory gusto upon the Brahminical reservations in the welcome accorded Mark Twain by members of the older New England inner circle; he is sure that the world is now having its laugh at the Brahmins. He reminds us also that, while Twain was still oh a kind of nervous probation in America, he had been received with unrestrained delight in England. But the right explanation of the hesitation on this side of the water does not seem to have occurred to him. The fact is that Twain was hailed with jubilation by Englishmen because he answered perfectly to their preconceptions of the American character and to their long-standing demand for something " indigenous." They could enjoy him, furthermore, with the same detached curiosity and glee that their ancestors at the Court of James I felt in the presence of Pocahontas—another typical American who, as we read, received marked attention from the Queen, and accompanied her to the Twelfth Night revels. We imagine that some gentlemen in Virginia were a little anxious lest it should be thought in England that all their wives were Indians—without deeming it at all necessary to apologize for Pocahontas; she was a lovely barbarian, to be sure, but she was truly representative only of the dusky background of their civilization. The Brahmins, correctly enough, looked upon Mark Twain, and will continue to look upon him, as a robust frontiersman, produced in the remote Jacksonian era, carrying into the courts of kings the broad laughter of the plains, and representing an America that, for them, is already historical and almost fabulous. But they should no more condescend to this Herculean humorist than to any other epic hero; they should accept him heartily as they accept Robin Hood and Charlemagne, the wily Odysseus and Dick Whittington, thrice Lord Mayor of London.

In the America that lies outside the chilly state of mind called New England, Mark Twain has rather won than lost friends by the savory earthiness, the naïve impudence, the lucky undisciplined strength of the folk hero. By his fearless revelation of the reaction of a frontiersman in contact with the riper aspects of civilization, he has appealed profoundly to the elements of the pioneer that have lurked in the hearts of most of his countrymen from the days of Captain John Smith to the days of Colonel Roosevelt. " Whenever I enjoy anything in art," he wrote to a friend, " it means that it is mighty poor. The private knowledge of this fact has saved me from going to pieces with enthusiasm in front of many a chromo." To ears outside of New England the sound of that is endearingly American. In his famous but somewhat heavy-handed attack upon a French critic's accounts of " these States," he declared that there is nothing " characteristically American " except drinking ice water. But on the occasion of a railway accident he remarked, " It is characteristically American—always trying to get along short-handed and save wages." If the eulogists of his humor held themselves to a strict inquisition, they would find themselves praising sometimes his legitimate triumphs and sometimes—with an admiration for success that is characteristically American—his infractions of the laws of taste. His humor not infrequently depends upon a disregard of proprieties, and occasionally it consists of little but a disregard of properties. An illustration may be found in the one-hundred-and-twenty-third chapter of the biography. The humor on this occasion consisted in reminding General Grant and his veterans of the Army of the Tennessee and the six hundred guests at a great and solemn banquet that once upon a time their grim commander-in-chief was wholly occupied in trying to get his great toe into his mouth—" and if the child is but the father of the man, there are mighty few who will doubt that he succeeded." The house, we are informed, came down with a crash, and General Sherman exclaimed, " I don't know how you do it! " That was humor befitting the Welsh giants of the Mabinogion or rather the bronzed revelers in Carson City. Only a very eminent American, speaking not in Boston but in Chicago could—in the characteristic American phrase— have " gotten away with it." It was a crime against taste, colossal, barbaric—or it would have been in any society which stood upon its dignity, recognized sacred superiorities, and exacted deferences.

Now the black frost which followed Mark Twain's after-dinner speech in Boston, and the thunder of applause which followed his similar after-dinner speech in Chicago indicate clearly enough, first, that he was out of place in Holmes's New England, and, secondly, that he was quite at home in Walt Whitman's leveled America. " I paint myriads of heads," cried Whitman, " but I paint no head without its nimbus of gold-colored light." At a banqueting table where every head is nimbused, what is elsewhere reprehended as indecorum passes for easy democratic familiarity. Among the descendants of the high priests of the Puritans Mark Twain discovered to his surprise that he was regarded as an unsanctified Philistine. On neither of these occasions was his "effrontery" a mere effusion of individual "impudence." It was rather an ingenuous assertion of the new democratic *camaraderie*—a rough western interpretation of the " brotherhood of man," which in the good-natured Mississippi Valley encourages the " hobo " in quest of a cup of coffee to ring the front door-bell and accost the lady of the house as " sister," or permits the colored porter to drop into a seat for a chat with the Pullman passenger, or prompts the Reverend " Billy " Sunday, the Henry Ward Beecher of that " section," to clap the Almighty on the back and to box the ears of the Prince of Darkness. In Boston Mark Twain spoke to an audience which freely entertained the abstract idea of equality but which was by no means ready to accept all these practical consequences of the fraternal ideal. In Chicago he spoke to an audience of veterans who in the Civil War had felt the kin-making physical touches of nature, and had lost some of their reverence for the starchy decencies and linen distinctions of formal society. In more or less conscious rebellion against the idea of the " grand style," which demands the representation of a military hero as mounted on a splendid charger with forefeet pawing the air, he brought down the house by a humorous stroke of the new " realism," which insists upon reminding the public that even a military hero is on a common footing with the average man in the possession and strategic manipulation of his great toe. The success of this effort may

perhaps not improperly be regarded as an omen of the
declining power of the New England tradition in
American literature—the partial eclipse of Holmes by
Mark Twain, of Longfellow by Whitman, of Hawthorne
by the Hoosier novelists, of Whittier by Edgar Lee
Masters. " Who are you, indeed," exclaims Whitman,
" who would talk or sing in America? " The antiphonal
voice replies:

> I swear I will have each quality of my race in myself.
> Talk as you like, he only suits These States whose manners
> favor the audacity and sublime turbulence of The States.

Humor, it is agreed, consists in contrasts and incon-
gruities, and the essence of Mark Twain's most characteristic humor consists in contrasting this typical nimbused American, compacted of golden mediocrities,
against the world—consists in showing the incongruity
of the rest of the world with this nimbused American.
In so far as that is true, it necessarily follows that the
heights and depths of humor are beyond the reaches of
Mark Twain's soul. His laughter is burly, not fine;
broad, not profound; and, in his earlier works, national,
not universal. When he that sitteth in the heaven
laughs, as we are assured that he does, he is not contrasting the year 1776 with the year 1300, nor the
President of the United States with Louis XVI, nor the
uncrowned sovereigns of Missouri with the serfs of
Europe. The comparison is intolerable; let us mark a
lowlier difference. When Puck in the *Midsummer
Night's Dream*, looks upon the bewildered Athenian
lovers and exclaims, " Lord what fools these mortals

be "; when Titania waking from magical sleep, murmurs
with drowsy amusement, " Methought I was enamoured
of an ass "—the mirth of these subtle creatures is
kindled by the contrast between the humanity of Bottom
and the Athenians, and the exquisite manners and passions of elfland. If Mark Twain had revised the play,
he would have had some Yankee boy in overalls making
sport of Puck and Titania; such, at any rate, is the
humor of *A Connecticut Yankee at King Arthur's Court*
and of *Captain Stormfield's Visit to Heaven.* It is said
that the last book he read was Carlyle's *French Revolution.* He must have found its picturesque and savage
denunciation of ancient shams very much to his taste;
but his own work shows little trace of its peculiar heart-
searching humor—the humor begotten by a reflective
comparison of the upstart, red-blooded pageant of
time's latest hour with the dim, grim phantasms of
history:

Charlemagne sleeps at Salzburg, with truncheon grounded,
only fable expecting that he will waken. Charles the
Hammer, Pepin Bow-legged, where now is their eye of
menace, their voice of command? Rollo and his shaggy
Northmen cover not the Seine with ships, but have sailed
off on a longer voyage. The hair of Tow-head (Tête
d'étoupes) now needs no combing; Iron-cutter (Taillefer)
cannot cut a cobweb; shrill Fredegonda, shrill Brunhilda,
have had out their hot life-scold, and lie silent, their hot
life-frenzy cooled. . . . They are all gone; sunk—down,
down with the tumult they made; and the rolling and
trampling of ever new generations passes over them; and
they hear it not any more forever.

Carlyle's humor has what we call historical depth;

he laughs at his contemporaries with a bygone eternity.
When Whitman asks that sardonic question, " Whom
have you slaughtered lately, European headsman? "
millions of strange shadows tend on him. He, too, is a
humorist and a grave one; he laughs prophetically—
with an eternity to come. Mark Twain, looking neither
before nor after, laughs, when he is in his popular vein,
with the present hour; and he cannot stand the comparison. Not by his subtlety nor his depth nor his
elevation but by his understanding and his unflinching
assertion of the ordinary self of the ordinary American
—" the divine average "—did Mark Twain become, as
some critics are now calling him, " our foremost man
of letters."

He was geographically an American; he knew his
land and its idioms at first hand—Missouri, the Mississippi River and its banks, Nevada, California, New
England, New York, the great cities. It was insuffi-
ciently recognized before his time that to love one's
country intelligently one must know its body, as well
as its mind. He had the good fortune to be born in the
West; so that, of course, he had to go east—otherwise
he might, instead of becoming an American, have remained a mere Bostonian or New Yorker all his life, and
never have learned to love Chicago and San Francico at
all. At various times and places, he was pilot, printer,
editor, reporter, miner, lecturer, author, and publisher.
But during the first half of his life, he went most freely
with " powerful uneducated persons, and with the
young, and with the mothers of families." The books
in which he draws upon his life in the West—*Tom*

Sawyer, Roughing It, Huckleberry Finn, and *Life on the Mississippi*—are almost entirely delightful. They are brimful of unreflective boyhood and youth, of rude energy and high spirits, of pluck and rough adventure; they are richly provincial and spontaneous; they spring luxuriantly out of their fresh native earth. One accepts them and rejoices in them as one accepts a bluff on the Mississippi or as one rejoices in a pine tree on a red spur of the Rockies.

It is when a frontiersman carries his virtues abroad that the lines of his character become salient. Mark Twain was a self-made man, of " small Latin and less Greek," deficient in historical sympathy and imagination, insensitive to delicate social differences, content and at home in modern workaday realities. I confess with great apprehension that I do not much care for his books of foreign travel. Like the story told on Whittier's birthday, they are " smart and saturated with humor "; but for some almost indefinable reason my emotions fail to enter into the spirit of the occasion. An uneasy doubt about the point of view binds my mirth as with a " black frost." I find myself concerned for my fellow-citizen, the author behind the books; beneath the surface gaiety the whole affair seems to be of appalling seriousness for us both. Ostensibly light-hearted burlesques of the poetical and sentimental volumes of travel, these books are in reality an amazingly faithful record of the way Europe and the Orient strike the " divine average "—the typical American— the man for whom the world was created in 1776. Wandering through exhumed Pompeii, he peoples its solemn

ruins with the American proletariat, and fancies that
he sees upon the walls of its theatre the placard, " Posi-
tively No Free List, Except Members of the Press."
He digresses from an account of the ascent of Vesuvius
to compare the prices of gloves, linen shirts, and dress
suits in Paris and in Italy.   At length arrived at the
summit of the mountain, he describes its crater as a
" circular ditch "; some of the party light their cigars in
the fissures; he descends, observing that the volcano is a
poor affair when compared with Kilauea, in the Sandwich Islands.   He visits the Parthenon in the night;
obviously, the memorable feature of the expedition was
robbing the vineyards on the way back to the ship.   The
most famous picture galleries of Europe are hung with
" celebrated rubbish "; the immemorial Mosque of St.
Sophia is the " mustiest barn in heathendom "; the Sea
of Galilee is nothing to Lake Tahoe.   The Mississippi
pilot, homely, naïve, arrogantly candid, refuses to sink
his identity in the object contemplated—that, as Cor-
poral Nym would have said, is the humor of it.   He is
the kind of traveling companion that makes you wonder
why you went abroad.   He turns the Old World into a
laughing-stock by shearing it of its storied humanity—
simply because there is nothing in him to respond to the
glory that was Greece, to the grandeur that was Rome—
simply because nothing is holier to him than a joke.
He does not merely throw the comic light upon counter-
feit enthusiasm; he laughs at art, history, and antiquity
from the point of view of one who is ignorant of them
and pretty well satisfied with his ignorance.   And, unless
I am very much mistaken, the " overwhelming major-

ity " of his fellow-citizens—those who made the success of *Innocents Abroad* and *A Tramp Abroad*—have laughed with him, not at him. So, too, unquestionably, in the nearly parallel case of the bludgeoning burlesque, *A Connecticut Yankee at King Arthur's Court.*

There is always a great multitude of what Matthew Arnold calls Philistines ready to rise up and hail as a deliverer any bold influential spokesman who will rail against the idea of " the saving remnant," and will assure the world that it is an idle affectation, an anaemic refinement, to pretend to admire the sort of things that Matthew Arnold urged us to admire. In Mark Twain's frequent excursions into literary criticism there is a note which escapes being demagogic only by being extravagantly and comically sincere. Let us take for example this little burst of revolt against the English classics in *Following the Equator:*

> Also, to be fair, there is another word of praise due to this ship's library: it contains no copy of the *Vicar of Wakefield,* that strange menagerie of complacent hypocrites and idiots, of theatrical cheap-john heroes and heroines, who are always showing off, of bad people who are not interesting, and good people who are fatiguing. A singular book. Not a sincere line in it, and not a character that invites respect; a book which is one long waste-pipe discharge of goody-goody puerilities and dreary moralities; a book which is full of pathos which revolts and humor which grieves the heart. . . .
>
> Jane Austen's books, too, are absent from this library. Just that one omission alone would make a fairly good library out of a library that hadn't a book in it.

When a reader of cultivated taste comes upon a

passage like that, he sighs and says, " Mark Twain
was not a literary critic " ; but when the " man in the
street " comes upon such a passage, he chuckles and
says, " Mark Twain was an honest man." As there are
always more men in the street than readers of cultivated taste, Mark Twain is justified by a large popular
majority. It thus appears that what endears a public
man to us is what he has in common with us—not his
occasional supereminences. It does not damage Franklin to say that he was not so graceful as Lord Chester-
field ; nor Lincoln to say that he was not so handsome
as Count D'Orsay ; nor Mr. Roosevelt to say that one
misses in his literary style I know not what that one
finds in the style of Walter Pater. Writing from Khar-
tum, our Lion hunter tells us that, in consequence of
hard service in camp, his pigskin books were " stained
with blood, sweat, gun oil, dust, and ashes." We have a
mystical feeling that this is very appropriate and beautiful—that an American's books ought to be stained
with gun oil and ashes. " Fear grace—fear delicatesse,"
cries the author of " Chants Democratic." It does not
damage Mark Twain with his constituency to say that
there was not a drop of the aristocrat in his veins.

His disrespect for aristocratic institutions and distinctions both in life and in literature is piquantly illustrated by his criticism of the French Revolution, Sir
Walter Scott, and the American South in *Life on the
Mississippi*.

Against the crimes of the French Revolution and of
Bonaparte may be set two compensating benefactions: the
Revolution broke the chains of the *ancien régime* and of the

Church, and made a nation of abject slaves a nation of free-men; and Bonaparte instituted the setting of merit above birth, and also so completely stripped the divinity from royalty that, whereas crowned heads in Europe were gods before, they are only men since, and can never be gods again, but only figure-heads, and answerable for their acts like common clay. Such benefactions as these compensate the temporary harm which Bonaparte and the Revolution did, and leave the world in debt to them for these great and permanent services to liberty, humanity, and progress.

Then comes Sir Walter Scott with his enchantments, and by his single might checks this wave of progress, and even turns it back; sets the world in love with dreams and phantoms; with decayed and degraded systems of government; with the silliness and emptiness, sham grandeurs, sham gauds, and sham chivalries of a brainless and worthless long-vanished society. He did measureless harm; more real and lasting harm, perhaps, than any other individual that ever wrote. Most of the world has now outlived a good part of these harms, though by no means all of them; but in our South they flourish pretty forcefully still. Not so forcefully as half a generation ago, perhaps, but still force-fully. There, the *genuine and wholesome civilization of the nineteenth century* (my italics) is curiously confused and commingled with the Walter Scott Middle-Age sham civilization, and so you have practical common-sense, progressive ideas, and progressive work, mixed up with the duel, the inflated speech, and the jejune romanticism of an absurd past that is dead, and out of charity ought to be buried. But for the Sir Walter disease, the character of the Southerner—or Southron, according to Sir Walter's starchier way of phrasing it—would be wholly modern, in place of modern and mediæval mixed, and the South would be fully a generation further advanced than it is. It was Sir Walter that made every gentleman in the South a major or a colonel, or a general or a judge, before the war; and it was

he, also, that made these gentlemen value the bogus decora-
tions. For it was he that created rank and caste down there,
and also reverence for rank and caste, and pride and
pleasure in them.

As this passage indicates, Mark Twain was a radical,
resolute, and rather uncritical democrat, committed to
the principles of the preamble to the Constitution, preserving a tang of Tom Paine's contempt for kings, and
not without a suggestion of the republican insolence
caricatured by Dickens in *Martin Chuzzlewit.* He did
not and could not give a " square deal " to the South
or to Scott or to Europe or to the Arthurian realm.
He refused all recognition to aristocratic virtues which
retard the complete establishment of the brotherhood
of man. He was not, like some more exquisite men of
letters, a democrat in his study and a snob in his drawing-room; he was of the people and for the people at
all times. His tender regard for the social contract
permeated his humor. It will be remembered that
Pudd'nhead Wilson earned his nickname and ruined his
chances as a lawyer for twenty years by an incomprehensible remark about a howling dog. " I wish I owned
half of that dog," said Wilson. " Why? " somebody
asked. " Because I would kill my half." No one
understood him—the sensitive, symbolic democracy of
the expression was too compact for their intelligence,
and they fell into a delicious discussion of how one-half
could be killed without injury to the other half. That,
to be sure, is also one of the problems of democracy;
but Wilson's implications were, I believe, both simpler
and deeper than that. In not molesting another man's

dog he showed the American reverence for property.
The American desire to be moderately well-to-do (Mr.
Roosevelt's "neither rich nor poor") he indicated by
desiring to own only half the dog. In saying that he
would kill his half he expressed his sacred and inalienable right to dispose of his own property as he chose,
while at the same time he recognized his neighbor's
sacred and inalienable right to let his half of the property howl. Indeed, I am not sure that he did not recognize that the dog had a certain property right in
howling.

With almost every qualification for a successful political career, Mark Twain could never have aspired to the
Presidency, for he was not a regular attendant at
church, a shortcoming, by the way, which interfered
seriously with Mr. Taft's campaign till his former pastor testified in the public prints that the candidate had
once at a church social taken the part of a fairy. In
religion, Twain appeared to be a mugwump, or, more
classically speaking, an agnostic over whom had fallen
the shadow of Robert Ingersoll of pious memory. The
irreligion of that generation is touched with a raw,
philistine rationalism, but is thoroughly honest. Like
all Americans, the author of *Tom Sawyer* received his
religious culture in the Sunday-school, but stumbled
over the book of Genesis and kindred difficulties, and was
"emancipated." The loss of faith which, in certain
conditions, is a terrible bereavement, was to him a blessed
relief; when the God of the old-fashioned Sunday-school
and the camp meeting ceases to terrify, he ordinarily
becomes a deadly bore. Having never known the mag-

nificent poetry of faith, he never felt the magnificent melancholy of unbelief. His experience was typical, however, and his very unspirituality was social. In his examination of Christian Science, he admitted that every man is entitled to his own favorite brand of insanity, and insisted that he himself was as insane as anybody. That was enough to assure most of us that he was sound on " all essentials."

" Be good and you will be lonesome " is, I suppose, one of Mark Twain's most widely quoted utterances in the field of morals. At first thought, one may wonder why this apparently Bohemian apothegm should have taken such hold upon the heart of a nation which above all things else adores virtue. But the difficulty disappears the instant one reflects that these seven words express by implication precisely the kind and temper of virtue that the nation adores. Like Wilson's observation on the dog, the saying is cryptic and requires explication. Mark Twain tells us in his autobiography that when he was a boy his mother always allowed about thirty per cent. on what he said for " embroidery " and so " struck his average." The saying means, as I take it, first of all, Don't lose your sense of humor as those do who become infatuated with their own particular hobbies in goodness. Calculate to keep about in the middle of the road, but make allowance for all reasonable shades of difference in taste and opinion. Don't be too good or you will find yourself in a barren and uninfluential minority of one. In America, whatever is not social is not virtue. Mark Twain seems to have felt that the New England Puritans were " too good to be true ";

that the American people could never get together on
the high levels of New England spirituality. In his
interesting series of dialogues, *What Is Man?*, he reduces all the motives of human conduct to self-interest;
but, like Benjamin Franklin, who set out from a similar
position, he reaches the conclusion that an enlightened
self-interest is not at war with the interests of others.
" Diligently train your ideals upward," he says, " and
still upward toward a summit where you will find your
chiefest pleasure in conduct which, while contenting you,
will be sure to confer benefits upon your neighbor and
the community." When he put his shoulder under the
debts of his bankrupt publishing house, he took a clear
stand on one of the essentials of a national " code."
In his chivalric treatment of Joan of Arc and Harriett
Shelley he showed the spirit animating another fundamental American tradition, which, it is to be hoped, our
iconoclasts will not be able to destroy. Fond of strong
language, careless of peccadilloes, tolerant of human
frailities though he was, his feet were "mortised and
tenoned " in domestic rectitude and common morality.

Mark Twain does not give us much help toward real-
izing our best selves; but he is a rock of refuge when the
ordinary self—" the divine average " is in danger. As
some one has said, " We cannot live always on the cold
heights of the sublime—the thin air stifles." We cannot flush always with the high ardor of the signers of
the Declaration, nor remain at the level of the address
at Gettysburg, nor cry continually, " O Beautiful! My
country! " Yet, in the long dull interspaces between
these sacred moments we need some one to remind us

that we are a nation. For in the dead vast and middle
of the years insidious foes are stirring—anaemic refinements, cosmopolitan decadencies, Teutonic heresies,
imperial lusts, fraud and corruption, the cold sickening
of the heart at reiterated expressions of unfaith in the
outcome of the democratic experiment. When our countrymen migrate because we have no kings or castles, we
are thankful to any one who will tell us what we can
count on. When they complain that our soil lacks the
humanity essential to great literature, we are grateful
even for the firing of a national joke heard round the
world. And when Mark Twain, robust, big-hearted,
gifted with the divine power to use words, makes us all
laugh together, builds true romances with prairie fire
and Western clay, and shows us that we are at one on
all the main points, we feel that he has been appointed
by Providence to see to it that the precious ordinary
self of the Republic shall suffer no harm.

Postscript

Good manuscripts are not often interred with the
bones of great writers, nor published after their death;
but Mark Twain, as his biographer explained to us,
lived under a somewhat stringent domestic censorship,
that of Mrs. Clemens, which renders his case exceptional.
The Mysterious Stranger, first published in 1916, one
surmises was suppressed and pigeonholed not because
it was below the author's literary standard, but because
it was regarded by some censor or other as indiscreet.
Literary discretion consists in continuing to write in

one's popular vein—consists in expressing the common-
sense of one's constituency.   When Mark Twain wrote
in his popular vein he expressed a fairly cheerful and
quite unabashed familiarity with the " buzzing, blooming confusion "—the habitual temper of his country-
men.   But *The Mysterious Stranger* he apparently
wrote to please himself; he expressed in it his personal
and intimate sense of an unsatisfactory world; he gave
vent to feelings too irregular, too bitter, and too subtle
to please all the lovers of Tom Sawyer and Huck Finn.
He revealed, in short, the undercurrent of his humor.
Upon one who is acquainted with his other works the
effect of this revelation is to deepen the note of his
gaiety throughout, making it appear the reflex of unex-
pectedly somber considerations.   Like the revelations
with regard to Charles Lamb's domestic affairs, like
certain cynical and pessimistic passages in the letters
of another characteristically American humorist, John
Hay, it lets one in to a temperament and character of
more gravity, complexity, and interest than the surfaces
indicated.

The artfulness of the book, in which illustrator and
publisher have had a part, sends one for comparison
to the *Travels of Lemuel Gulliver*.   The point is, as I
have proved by experiment, that a boy of nine can read
this brightly pictured magical romance of the sixteenth
century with delight and without undesirable stimula-
tion.   He will take pleasure with the three lads of Eseldorf (he probably will not Anglicize the name of this
Austrian village) in the ingenious marvels wrought by
the mysterious stranger.   He will be gently touched in

his compassionate instincts by the witch-hunting scenes
and by the strange pathos of sudden death supernatur-
ally foreseen. But he will not raise embarrassing religious or metaphysical questions, for the air of enchant-
ment and romance intervenes between this fiction and
the world of his serious concern. He will ingenuously
accept Eseldorf as an unusually animated province of
wonderland. He will be quite unconscious that he has
read a book written at his elders, a book steeped in
irony, a dangerous " atheistical " book, presenting a
wholly unorthodox view of the devil and a biting
arraignment of the folly and brutality of mankind.

Mark Twain was one of many men of his generation
who early received an untenable conception of God,
tried the conception by human standards, and dismissed
it as untenable. There are two priests and an astrologer
in Eseldorf; but there is no God. His functions are
pretty completely taken over by the mysterious stranger
who candidly announces himself as Satan, nephew to the
well-known gentleman of that name. He is a well-fa-
vored and winsome youth with a " winy " invigorating
atmosphere. Essentially he is the incarnation of vital
force, the creative power in the universe. Knowing
all things, having power over all things, he despises
man and is mildly amused by him, looks down upon him
as an elephant looks down upon a red spider, sends him
to death or torment without malice and without a pang.
His conduct shines in comparison with that of man; for
though he is without good-will, he is without ill-will
also, and he has intelligence and power. In comparison
with the conduct of man, moreover, the conduct of dumb

animals shines; for though they lack some useful faculties, they are blest in freedom from the " Moral Sense "
—that terrible human faculty which organizes and legal-
izes and perpetuates cruelty and folly.

It is not " tonic " to look at men through the eyes
of the mysterious stranger; to him " their foolish little
life is but a laugh, a sigh, and extinction; and they have
no sense. Only the Moral Sense." He alters a link in
the life of one of the lads of Eseldorf, to whom he has
taken a fancy, so that he shall drown; this alteration,
he explains to the boy's playmates, is a real kindness,
for " he had a billion possible careers, but not one of
them was worth living." He shows to the boys a vision
of human history; they see Caesar invade Britain—
" not that those barbarians had done him any harm, but
because he wanted their land, and desired to confer the
blessings of civilization upon their widows and orphans."
" You see," says Satan, " that you have made continual
progress. Cain did his murder with a club; the Hebrews
did their murders with javelins and swords; the Greeks
and Romans added protective armor and the fine arts
of military organization and generalship; the Christian
has added guns and gunpowder; a few centuries from
now he will so greatly have improved the deadly effec-
tiveness of his weapons of slaughter that all men will
confess that without Christian civilization war must
have remained a poor and trifling thing to the end of
time."

Relief from this irony and cynicism is, of course, not
afforded by the presence of Satan or Nature in the
romance. The relieving contrast to the folly and

cruelty depicted is in the felt presence of the chivalrous heart and mind of Mark Twain himself, in his definite conception of certain evils to be removed, in his hopefulness about the possibility of removing them. The wicked world visited by the mysterious stranger is, after all, sixteenth-century Austria—not these States. What Mark Twain hated was the brutal power resident in monarchies, aristocracies, tribal religions, and—minorities bent on mischief, and making a bludgeon of the malleable many. His passion of hatred for oppression and unreason was never more cuttingly phrased than in this posthumous volume. The intensity of his vision of evil has subdued and darkened his laughter—has given it a note almost like despair; it is the laughter of an often-outraged believer in liberty, democracy, and loving-kindness.

II

THE UTOPIAN NATURALISM OF H. G. WELLS

(BEFORE THE WAR)

IT is a singularly incurious person who has never looked into the books of H. G. Wells; for through his innumerable pages swarm the figures, flash the colors, hum the voices of strictly contemporary life. Though he is on the brink of fifty, he remains the copious and incessant spokesman for the Younger Generation which he has stung into consciousness of itself. He helps us also to understand the stupidity of our fathers and the absurdity of our mothers. When Ann Veronica, in the novel bearing her name, announces her intention of attending an unchaperoned dance in London and spending the remnant of the night in a hotel, her aunt packs an entire " system of ideas " into the little apprehensive phrase, " But, my dear!" If you feel that the exclamation is delightfully ridiculous, you may consider yourself of the Younger Generation. If you elevate pained eyebrows with the aunt, you must set yourself down as Victorian.

When the Queen's great reign closed with her death in 1901, Mr. Wells did not go so far as to insist that the bones of her statesmen should be hung in chains and the ashes of her men of letters scattered to the winds.

But he recognized, as did the court poets at the Restoration, that the readiest way to brighten a new epoch is to blacken its predecessor; violating the Victorians was an expedient justified, to adapt a military expression, by literary necessity. Accordingly he has put into circulation the popular epithets for the politics, religion, art, and morals which prevailed in the " dingy, furtive, canting, humbugging, English world " of our fathers, with its " muddled system," its " emasculated orthodoxy," its " shabby subservience," its " unreasonable prohibitions," its " meek surrender of mind and body to the dictation of pedants and old women and fools." At the same time he has been giving currency to the catchwords of the new era: " scientific method," " research," " efficiency," " cooperation," " publicity," " constructive statesmanship," " socialism," " eugenics," " feminism," " aviation." When we open his works of fiction, we find the Victorian muddler, the prig, the standpatter, and the prude making way for the clear-eyed theorist with the " white passion of statecraft," the titled lady with a penchant for breaking plate glass, the inconoclastic journalist in greenish-gray tweeds and art-brown tie, the independent young schoolgirl who dares to say " damn." And we are feelingly persuaded that we are moving, or that the world has rolled on and left us behind.

A writer so full of tendency as Mr. Wells, constantly setting father against son and son against father, is obviously something more or less than a novelist, quite irrespective of his sociological treatises. In the state of literary manners existing under George V, it is a bit difficult, however, to determine whether a man of letters who comes forward with a new order of ideas is a humbug or a philosopher. While I was pondering this delicate essential question in the case of Mr. Wells, there came into my hands a study [1] of the man and his works by a critic of the younger generation, Mr. Van Wyck Brooks, which helped me out of an embarrassing situation. " Grotesque and violent as it may at first appear," says Mr. Brooks, " I believe that in the future Wells will be thought of as having played toward his own epoch a part very similar to that played by Matthew Arnold."

I was glad to be assured that Mr. Wells's air of passionate earnestness and transparent candor was not merely an aspect of his literary technique. And I seized eagerly upon the suggested parallelism; for, as I said to myself, if Wells is the Arnold of our time, by instituting a series of comparisons between the two men we may measure the " march of mind " in the post-Victorian period, and demonstrate the superiority of the ideas open to our young people over those set before their elders. But as I glanced down the page, I perceived that the likeness of Arnold and Wells was not limited to their general function in bringing home to the English mind " a range of ideas not traditional in it." That likeness extends, it seems, to " their specific attitudes toward most of the branches of thought and action they have concerned themselves with. Wells on Education, on Criticism, on Politics, and the nostrums of Liberalism; Wells, even on Religion, continues the

[1] *The World of H. G. Wells.* By Van Wyck Brooks. New York.

propaganda of Arnold. Everywhere in these so super-ficially dissimilar writings is exhibited the same fine dis-satisfaction, the same faith in ideas and standards, the same dislike of heated bungling, plunging, wilfulness, and confusion; even the same predominant contempt for most things that are, the same careful vagueness of ideal."

Though I share the critic's desire to relate Mr. Wells in some way to his predecessors, I was reluctant to acquiesce in the implications of this series of compari-sons. For one point I supposed was entirely certain—that Wells repudiated the Victorians; and here was Mr. Brooks making him out the spiritual son and heir of one of their leading representatives. With a little effort, I believed, a spiritual ancestor with a more appealing likeness to his descendant could have been discovered outside the age of compromise and muddle. Arnold, as I thought, was disqualified for the relationship by char-acteristics which he shared with most of the reforming novelists of his sluggish period. I refer to their habit of dealing, " confusedly," no doubt, with realities, and to the modesty of their enterprises. Dickens, Kingsley, Reade, Mrs. Stowe, and the rest—they did not seek to make the world over, but only to accomplish a few simple things like abolishing slavery, sweat-shops, Corn Laws, the schools of Squeers, imprisonment for debt, the red tape of legal procedure, the belief in pestilence and typhoid as visitations of God—and all that sort of pid-dling amelioration.

What Wells required in the way of an ancestor was a man with a large free gesture, like Godwin or Rousseau, sweeping away the Dædalian labyrinth of existing society, and with a few bold strokes chalking out a new social order. Shelley might serve; he was like Wells in striving " to bring home to the English mind a range of ideas not traditional in it "; and he showed other points of similarity. In both Shelley and Wells we find the same fierce railing at conventional and customary things, the same eager projecting and reforming temper, the same childlike faith in the possibility of refashioning human nature, the same absorbed interest in sex, and the same abandonment of an eagerly pursued science for the sake of writing romances.

Though in these general respects Shelley was like Wells, Shelley was not in the least like Arnold, who, as will be remembered, dismissed him as a beautiful but ineffectual angel. I was thus driven to conclude that the really decisive likeness which Mr. Brooks saw between Wells and Arnold was not in their general function and temper, but in " their specific attitudes toward most of the branches of thought and action they have concerned themselves with." Yet having by this time conceived a partiality for my own literary parallel, I subconsciously ran it out alongside that of Mr. Brooks, while I was examining his contention that the prophet of the Younger Generation has continued the propaganda of the " elegant Jeremiah " of the Victorians.

Wells, we are told, continues the propaganda of Arnold with regard to education. The error involved here could have been made only in an age more concerned about its educational machinery than about its educational product. It is perfectly true that both

Wells and Arnold wish the state to organize and standardize instruction.   The vital question, however, is whether they agree upon what the state schools are to teach, and upon what is the " objective " of teaching.

It will hardly be disputed that if educators have anything in common it is the desire of each to reproduce his own educational species.   Wells was trained at the Royal College of Science in physics, chemistry, astronomy, geology, and botany; Arnold was trained at the University of Oxford in the traditional classical disciplines.   Wells belongs indubitably to the scientific species of educator, distinguished by its devotion to original research and by its steadfast belief that the crown of human endeavor is an extension of the boundaries of knowledge.   Arnold belongs indubitably to the humanistic species of educator, distinguished by the importance it attaches to the assimilation of classical experience in the attainment of its highest end, the perfection of the individual character.

When Wells outlines a model course for the schools of the future, he discards Greek and Latin, and prescribes as the " backbone " of a sound curriculum as much mathematics as possible, English, and the natural sciences.   When Arnold, after thirty years' experience as inspector of schools, delivers in America the essence of his educational ideas, he tells us that for most men a little mathematics suffices; that Greek will be " increasingly studied as men increasingly feel the need in them for beauty and how powerfully Greek art and literature can serve this need "; and that if there is to be a separation and option between humane letters and natural

sciences, the majority of men would do well " to choose
to be educated in humane letters rather than in the
natural sciences." For, argues Arnold, humane letters
help a man's soul to get soberness, righteousness, and
wisdom; while in the sphere of conduct, which is three-
fourths of life, the natural sciences are comparatively
impotent, leaving the moral nature undisciplined and
inclined to caprice and eccentricity. Arnold maliciously
cites the case of Faraday, that eminent man of science,
who was a Sandemanian; one thinks also of Shelley, who
emerged from his passionate study of chemistry at
Oxford, declaring that the happiness of the human race
depends upon the adoption of a vegetable diet; and one
remembers the many heroes and heroines of Wells who
have been bred on the natural sciences, and how they
apply their zoological observations to the conduct of
life. If, finally, we recall together the fact that Wells
is a pupil and disciple of Huxley, and the fact that
Arnold's *Science and Literature* is rather explicitly an
attack upon the new educational programs inspired by
Huxley, it should be clear that Wells came into the
world to condemn the educational ideas of Arnold.

It is true that both Wells and Arnold insist upon the
importance of fearless criticism—the free play of ideas
upon all the subjects which concern us. But here again,
before we agree that one continued the work of the
other, it is essential to know the standpoint adopted,
the method pursued, and the object contemplated by
each.

At the risk of verbal absurdity one is obliged to say
that Wells as critic takes his stand with the future

behind him; that he retreats into the future for light on the problems of the present; and that the object of his criticism is to enable us to see things as in themselves they really are not. And, to continue the Hibernian contrast, Arnold takes his stand with the past behind him; he turns to history for light on the questions of the day; and his object, as he never tires in repeating, is to enable us to see things as in themselves they really are.

This wide difference in critical object, method, and standpoint arises from the fundamental opposition between, let us say, the pseudo-scientific and the humanistic outlook upon life. Wells, whose philosophy took shape in the biological laboratory as under the microscope the bounds which seemed to hold individuals in fixed species disappeared and everything merged in everything else by an infinite scale of infinitesimal differences—Wells is profoundly impressed by the *uniqueness* of every atom in the universe, and hence by the impossibility of formulating any law valid for any two atoms. Arnold, whose philosophy took shape as he studied the moral rather than the physical history of man, is profoundly impressed by the *identity* of human passions and human needs in Palestine, Greece, and England; and hence by the possibility of discovering law valid for civilized men everywhere and at all times.

We have here an explanation of the curious fact that the critic of scientific training abandons the " scientific method " and proceeds from the unknown to the known, while the critic trained in humane letters adopts the " scientific method " and proceeds from the known to the unknown. I mean that Wells, in his skepticism of

the categories established by the intellect, throws reason
overboard, and commits the steerage of his course to
a self-willed, egoistic, anarchical imagination. " I make
my beliefs," he says, " as I want them. I do not attempt
to go to fact for them. I make them thus and not thus
exactly as an artist makes a picture so and not so."
For Arnold, who retains his faith in the intellect, truth
is not something to be created, but something to be
ascertained. Between the two critics yawns this gulf:
Wells seeks to make whim and the will of Wells prevail,
while Arnold seeks to make " right reason and the will
of God " prevail.

This distinction holds between the political fantasies
of Wells as set forth in his various Utopian essays, and
the political and social criticisms of Arnold as set forth
in his essays on Democracy, Equality, British Liberalism, and Culture and Anarchy. In the one case, a
lyrical voice cries, like the Persian poet, " Come, let us
drink wine, and crown our heads with roses, and break
up the tedious roof of heaven into new forms." In the
other case, a sober, persistent Englishman says, " Let
us try to look at this nineteenth century of ours steadily
and determine what can be done; let us straighten a
little here, and level a little there, and elevate a little
everywhere."

A specious likeness is perhaps observable in the fact
that both Wells and Arnold advocate extending the
powers of the state. The likeness itself becomes a
difference the moment one reflects that Arnold recommended an increase of governmental action in a time
of *laissez-faire* Liberalism and radical Individualism,

and that Wells advocates an increase of governmental action in a time when an English statesman is telling us that " we are all Socialists nowadays." It is not the function of a political critic, as Arnold reminds us, to carry coals to Newcastle.

The difference widens as soon as one considers the uses to which Wells and Arnold propose to put the enlarged powers of the state. Wells, having the courage of his sanguine imagination, desires to make the state a magnificent reservoir of science and energy and capital, " which will descend like water that the sun has sucked out of the sea," which will do away with the necessity of poverty and labor and pain, and which will abolish " the last base reason for any one's servitude or inferiority." Arnold, who prefers to retain some contact with the realities of life, phlegmatically lays down a very simple principle defining the limits of state action: " To use the state is simply to use cooperation of a superior kind. All you have to ask yourselves is whether the object for which it is proposed to use this cooperation is a rational and useful one, and one likely to be best reached in this manner. Professor Fawcett says that Socialism's first lesson is that the working-man can acquire capital without saving, through having capital supplied to him by the state, which is to serve as a fountain of wealth perennially flowing without human effort. Well, to desire to use the state for that object is irrational, vain, and mischievous. Why? Because the object is irrational and impossible."

What more need be said of the New Republic and other ships of state which Wells, like Shelley launching his paper boats on the pond in Kensington Gardens, lets drift down the stream of time? What more need be said but that Wells himself, like Shelley in his later years, has begun to despair of transforming the world by state intervention, and is transferring his faith to the redemptive power of the " beautiful moral idealisms " embodied in his own novels!

Nowhere, however, does the irreconcilable opposition of Wells and Arnold appear more distinctly than in their respective attitudes toward morality, and in particular toward " sexual morality." In the latter field, the Bosnia of the moral world, Wells has been an incessant dropper of bombs. Arnold, in general, maintained the despised Victorian " reticence." One recalls, nevertheless, significant passages in his letters expressing apprehensions for the future of France on the score of the " social evil." And one recalls his equally significant declaration that Dowden's *Shelley* makes one feel " sickened for ever of the subject of irregular relations."

To this humanistic moralist of the Victorians morality seems a settled and simple matter. He holds that in the course of some thousands of years of civilized society the elementary principles of conduct have been adequately tested, and are now to be unequivocally accepted. They constitute a standard of " right reason " outside themselves, to which we should vigorously subject our treacherous individual sensibilities. By adopting these principles the individual acquires a character, becomes a member of civil society, and performs the first duty of man, which is to perpetuate in and through himself the moral life of the race.

The zoological moralist of the Younger Generation holds that morality is a new, complex, experimental science with its work all before it and only a vague generalization fresh from Mr. Wells' laboratory to guide it. In order to get society upon a sound moral basis, says Mr. Wells, it is essential " to reject and set aside all abstract, refined, and intellectualized ideas as starting propositions, such ideas as right, liberty, happiness, duty, or beauty, and *to hold fast to the fundamental assertion of life as a tissue and succession of births.*" How Sairey Gamp would have enjoyed that " tissue and succession of births "! Upon this striking obstetrical truth Mr. Wells proposes to hang Moses and all the prophets. Then he will erect upon it the new morality.

Since life is fundamentally a tissue and succession of births, it appears to follow that the first duty of man is to perpetuate not the moral but the physical life of the race. Since " we don't know what to breed for," orthodox eugenics is all astray. Since scientific man-breeding, or zoological ethics, is still in its infancy, it behooves us to encourage all sorts of experimentation in procreation, cohabitation, the rehabilitation of natural children, the state subsidization of mothers, and perhaps also of lovers. In the new society, instead of the Victorian convention which precluded the married man from investigation in this field, we shall have freedom for various sex-associations, and, consequently, for enriching emotional discoveries in what are now the dull years of domestic fidelity and emotional hebetude. Mr. Wells is rather fond of turning the tables upon the naughty dramatists of the Restoration, who, as every one knows, exalted the bachelor at the expense of the married man. In *Ann Veronica*, for example, and *The New Machiavelli*, it is the bachelor who is the cad and the *cornuto*; it is the married man who knows how to strike the emotional diapason.

It may be objected that it is idle to promise a future in which a man may love any woman he pleases, since all history teaches that a man has his life-work cut out for him if he pleases any woman he loves. Mr. Wells does not care what history teaches. It may be pointed out that experimentation in irregular relations is not a novelty; that it is now, and always has been, widely practiced; and that the experience of mankind has generally proved it disastrous. Mr. Wells does not care what the experience of mankind has proved. If you assure him that it is not a question of social " systems," but of human nature, if you insist that irregular relations under any system quite regularly beget that " vehement flame " of jealousy which the wise man of Israel says is " cruel as the grave," you do not abate his enthusiasm one jot. He is a man of imagination. He makes his beliefs as he wants them. If they clash with immutable things in this world, he creates another world. He has heard of jealousy; but he intends to abolish it. He intends to create a new society in which one can make love to another man's wife without exciting the jealousy of her husband. This is the inspiriting message of *Passionate Friends*, which closes with these words: " I will not be content with that compromise of jealousies which is the established life of human-

ity today. I give myself—to the destruction of jealousy
and of the forms and shelters and instruments of
jealousy, both in my own self and in the thought and
laws and usage of the world."

Precisely Shelley's idea when he magnanimously invited his wife to join him and Mary Godwin in Switzer-
land. And she, poor wretch, dumbly criticized his idea
from the bottom of the Serpentine.

The defect in Wells's religion which distinguishes it
from the religion of Arnold is exactly the defect in his
morality, namely, the lack of any principle of control.
Here again, he cries, we are in a field for free experimentation; nothing has been determined; " religion and
philosophy have been impudent and quackish—quackish!" And so, while for Arnold religion is something
which binds and limits, religion for Wells is something
which looses and liberates. Arnold rejects dogmatic
theology, but he writes three books to justify the
Hebraic faith in an Eternal, not ourselves, which makes
for righteousness, and to extol the " method " and the
" sweet reasonableness " of Jesus. Wells rejects dogmatic theology and all our inheritance from the Hebrews
—except their turn for business organization; his sub-
stitute for " morality touched with emotion " is a hot
fit of enthusiasm for social progress excited by fixed
meditation upon the Utopian projections of his own
fancy.

For Arnold, the men of true religious insight are
Jesus, Marcus Aurelius, St. Francis, the author of the
Imitations, Spinoza, who all consent together that " the
Kingdom of God is within you." Wells designates this

conception in the case of Marcus Aurelius as " a desire
for a perfected inconsequent egoism." There is something to be said for a religion which produces a perfected egoism like that of Aurelius. But Wells, in the
temper of Shelley and other social revolutionists, insists
that " salvation's a *collective* thing," to be accomplished
somewhere in the social environment, beyond the borders
of the individual soul. The logical product of the sentimental altruism of Wells may be seen in the hero of
almost any of his later novels—in the hero, for example,
of *Tono-Bungay,* whom his creator quite accurately
characterizes as a " spiritual guttersnipe in love with
unimaginable goddesses."

With all its fervor for perfecting mankind in the
mass, the religion of Wells somehow fails to meet the
needs of the individual man. It helps every one but its
possessor. He has struggled with this problem, but he
has not brought to his task the resources of the religious
sages; he has approached it with only the resources of
the scientific perfectibilians. He has felt, as we all have
felt, the dumb and nameless pain which throbs at the
heart of our being as we march or mince or creep or
crowd through the welter of cross-purposes, wars, poverty, dreadful accidents, disease, and death, which we
call our life. If you ask him how to assuage that pain,
he answers that we must apply scientific methods to
make mankind pacific, intelligent, well, and wealthy. If
you ask him why his hero, Trafford in *Marriage,* who is
already wealthy, well, intelligent, and pacific, still feels
the throbbing pain, he replies, " That is because Trafford has a developed social consciousness, and cannot

enter into felicity until there is a like felicity for all men to enter."

Now, did Mr. Wells possess not the insight of the religious sages, but just the sober human experience of a pagan like Horace, he would know that though all men entered his earthly paradise of lacquered ceilings, white-tiled bathrooms, Turkey rugs, scientific kitchens, motor-boats, limousines, and Victrolas, still in their poor worm-infested breasts would dwell " black care," still would they remain spiritual guttersnipes in their scientific Elysium. And if Mr. Wells consulted Arnold or the spiritual physicians who have effectually prescribed for the essential malady of living, he would be told that inner serenity springs from self-collection, self-control, and, above all, from the Hebraic sense of personal righteousness, which is the beginning of religious wisdom.

Here and there through the works of Wells there is a glint of skepticism, a flash of self-mockery, which makes one wonder to what extent he himself feels the confidence of the young people who look to him as their saviour. But I have deliberately renounced inquiry into the essential sincerity of his radicalism. I have presented him in the rôle that captivates his admirers, not as an empty resonator for a bewildered and discontented multitude, but as a glowing, eloquent, sanguine leader of the generation which is pressing for a place in the sun. I have exhibited him rising in adorable, unworldly innocence to arraign a social system under which two and two make only four, and water refuses to run up hill, and a child cannot eat his cake and keep it, and fire

will not refrain from burning, nor the lion and the lamb
lie quietly together, nor sober people take seriously his
fairy tales of science, sex, and sociology. If my analysis
is correct, I have detached him from Arnold, and established his connection with Shelley. This service should
be grateful to him and to his followers; for I have denied
him the rank of a Victorian critic only that I might
elevate him to the rank of a Georgian angel.

(SINCE THE WAR)

What transformation has the war wrought in the
protean shape of Mr. Wells?

If there is anything fixed in his convictions it is his
belief that at about the period of his literary advent the
world began to spin down the ringing grooves of change
into an orderly and luminous future. As the advance
agent of progress and the bosom friend of posterity he
was more or less under obligation to interpret the European upheaval as a stage in a happy evolutionary process. Accustomed to thinking on a large scale, he at once
spread out before him the map of the world and indulged
himself in his favorite recreation of prophesying. In
his volume of prognostications, *What Is Coming?*
(1916) he attempted a serious and realistic forecast
based upon an analysis of existing forces and tendencies.
The war had somewhat shocked and embittered him, but
on the whole its first effect was to strengthen his cheerful self-confidence. It promised, he thought, to further
in its own way the political and social changes which he
had always regarded as necessary preliminaries to the

millennium. The responsibility for the débâcle—and thus for the forward lunge of civilization—he placed to the credit of the militaristic misrulers and the " cultivated rancid nationalism " of Germany. He saw the possibility of a permanent settlement of Europe in the overthrow of the Hohenzollern Empire. Since in the present style of warfare a decisive and shattering victory was not to be expected, he declared that the reduction of the Central Powers must be continued, after arms were laid down, by an economic alliance. This program would necessitate the retention and the extension of the present strong governmental control of industries, commerce, and transportation. The Central Powers would be obliged to adopt similar measures, and a third great alliance of the Americas was fairly predictable. Among these three great groups of nations tremendous conflicts would ensue. Yet in these grand divisions questions of race, nationality, and sovereignty would inevitably lose their exacerbating acuteness. The way would be gradually cleared for the federation and socialization of the nations and the scientific world-state, which has always floated like a beautiful mirage on the far horizon of Mr. Wells's soul. The hopes of humanity thus depended, as Mr. Wells felt in the earlier stages of the war, upon vast political and social alterations, dictated by military necessity, imposed by military force, and equivalent in their total effect to what a neutral observer might have called the " Germanization " of the world.

Desperate Liberals on every hand have said: " We must fight fire with fire. We abhor the spirit of modern Germany; but in order to defeat Germany we must *temporarily* imitate Germany." Mr. Wells, however, desired the defeat of the Germans and at the same time the permanent and universal triumph of German organization. It had been his constant day-dream to get Humanity into the Promised Land *en masse,* and not ten thousand years hence, but swiftly, soon, in the next fifty years, in the next decade, soon enough to permit his writing a novel entitled " Beyond Jordan." Humanity apathetically dillydallied in the wilderness. Humanity refused to march sweetly and smoothly and moved as by one common thought—and that Mr. Wells's. The war revealed to him the methods of " reformers " who get results. Snatching at military necessity as an obviously effective goad to indolent and divers-minded men, he grasped at last the missing essential in a scientific socialist Utopia—a coercive force.

He and other honest men maintain that military coercion is a temporary expedient and that Germany is a needlessly imperfect model. He reassuringly declares that the Kaiser and the Prussian oligarchy and the German army are curious archaisms, unnecessary and removable excrescences upon the " modern scientific State." But this, I think, is one of the great contemporary illusions. Army, oligarchy, and Kaiser, or their equivalents, are the causes and conditions of such a state—are the indispensable clubs of cooperation and efficiency and impassioned concerted mass action. It is idle to point to the accomplishment of " democratic " England so long as England is at war, for England has to all intents and purposes temporarily abandoned democracy. Government in war-time is, if effective, government while the people hold their breath, government under artificial conditions maintained by a quite abnormal and, in the long run, unendurable surrender of individual liberty, will, property, and life. When the objects of existence are simplified by the extraordinary stress of a great war to the production of munitions, provisions, and transportation, the obvious demand is for expert governmental control; the cry goes up for a " dictator." The moment peace is made and the abnormal diversity and multiplicity of individual human interests are again free to assert themselves, democrats will recall to secure what rights governments are instituted among men. John Smith will inquire again in his old skeptical democratic fashion where is the government official who is more expert than John Smith in managing his own life and liberty and in directing his own pursuit of happiness. The temporary unity and solidarity of the *volonté générale* will disappear. The will of the governors will lose its identity with the will of the governed. Only an iron fist will be able to buffet them out of the " rotten " individualism which distinguishes a true democracy from a military autocracy.

" We are beginning to agree," says Mr. Wells, " that reasonably any man may be asked to die for his country; what we have to recognize is that any man's proprietorship, interests, claims, or rights may just as properly be called upon to die." Our prophet counts heavily upon the immense burden of the war debt and the trained sacrificial spirit of the soldiers returning to civil life to strengthen and continue in the years of peace this readiness to surrender all to the State. Under dire necessity the mood may persist in some degree through the period of reconstruction; and we shall hear eloquent and heroic-sounding voices urging us to despise the individual and to glorify the national life. Yet we may certainly reckon on a powerful reaction after the war against the abstract idealism and the concrete brutality of " politically-minded men." Times like these in which we are living may hear with little show of horror the Napoleonic question, " What are a million lives to a man like me?" or—to modernize the query—" What are the lives of all your sons in comparison with the perpetuity of the State?" But human nature will return to its deep-seated belief in certain inalienable individual human rights; and millions of young men in Europe who are doomed to go maimed and stumping through their prime will soon be looking a little wistfully about to discover whether there is any land left in the world where a man may live and let live. In the moment that the all-sanctifying military necessity relaxes, some at least of the " moral " qualities which, in the stress of war, governments stamp with the highest values will be popularly rated like Confederate " shinplasters "; and plain people, chafing under orders to march in directions which they have not determined, will be praying again to the shiftless and inefficient gods of the Victorians to preserve them from too much government.

Mr. Britling Sees It Through owes its success in this country largely to the fact that Mr. Wells reacts in it against his own prophecies of the salvation of the world by military force, economic necessity, and the alteration of the map. The prophetic book was a typical product of his speculative reason, influenced by the current exaltation of mechanical efficiency, and reiterating in great part his earlier prophecies. The novel was the result of his actual experiences in a war waged by a mechanically efficient nation against its more or less inefficient neighbors. In the first shock of the conflict Mr. Britling of course cries out: " Oh why, my fellow-Britons, did you not render yourselves mechanically efficient as Rudyard Kipling, and Mr. H. G. Wells, and other foresighted gentlemen long ago urged you to do." But as the war goes on Mr. Britling enters upon grave reconsiderations. The central interest of the book is in its exhibition of something like spiritual commotion, in the midst of which there appear profound doubts of naturalistic morality and mechanical efficiency, our modern instrument of salvation.

The masterpiece is of course Mr. Britling, who is transparently Mr. Wells himself, portrayed with unprecedented frankness. Most of his important portrait-painting is done from the same model, but his practiced hand has never before produced so engaging a likeness of himself. I am not speaking of his private life, of which I know nothing, but of his ideas, his sympathies, his character as a man of letters. What one enjoys in Mr. Wells is his curiosity, his vivacity, his hopefulness, his bright eagerness to clasp the wide universe in one heart-satisfying embrace. What one deplores in him is his hodgepodge of sex and politics, his passion for chimeras, his habit of supping on the east wind, his unwillingness to grow up at last and cheerfully adjust himself to the generally recognized fact that there is

no pot of gold at the end of the rainbow. Aspiring,
visionary, and diffuse, he makes himself adored by radicals of one-and-twenty and by middle-aged women with
imaginations unappeased by experience. But he dis-
appoints those who expect an intellectual leader to find
his own center, make up his mind, and come to conclusions. To those who look for fruit in the fall of the
year he offers a new crop of blossoms. He has made a
god of " becoming." His intellectual fluency and ver-
satility have been his undoing, giving him ever the
appearance of an unstable, an unformed power, a nebu-
lous nucleus of dissolving impulses. Mr. Chesterton
once remarked that one can hear Mr. Wells growing
overnight. The war has been a long and a formative
night, and Mr. Wells has come out of it with one book
which can stand the light of common day. The fact is,
apparently, that he has at last, to borrow his own
figure, " felt in his skin " what he has only been dreaming about for the last quarter of a century. He has felt
in his skin what is wrong with the world.

The effect of futility in a great many of his novels
is directly traceable to his endeavor to persuade us that
something which is in fact of very little importance is
of very great importance. I refer to the philanderings
of his fervent heroes and heroines. In order that some
fervent hero or heroine might philander for six months
or a year, and philander in tranquility, he has repeatedly tried to persuade us that human nature should be
altered and the world reconstructed. Now, the world
needs reconstitution, and human nature needs alteration; but not for that purpose. It was difficult, indeed,

to believe that a man with Mr. Wells's wholesome comic sense could seriously weigh or consider that purpose; or fail to see the absurdity of clamoring for order, measure, and control in the external world while reserving a silly, sentimental, yet tremendously destructive anarchy in the heart. It was almost necessary to believe that in employing the bait used by the lower order of socialists he was inspired less by a desire to reform the world than by a desire to make his trap irresistibly captivating to unappeased middle-aged women and radicals of one-and-twenty.

Well, in this respect the great war, with its multitudinous public and private calamities pressing daily nearer to the heart of the household at Matchings Easy, provokes in Mr. Britling a revulsion of feeling. Through the first selfish panic of the civil population hoarding their gold and buying up bread and tinned sardines; through the days when one watched with growing astonishment, yet with an aloof spectatorial air, the thunderous trampling and rush of the Germans toward Paris; through the period of agitated unpreparedness and the apathetic recruiting and the drilling without uniforms or rifles; through the Churchill-excursions to Constantinople; through the tedious wintry sieges; through the months when the villages of England filled with Belgian exiles and with wounded sons and with English widows and orphans, sleeping and shuddering under the peril of infested skies—through all this commotion the distinguished speculative author, Mr. Britling, settles slowly earthwards till his feet are planted upon the " realities of life." Incidentally his eighth affair of the

heart, which in the piping times of peace would have
required to be elaborated into one of his soulful romances, sinks into exactly the place of contemptible
insignificance which it deserves.

With a new sense of values Mr. Wells turns upon
himself, in the person of Mr. Britling, and humorously
analyzes that fascinating romantic temperament to
which in his previous novels he has been so indulgent:

The mysterious processes of nature that had produced
Mr. Britling had implanted in him an obstinate persuasion
that somewhere in the world, from some human being, it
was still possible to find the utmost satisfaction for every
need and craving. He could imagine, as waiting for him,
he knew not where, a completeness of understanding, a perfection of response, that would reach all the gamut of his
feelings and sensations from the most poetical to the most
entirely physical, a beauty of relationship so transfiguring
that not only would she—it went without saying that this
completion was a woman—be perfectly beautiful in its
light, but what was manifestly incredible, that he too would
be perfectly beautiful and quite at ease.

There is what I have called the unrealistic and
Shelleyan emotional tendency in the prophet of the
Younger Generation. Now hear Mr. Wells's realistic
and disillusioning comment upon that tendency:

This persuasion is as foolish as though a camel hoped
that some day it would drink from such a spring that it
would never thirst again. For the most part Mr. Britling
ignored its presence in his mind, and resisted the impulses
it started. But at odd times, and more particularly in the
afternoon and while traveling and in between books [fairly

often by this account] Mr. Britling so far succumbed to this strange expectation of a wonder round the corner that he slipped the anchor of his humor and self-contempt and joined the great cruising brotherhood of the Pilgrims of Love. . . .

For some years the suspicion had been growing in Mr. Britling's mind that in planting this persuasion in his being, the mysterious processes of Nature had been, perhaps for some purely biological purpose, pulling, as people say, his leg; that there were not these perfect responses, that loving a woman is a thing one does thoroughly once for all—or so— and afterwards recalls regretfully in a series of vain repetitions, and that the career of a Pilgrim of Love, so soon as you strip off its undulous glamor, is either the most pitiful or the most vulgar and vile of perversions from the proper conduct of life.

What does all this mean but that Mr. Wells is relaxing his hold upon his grand elementary moral conception of life as a " tissue of births." As a Utopian naturalist he had advocated the harmonization of conscience with what he now almost contemptuously designates as Nature's " purely biological purpose." He now implicitly recognizes human purposes which properly run counter to the biological purpose, and human ideals which properly oppose the mysterious instincts conspiring to pull, as people say, one's leg. Mr. Wells has been guilty here of another betrayal of the Younger Generation. He threatens to lead the young people back into the abandoned region of " abstract, refined, and intellectualized ideas "—such ideas as right, liberty, happiness, duty, and beauty, in behalf of which, indeed, they are now shedding their blood.

It may be objected that the quasi-official philosophy of modern Germany fortifies its warriors without resort to the old moral abstractions. It gets the fighting virtues by sternly inculcating the subordination of personal instincts to the imperious needs of the species. It has heard Nature murmuring to herself in the still watches of the night " *Deutschland über alles*," and it has resolutely harmonized conscience with the Great Mother's biological purpose, her mysterious passion for the segregation, triumph, and perpetuity of the German race. At some time in the course of the war, one conjectures, it must have rushed upon Mr. Wells with a shock that the German " morality " is Wellsian theory adapted to circumstances by practical men, that German efficiency is the realization of his life-long dreams, that modern Germany is, in short the naturalistic Wellsian Utopia militant. It must have occurred to him with horrible searchings of the heart that there at last at his door, effectively operating, was the machinery for " railroading " mankind into the scientific millennium. Why should he seek to destroy it? Because it was not English? That doubtless was the cause of his first instinctive gesture of wrath and indignation. He had accustomed himself to thinking of the road into the Promised Land as built and operated by Englishmen. Accordingly he joined in the popular clamor, which may be summarized as follows: " The German machine is the best ever devised. Therefore we must utterly destroy it. And we must build one of our own exactly like it. The Germans are scoundrels. We are honest men." Into this logic of jealousy Mr. Wells was plunged by the fact

that he and the Germans worshiped the same gods, and
founded their " morality " upon the same naturalistic
principles. Had he not in *The Discovery of the Future*
scoffed at the legal type of mind which reveres the past,
stands upon promises, abides by treaties, and quibbles
about who began the fighting? Had he not glorified the
" creative mind " with visions of empire, with the " will
to live," jesuitically making morality a means to its
end, boldly trampling over prohibitions to its goal,
cheerily letting the dead past bury its dead? How could
he distinguish his attitude of mind from that of the alien
enemy? Only by abandoning his " atheistical " followers, renouncing his worship of machinery, and shifting
his moral center.

On the publication of *Mr. Britling* it was widely
heralded through the press that Mr. Wells had " discovered God." It would have been more accurate to say
that Mr. Wells was fumbling for God. He was reaching out, with manifest symptoms of spiritual distress, for a power apart from the brutal rush and conflict of natural forces. He brought in an incoherent report of a vague spiritual reality mistily en-
compassing the field " where ignorant armies clash by
night."

The " inwardness " of Mr. Wells's reaction to the war
after his " discovery of God " may perhaps be suggested
by the words which come into Mr. Britling's mind as he
stands on the scene of a Zeppelin raid:

Some train of subconscious suggestion brought a long forgotten speech back into Mr. Britling's mind, a *speech that
is full of that light which still seeks so mysteriously and*

*indefatigably to break through the darkness and thickness
of the human mind.*

He whispered the words.   No unfamiliar words could
have the same effect of comfort and conviction.

He whispered it of those men whom he still imagined
flying far away there eastward, through the clear freezing
air beneath the stars, those muffled sailors and engineers
who had caused so much pain and agony in this little town.

"Father, forgive them, for they know not what they do."

Is this hypocrisy and an insufferable literary pose on
the part of Mr. Britling?   Or is it just as sincere as his
son's "Damn the Kaiser—and all fools"?   One accepts
its sincerity.   For Mr. Britling has been taking medi-
cine, bitter and purgative, to his soul's great good.   He
has brought "the Zeppelin raids, with their slow cres-
cendo of blood-stained futility," into connection with
"the same kind of experience that our ships have in-
flicted scores of times in the past upon innocent people
in the villages of Africa and Polynesia."   These terrible
incursions were a part of that mechanical "efficiency"
which the Germans had and the English had not, but
which Mr. Wells and other imperially-minded men had
long been urging upon the English as the way of salvation.   It was *not* the way!   That was the truth glim-
mering in Mr. Britling's mind.   It was the way to something—perhaps to *more* efficiency, but not to salvation.
That lay at the end of a route which the footsteps of
the imperial dream have never trod.   It lay perhaps
somewhere in the valley of self-humiliation beyond the
range of those who put their trust in the legs of man or
in chariots and horses.   Mr. Britling took his first step

toward it by honestly " no longer thinking of the Germans as diabolical. They were human; they had a case. It was a stupid case, but our case, too, was a stupid case. How stupid were all our cases! What was it we missed? Something, he felt, very close to us, and very elusive. Something that would resolve a hundred tangled oppositions."

Mr. Wells and Mr. Britling have written in the course of the war a good many pamphlets on what should be done after it. Mr. Britling criticizes his contributions thus:

" Dissertations," said Mr. Britling.
Never had it been so plain to Mr. Britling that he was a weak, silly, ill-informed, and hasty-minded writer, and never had he felt so invincible a conviction that the Spirit of God was in him, and that it fell to him to take some part in the establishment of a new order upon the earth; it might be the most trivial part by the scale of the task, but for him it was to be now his supreme concern.

The criticism in this paragraph was severe but not wholly undeserved, and the promise of amendment which it offered was illusory, as Mr. Wells promptly demonstrated by the publication of *God The Invisible King*, a book as hasty and ill-informed as anything that he has written. Apparently he was elated by the impression made upon his readers by Mr. Britling's religious experiences but mistaken about the nature of the impression. *Mr. Britling Sees It Through* was an arresting social phenomenon. " Mark," one said to oneself, " this interesting indication of the law of man's spirit. In the hour of overwhelming trial and bewildering disasters he gropes instinctively for a rock of refuge, for the permanent amid the transitory, for the eternal which we call God. So pervasive is the present sense of need that it takes hold upon the mind even of H. G. Wells, who probably knows less of the nature of God than any author of his eminence now living." Such was our impression of his conversion. But Mr. Wells, hearing the wide murmur of interest in the one " naturalist " that had repented, leaped to the conclusion that he, single-handed, had made a great light break upon a world waiting in outer darkness for his private illumination. Far from admitting that he has returned to the " fold," he naïvely lifts up his voice and invites the fold to turn to him. There is not a grain of humility in this new apostle. Standing in the midst of Mars' Hill he radiantly offers us a copy of his new book, saying in effect: " Whom therefore ye ignorantly worship, him declare I unto you."

There is unquestionably an abundance of magnanimous impulse in *God The Invisible King*, and its presence tempts the benevolent critic to exclaim, " Let the devil fly away with its faults." But Mr. Wells himself teaches us no such 'critical forbearance. Every time that he writes a book he condemns all his predecessors. His occasional tributes to other men go to his contemporaries. And each new message of his cancels his previous messages. He has no base of supplies; he keeps open no line of communication with the past. He is still the grandiose and romantic dreamer bent upon bringing forward a brand-new scheme for the salvation of the world. A few years ago it was world-socialism; a little later it was world-aristocracy; today it is world-theocracy. What it will be tomorrow no man knows, but every man can guess that it will be something different and equally evanescent. Every reflecting man can guess this, because the problem which Mr. Wells sets himself is insoluble to the point of absurdity, namely, the establishment of a government of the world by anarchists. Like all men of anarchical temper, he constantly oscillates between absolute despotism and absolute liberty, and never stops at the point of rest between the extremes. The problem presented in *God The Invisible King* is precisely: How to bring about " the kingdom of God on earth " by complete and universal anarchy in religion. I have misstated the case. Every anarchist is by nature a despot. Mr. Wells's anarchy is not to be quite complete and universal. " Had I the plantation of this isle," says old Gonzalo in *The Tempest*, " and were the king on't, I would by contraries execute all things," and a little later he adds that on the island there should be no *sovereignty*. The end of his speech, as a bystander remarks, forgets its beginning. Mr. Wells's anarchy, like the amiable Gonzalo's, is qualified by the absolute despotism of its would-be creator. In the " kingdom of God on earth " he very firmly rules that there shall be no churches, no priests, no Bibles, no creeds; and happy is the man *cuius oblectatio est in lege H. G. Wells, et qui de lege illius meditatur interdiu ac noctu.*

Compared with Mr. Wells, the Reverend Billy Sunday walks humbly and reverently before God and the history of human experience. Billy Sunday, knowing that religion is what binds us to righteousness, seeks to fill the emotions with love and fear of God and hatred and fear of the devil in order to bind his hearers to the ten major laws delivered by Moses. His religion is founded upon a rock, which he does not imagine is of his discovery or invention. Mr. Wells has invented his God, but he has not yet invented his righteousness; and that singular omission leaves his deity out of all characteristic employment. He does not even pretend to know what righteousness is. Furthermore he profoundly objects to being bound by anything. Accordingly he makes a clean sweep of all religious authorities and all scriptures which, as " revealed " truth or as potent poetical symbol, have proved through generation after generation their regulative efficiency in human affairs. In their stead he offers his sketch of the Invisible King made in his own image early in 1917—a Utopian enthusiast whose function is not to bind and regulate but to fling the reins on the neck of enthusiasm. The Invisible King is no meddler, like the God of the Hebrews, in a man's private affairs: " We have to follow our reason as our sole guide in our individual treatment of all such things as food, and health, and sex." Mr. Wells modifies this principle in another place by telling us that when in doubt about some nice point of conduct we may consult our family physician; and this permission or advice seems justified by the fact that " our spiritual nature follows our bodily as a glove follows the hand." Souls craving more light are recommended to consult the author's *First and Last Things*. If by chance any apostle of the new faith insists upon having a background for his religion, let him turn to the Koran rather than to the Bible. The Koran is a better source; for " Islam was never saddled with a creed."

As Mr. Wells warms to his task of composition, the spirit of prophesy descends upon him, and he begins to declare what things this churchless, creedless, lawless faith is going to accomplish in the world. The tangle of contradictions into which he falls is amusing. " We of the new faith " reject Christ because he was only " a saint of non-resistance." And yet, continues our angelic doctor gravely, " there is a curious modernity about very many of Christ's recorded sayings." " Our faith," however, as distinguished from Christianity is militant. Apparently " we " have conceived the quite novel idea of redeeming the world from sin by the effusion of blood! Ours is a militant faith; yet it is absolutely unorganized: " it is for each man to follow his own impulse, and to speak to his like in his own fashion." The intelligent reader will at once perceive what an advantage that gives " us " over, let us say, Catholic Christendom. Our faith is unorganized; " and yet "—here, I submit, Mr. Wells's trust in religious anarchy touches the cloudy borders of sublimity—" and yet in a few score years the faith of the true God will be spreading about the world. The few halting confessions of God that one hears here and there today, like that little twittering of birds which comes before the dawn, will have swollen to a choral harmony."

The fine and sound things in this book I have not much emphasized. They are exhortations to " repent-

ance," " consecration," " self-sacrifice," labor for the
" kingdom of God on earth." Mr. Wells's impression
that they are new is as " curious " as the " modernity of
very many of Christ's recorded sayings." They may
of course be heard in any orthodox pulpit in the course
of a month's sermons—with due credit given for their
origination and some attempt made to render their
meaning definite and their application practical. As
Mr. Wells handles them they tend only to create a vague
diffusive emotion. It is better for him to think of them
as of his own confection than for him not to think of
them at all; but as a matter of fact the chief contribu-
tive element in his testament is his peculiarly sanguine
and mellifluous egotism. If he could only bring himself
to acknowledge now and then that ideas may be true and
useful even though they have always been recognized
as such, he might occasionally find the whole force of
ancient traditions gathering behind him and supporting
his advance into the future. His passion for dynamit-
ing his own rear and sallying out on that long march
with only his " personal luggage " betokens not an intellectual leader but an intellectual madcap. It is a fine
feather in the bonnet of a writer of naturalistic fiction
to create and bring out between novels a perfectly new
divinity, and one so amiable as the Invisible King. But
I, for one, find that his prophecy of the kingdom of this
pleasant Utopian has only given me a particular relish
for rereading the ninetieth and the ninety-first Psalms.

III

THE BARBARIC NATURALISM OF
THEODORE DREISER

THE layman who listens reverently to the reviewers discussing the new novels and to the novelists discussing themselves can hardly escape persuasion that a great change has rather recently taken place in the spirit of the age, in the literature which reflects it, and in the criticism which judges it. The nature of the supposed revolution may be briefly summarized.

The elder generation was in love with illusions, and looked at truth through a glass darkly and timorously. The artist, tongue-tied by authority and trammeled by aesthetic and moral conventions, selected, suppressed, and rearranged the data of experience and observation. The critic, " morally subsidized," regularly professed his disdain for a work of art in which no light glimmered above " the good and the beautiful."

The present age is fearless and is freeing itself from illusions. Now, for the first time in history, men are facing unabashed the facts of life. ' Death or life," we cry, " give us only reality! " Now, for the first time in the history of English literature, fiction is become a flawless mirror held up to the living world. Rejecting nothing, altering nothing, it presents to us—let us take our terms from the bright lexicon of the reviewer—a

" transcript," a " cross-section," a " slice," a " photo-graphic " or "cinematographic " reproduction of life. The critic who keeps pace with the movement no longer asks whether the artist has created beauty or glorified goodness, but merely whether he has told the truth.

Mr. Dreiser, in his latest novel, *The Genius,* describes a canvas by a painter of this austere modern school: " Raw reds, raw greens, dirty gray paving stones—such faces! Why, this thing fairly shouted its facts. It seemed to say: ' I'm dirty, I am commonplace, I am grim, I am shabby, but I am life.' And there was no apologizing for anything in it, no glossing anything over. Bang! Smash! Crack! came the facts one after another, with a bitter, brutal insistence on their so-ness." If you do not like what is in the picture, you are to be crushed by the retort that perhaps you do not like what is in life. Perhaps you have not courage to confront reality. Perhaps you had better read the chromatic fairy-tales with the children. Men of sterner stuff exclaim, " Thank God for a realist! "

Mr. Dreiser is a novelist of the new school, for whom we have been invited off and on these fourteen years to " thank God "—a form of speech, by the way, which crept into the language before the dawn of " modern " realism. He has performed with words what his hero performed with paint. He has presented the facts of life " one after another with a bitter, brutal insistence on their so-ness," which marks him as a " man of the hour," a " portent "—the successor of Mr. Howells and Mr. James? In the case of a realist, biographical details are always relevant. Mr. Dreiser was born of German-American parents in Terre Haute, Indiana, in 1871. He was educated in the Indiana public schools and at the State University. He was engaged in newspaper work in Chicago, St. Louis, New York, and elsewhere, from 1892 to 1910. He has published two books of travel: *A Traveller At Forty*, 1913, and a *Hoosier Holiday*, 1916, which, without the support of his fiction, would entitle him to dispute with Mr. Viereck for the title of vulgarest voice yet heard in American literature; also a collection of one-act dramas, *Plays of the Natural and Supernatural*, 1916. But he has laid reality bare for us most generously in his five novels, published as follows: *Sister Carrie*, 1901; *Jennie Gerhardt*, 1911; *The Financier*, 1912; *The Titan*, 1914; and *The Genius*, 1915. These five works constitute a singularly homogeneous mass of fiction. I do not find any moral value in them, nor any memorable beauty—of their truth I shall speak later; but I am greatly impressed by them as serious representatives of a new note in American literature, coming from that "ethnic" element of our mixed population which, we are assured by competent authorities, is to redeem us from Puritanism and insure our artistic salvation. They abundantly illustrate, furthermore, the methods and intentions of our recent courageous veracious realism. Before we thank God for it let us consider a little more closely what is offered us.

The first step toward the definition of Mr. Dreiser's special contribution is to blow away the dust with which the exponents of the new realism seek to becloud the perceptions of our "reverent layman." In their main pretensions there are large elements of conscious and unconscious sham.

It should clear the air to say that courage in facing and veracity in reporting the facts of life are no more characteristic of Theodore Dreiser than of John Bunyan. These moral traits are not the peculiar marks of the new school; they are the marks common to every great movement of literature within the memory of man. Each literary generation detaching itself from its predecessor—whether it has called its own movement Classical or Romantic or what not—has revolted in the interest of what it took to be a more adequate representation of reality. No one who is not drunken with the egotism of the hour, no one who has penetrated with sober senses into the spirit of any historical period anterior to his own, will fall into the indecency of declaring his own age preeminent in the desire to see and to tell the truth. The real distinction between one generation and another is in the thing which each takes for its master truth—is in the thing which each recognizes as the *essential* reality for it. The difference between Bunyan and Dreiser is in the order of facts which each reports.

It seems necessary also to declare at periodic intervals that there is no such thing as a " cross-section " or " slice " or " photograph " of life in art—least of all in the realistic novel. The use of these catchwords is but a clever hypnotizing pass of the artist, employed to win the assent of the reader to the reality of the show, and, in some cases, to evade moral responsibility for any questionable features of the exhibition. A realistic novel no more than any other kind of a novel can escape being a composition, involving preconception, imagination, and divination. Yet, hearing one of our new realists expound his doctrine, one might suppose that writing a novel was a process analogous to photographing wild animals in their habitat by trap and flashlight. He, if you will believe him, does not invite his subjects, nor group them, nor compose their features, nor furnish their setting. He but exposes the sensitized plate of his mind. The pomp of life goes by, and springs the trap. The picture, of course, does not teach nor preach nor moralize. It simply re-presents. The only serious objection to this figurative explanation of the artistic process is the utter dissimilarity between the blank impartial photographic plate, commemorating everything that confronts it, and the crowded, inveterately selective mind, which, like a magnet, snatches the facts of life that are subject to its influence out of their casual order and redisposes them in a pattern of its own.

In the case of any specified novelist, the facts chosen and the pattern assumed by them are determined by his central theory or " philosophy of life "; and this is precisely citicism's justification for inquiring into the adequacy of any novelist's general ideas. In vain, the new realist throws up his hands with protestations of innocence, and cries: " Search me. I carry no concealed weapons. I run life into no preconceived mold. I have no philosophy. My business is only to observe, like a man of science, and to record what I have seen." He cannot observe without a theory, nor compose and record his observations without betraying his theory to any critical eye.

As it happens, the man of science who most profoundly influenced the development of the new realistic novel, Charles Darwin, more candid than the writers of "scientific" fiction, frankly declared that he could not observe without a theory. When he had tentatively formulated a general law, and had begun definitely to look for evidence of its operation, then first the substantiating facts leaped abundantly into his vision. His *Origin of Species* has the unity of a work of art, because the recorded observations support a thesis. The French novelists who in the last century developed the novel of contemporary life learned as much, perhaps, from Darwin's art as from his science. The technique of fiction imitated the procedure of scientific research. Balzac had emphasized the relation between man and his social milieu; the Goncourts emphasized the importance of extensive "human documents"; Zola emphasized the value of scientific hypotheses. He deliberately adopted the materialistic philosophy of the period as his guide in observation and as his unifying principle in composition. His theory of the causes of social phenomena, which was derived largely from medical and physiological treatises, operated like a powerful magnet among the chaotic facts of life, rejecting some, selecting others, and redisposing them in the pattern of the *roman naturaliste*. Judicious French critics said: "My dear man," or words to that effect, "your representations of life are inadequate. This which you are offering us with so earnest an air is not reality. It is your own private nightmare." When they had exposed his theory, they had condemned his art.

Let us, then, dismiss Mr. Dreiser's pretensions to superior courage and veracity, the photographic transcript, and unbiassed service of truth; and let us seek for his definition in his general theory of life, in the order of facts which he records, and in the pattern of his representations.

The impressive unity of effect produced by Mr. Dreiser's five novels is due to the fact that they are all illustrations of a crude and naïvely simple naturalistic philosophy, such as we find in the mouths of exponents of the new *Real-Politik*. Each book, with its bewildering mass of detail, is a ferocious argument in behalf of a few brutal generalizations. To the eye cleared of illusions it appears that the ordered life which we call civilization does not exist except on paper. In reality our so-called society is a jungle in which the struggle for existence continues, and must continue, on terms substantially unaltered by legal, moral, or social conventions. The central truth about man is that he is an animal amenable to no law but the law of his own temperament, doing as he desires, subject only to the limitations of his power. The male of the species is characterized by cupidity, pugnacity, and a simian inclination for the other sex. The female is a soft, vain, pleasure-seeking creature, devoted to personal adornment, and quite helplessly susceptible to the flattery of the male. In the struggles which arise in the jungle through the conflicting appetites of its denizens, the victory goes to the animal most physically fit and mentally ruthless, unless the weaklings, resisting absorption, combine against him and crush him by sheer force of numbers.

The idea that civilization is a sham, Mr. Dreiser sometimes sets forth explicitly, and sometimes he conveys it by the process known among journalists as " coloring the news." When Sister Carrie yields to the seductive drummer, Drouet, Mr. Dreiser judicially weighs the advantages and disadvantages attendant on the condition of being a well-kept mistress. When the institution of marriage is brushed aside by the heroine of *The Financier*, he comments " editorially " as follows: " Before Christianity was man, and after it will also be. A metaphysical idealism will always tell him that it is better to preserve a cleanly balance, and the storms of circumstance will teach him a noble stoicism. Beyond this there is nothing which can reasonably be imposed upon the conscience of man." A little later in the same book he says: " Is there no law outside of the subtle will and power to achieve? If not, it is surely high time that we knew it—one and all. We might then agree to do as we do; but there would be no silly illusion as to divine regulation." His own answer to the question, his own valuation of regulation, both divine and human, may be found in the innumerable contemptuous epithets which fall from his pen whenever he has occasion to mention any power set up against the urge of instinct and the indefinite expansion of desire. Righteousness is always " legal "; conventions are always " current "; routine is always " dull "; respectability is always " unctuous "; an institution for transforming schoolgirls into young ladies is presided over by " owl-like conven-

tionalists "; families in which the parents are faithful
to each other lead an " apple-pie order of existence "; a
man who yields to his impulses yet condemns himself for
yielding is a " rag-bag moralistic ass." Jennie Gerhardt, by a facile surrender of her chastity, shows that
" *she could not be readily corrupted by the world's selfish
lessons* on how to preserve oneself from the evil to come."
Surely this is " coloring the news."

By similar devices Mr. Dreiser drives home the great
truth that man is essentially an animal, impelled by
temperament, instinct, physics, chemistry—anything
you please that is irrational and uncontrollable. Sometimes he writes an " editorial " paragraph in which the
laws of human life are explained by reference to the
behavior of certain protozoa or by reference to a squid
and a lobster fighting in an aquarium. His heroes and
heroines have " cat-like eyes," " feline grace," " sinuous
strides," eyes and jaws which vary " from those of the
tiger, lynx, and bear to those of the fox, the tolerant
mastiff, and the surly bulldog." One hero and his mistress are said to " have run together temperamentally
like two leopards." The lady in question, admiring
the large rapacity of her mate, exclaims playfully:
" Oh, you big tiger! you great, big lion! Boo! " Courtship as presented in these novels is after the manner of
beasts in the jungle. Mr. Dreiser's leonine men but
circle once or twice about their prey, and spring, and
pounce; and the struggle is over. A pure-minded
serving-maid, who is suddenly held up in the hall by a
" hairy, axiomatic " guest and " masterfully " kissed
upon the lips, may for an instant be " horrified, stunned,

like a bird in the grasp of a cat." But we are always assured that " through it all something tremendously vital and insistent " will be speaking to her, and in the end she will not resist the urge of the *élan vital.*   I recall no one of the dozens of obliging women in these books who makes any effective resistance when summoned to capitulate. " *The psychology of the human animal,* when confronted by these tangles, these ripping tides of the heart," says the author of *The Titan,* " has little to do with so-called reason or logic." No; as he informs us elsewhere in endless iteration, it is a question of chemistry. It is the " chemistry of her being " (that of the female in question) which rouses to blazing the ordinarily dormant forces of Eugene Witla's sympathies in *The Genius.* If Stephanie Platow is disloyal to her married lover in *The Titan,* " let no one quarrel " with her. Reason: " She was an unstable chemical compound."

Such is the Dreiserian philosophy.

By thus eliminating distinctively human motives and making animal instincts the supreme factors in human life, Mr. Dreiser reduces the problem of the novelist to the lowest possible terms. I find myself unable to go with those who admire the powerful reality of his art while deploring the puerility of his philosophy. His philosophy quite excludes him from the field in which the great realist must work. He has deliberately rejected the novelist's supreme task—understanding and presenting the development of character; he has chosen only to illustrate the unrestricted flow of temperament. He has evaded the enterprise of representing human conduct; he has confined himself to a representation of animal behavior. He demands for the demonstration of his theory a moral vacuum from which the obligations of parenthood, marriage, chivalry. and citizenship have been quite withdrawn or locked in a twilight sleep. At each critical moment in his narrative, where a realist like George Eliot or Thackeray or Trollope or Meredith would be asking how a given individual would feel, think, and act under the manifold combined stresses of organized society, Mr. Dreiser sinks supinely back upon the law of the jungle or mutters his mystical gibberish about an alteration of the chemical formula.

The possibility of making the unvarying victoriousness of jungle-motive plausible depends directly upon the suppression of the evidence of other motives. In this work of suppression Mr. Dreiser simplifies American life almost beyond recognition. Whether it is because he comes from Indiana, or whether it is because he steadily envisages the human animal, I cannot say; I can only note that he never speaks of his men and women as " educated " or " brought up." Whatever their social status, they are invariably " raised." Raising human stock in America evidently includes feeding and clothing it, but does not include the inculcation of even the most elementary moral ideas. Hence Mr. Dreiser's field seems curiously outside American society. Yet he repeatedly informs us that his persons are typical of the American middle class, and three of the leading figures, to judge from their names—Carrie Meeber, Jennie Gerhardt, and Eugene Witla—are of our most highly " cultured " race. Frank Cowperwood, the hero of two novels, is a hawk of finance and a rake almost from the cradle; but of the powers which presided over his cradle we know nothing save that his father was a competent officer in a Philadelphia bank. What, if anything, Carrie Meeber's typical American parents taught her about the conduct of life is suppressed; for we meet the girl in a train to Chicago, on which she falls to the first drummer who accosts her. From the bosom of a typical middle-class American family, Eugene Witla emerges in his teens with a knowledge of the game called post-office, takes the train for Chicago, and without hesitation enters upon his long career of seduction. Jennie Gerhardt, of course, succumbs to the first man who puts his arm around her; but, in certain respects, her case is exceptional.

In *Jennie Gerhardt* Mr. Dreiser ventures a disastrous experiment at making the jungle-motive plausible without suppressing the evidence of other motives. He provides the girl with pious Lutheran parents, of fallen fortune, but alleged to be of sterling character, who " raise " her with utmost strictness. He even admits that the family were church-goers, and he outlines the doctrine preached by Pastor Wundt: right conduct in marriage and absolute innocence before that state as essentials of Christian living; no salvation for a daughter who failed to keep her chastity unstained, or for the parents who permitted her to fall; Hell yawning for all such; God angry with sinners every day. " Gerhardt and his wife, and also Jennie," says Mr. Dreiser, " accepted the doctrines of their church without reserve." Twenty pages later Jennie is represented as yielding her virtue in pure gratitude to a man of fifty, Senator Brander, who has let her do his laundry and in other ways has been kind to her and her family. The Senator suddenly dies; Jennie expects to become a mother; Father Gerhardt is broken-hearted; and the family moves from Columbus to Cleveland. The first episode is perhaps not altogether incredibly presented as a momentary triumph of emotional impulse over training—as an " accident." The incredible appears when Mr. Dreiser insists that an accident of this sort to a girl brought up in the conditions stated is not necessarily followed by any sense of sin or shame or regret. Upon this simple pious Lutheran he imposes his own naturalistic philosophy, and, in analyzing her psychology before the birth of her illegitimate child, pretends that she looks forward to the event " without a murmur," with " serene, unfaltering courage," " the marvel of life holding her in a trance," " with joy and satisfaction," seeing in her state " the immense possibilities of racial fulfilment." This juggling is probably expected to prepare us for her instantaneous assent, perhaps a year later, when a healthy magnetic manufacturer, who has seen her perhaps a dozen times, claps his paw upon her and says, " You belong to me," and in a perfectly cold-blooded interview, proposes the terms on which he will set her up in New York as his mistress. Jennie, who is a fond mother and a dutiful daughter, goes to her pious Lutheran mother and talks the whole matter over with her quite candidly. The mother hesitates—not on Jennie's account, gentle reader, but because she will be obliged to deceive old Gerhardt; " the difficulty of telling this lie was very great for Mrs. Gerhardt "! But she acquiesces at last. " I'll help you out with it," she concludes—" with a little sigh." The unreality of the whole transaction shrieks.

Mr. Dreiser's stubborn insistence upon the jungle-motive results in a dreary monotony in the form and substance of his novels. Interested only in the description of animal behavior, he constructs his plot in such a way as to exhibit the persistence of two or three elementary instincts through every kind of situation. He finds, for example, a subject in the career of an American captain of industry, thinly disguised under the name of Frank Cowperwood. He has just two things to tell us about Cowperwood: that he has a rapacious appetite for money; and that he has a rapacious appetite for women. In *The Financier* he " documents " these truths about Cowperwood in seventy-four chapters, in each of which he shows us how his hero made money or how he captivated women in Philadelphia. Not satisfied with the demonstration, he returns to the same thesis in *The Titan*, and shows us in sixty-two chapters how the same hero made money and captivated women in Chicago and in New York. He promises us a third volume, in which we shall no doubt learn in a work of sixty or seventy chapters—a sort of huge club-sandwich composed of slices of business alternating with erotic episodes—how Frank Cowperwood made money and captivated women in London. Meanwhile Mr. Dreiser has turned aside from his great " trilogy of desire " to give us *The Genius*, in which the hero, Witla, alleged to be a great realistic painter, exhibits in 100 chapters similarly sandwiched together, an appetite for women and money indistinguishable from that of Cowperwood. Read one of these novels and you have read them all. What the hero is in the first chapter, he remains in the one hundred and first and the one hundred and thirty-sixth. He acquires naught from his experiences but sensations. In the sum of his experience there is nothing of the impressive mass and coherence of activities bound together by principles and integrated in character, for all his days have been but as isolated beads loosely strung on the thread of his desire. And so after the production of the hundredth document in the case of Frank Cowperwood, one is ready to cry with fatigue: " Hold! Enough! We believe you. Yes, it is very clear that Frank Cowperwood had a rapacious appetite for women and for money."

If at this point you stop and inquire why Mr. Dreiser goes to such great lengths to establish so little, you find yourself once more confronting the jungle-motive. Mr. Dreiser, with a problem similar to De Foe's in *The Apparition of Mr. Veal*, has availed himself of De Foe's method for creating the illusion of reality. The essence of the problem for both these authors is the certification of the unreal by the irrelevant. If you wish to make acceptable to your reader the incredible notion that Mrs. Veal's ghost appeared to Mrs. Bargrave divert his incredulity from the precise point at issue by telling him all sorts of detailed credible things about the poverty of Mrs. Veal's early life, the sobriety of her brother, her father's neglect, and the bad temper of Mrs. Bargrave's husband. If you wish to make acceptable to your reader the incredible notion that Aileen Butler's first breach of the seventh article in the decalogue was " a happy event," taking place " much as a marriage might have," divert his incredulity by describing with the technical accuracy of a fashion magazine not merely the gown she wore on the night of Cowperwood's reception, but also with equal detail the half-dozen other gowns that she thought she might wear, but did not. If you have been for three years editor-in-chief of the Butterick publications you can probably persuade your readers that you are a master of the subject, and having acquired credit for expert knowledge in matters of dress and millinery, you can now and then emit unchallenged a bit of phliosophy such as " Life cannot be put in any one mold, and the attempt may as well be abandoned at once. . . . Besides, whether we will or not, theory or no theory, the large basic facts of chemistry and physics remain." None the less, if you expect to gain credence for the notion that your hero can have any woman in Chicago or New York that he puts his paw upon, you had probably better lead up to it by a detailed account of the street-railway system in those cities. It will necessitate the loading of your pages with a tremendous baggage of irrelevant detail. It will not sound much like the fine art of fiction. It will sound more like one of Lincoln Steffens's special articles. But it will produce an overwhelming impression of reality, which the reader will carry with him into the next chapter where you are laying bare the " chemistry " of the human animal.

It would make for clearness in our discussions of con-

temporary fiction if we withheld the title of " realist "
from a writer like Mr. Dreiser, and called him, as Zola
called himself, a " naturalist." While asserting that
all great art in every period intends a representation
of reality, I have tried to indicate the basis for a working distinction between the realistic novel and the naturalistic novel of the present day. Both are representations of the life of man in contemporary or nearly
contemporary society, and both are presumably composed of materials within the experience and observation
of the author. But the realistic novel is a representation based upon a theory of human conduct. If the
theory of human conduct is adequate, the representation constitutes an addition to literature and to social
history. A naturalistic novel is a representation based
upon a theory of animal behavior. Since a theory of
animal behavior can never be an adequate basis for a
representation of the life of man in contemporary
society, such a representation is an artistic blunder.
When half the world attempts to assert such a theory,
the other half rises in battle. And so one turns with
relief from Mr. Dreiser's novels to the morning papers.

IV

THE REALISM OF ARNOLD BENNETT

In discussing the work of Mr. Dreiser, I have offered a protest against the confusion which results from calling all novelists who deal with contemporary life realists; and I have proposed, as a means of making useful and important distinctions among them, a scrutiny of the bundle of general ideas which constitute for each his "working philosophy," and which, as I maintained, necessarily underlie the artistic representation of each and in considerable measure determine its form. When I had traced the lack of verisimilitude in the Dreiserian novel to Mr. Dreiser's perverse and libellous "theory of animal behavior" and, on that basis, had proposed to desgnate him as a naturalist, I felt the need of supplementing my argument by exhibiting the relationship, in some popular exemplar, between genuine realism and a "respectable theory of human conduct."

Arnold Bennett at once appeared in at least one respect to be a promising candidate for the position. His works, to be sure, are of very unequal value; for, frankly writing to live, he has diversified the production of masterpieces by the quite unscrupulous production of pot-boilers. Yet all sorts of good judges unite in declaring that his best novels—*The Old Wives' Tale* and the Clayhanger trilogy, including *Clayhanger, Hilda*

Lessways, and *These Twain*—produce upon them an unprecedented impression of reality. These books, we are told, challenge and endure comparison not with other books but with life itself. Their " transcript " of Five Towns society is so full, detailed, and accurate that it may be used by the student of human nature almost as confidently as first-hand observation. I was glad to find general agreement on this point, for it relieved me of the task of justifying my own conviction that Mr. Bennett is, in effect, a realist.

The only objection that I saw to the choice of Mr. Bennett as a contemporary realist was that the very critics who praise the reality of his representations insist sternly that he has no " philosophy in life," that he represents no ideal, that he does not " interpret " his facts, that his value resides wholly in the energetic integrity of his transcript. Mr. Darton, himself a novelist, says in his recent study of his fellow craftsman: " In the Five Towns novels there is no ideal. There is no criticism. There is no tradition or philosophy of society. There is nothing but life as the people described live it and see it and feel it." This is highly interesting, if it is true. If it is true, it disposes of my contention that an artist cannot observe without a theory. If it is true, it should suggest to the younger generation of novelists who are looking to Mr. Bennett as their master the wisdom of making all haste to get rid of their ideas.

Mr. Darton's assertion that Arnold Bennett's work has no value save that of mere representation was anticipated by Henry James in his discussion of the " new novel " in 1914, and was by him extended to an entire group of the younger writers, of which he specified Mr. Bennett and Mr. Wells as the leaders. The distinguishing characteristic of the group, according to Mr. James, is " saturation." By this he means, as I take it, that all these novelists, and to a high degree their leaders, are masters of the materials of their art. They know with extraordinary completeness and detail what they are talking about, but when they have made us see what they have seen, they yield us no further satisfaction. They squeeze the sponge or, as Mr. James puts it, the " orange "; this gives us an " expression of life." Expectant but disappointed criticism cries: " Yes, yes,—but is this all? These are the circumstances of the interest—we see, we see; but where is the interest itself, where and what is its center, and how are we to measure it in relation to that? "

I cannot follow a critic who finds Wells and Bennett alike in their dominant value, and, what is far more interesting, neither can Mr. Wells! Stung to the quick of his celestial mind by the polite implication that he is only a thoroughly immersed sponge, he has retorted in his semi-pseudonymous *Boon*, 1915, with a scathing criticism and a " take-off " on Mr. James, whom he links with Mr. George Moore by virtue of their sterile aestheticizing. *That* is *their* dominant " value "—their central " interest." His own central interest, as he reasserts with more than customary vehemence and formlessness, is the expression of his yearning for a life a divine efficiency and divine ecstacy. He has a theory of conduct which has developed out of that romantic yearning; and his representations of life in fiction are experimental illustrations of that theory. It is quite absurd to charge an author with " mere representation," who almost invariably bursts the outlines of his hero, disrupts his narrative in mid-career, shatters the illusion of reality, and buries all the characters under the avalanche of his own personal dreams and desires. Mr. Wells, in brief, cherishes a " philosophy of life " which makes it impossible for him to write a realistic novel. He is dedicated to romance. His high calling is to write pseudo-scientific fantasies and fairy tales of contemporary society.

Mr. Wells in *Boon* incidentally repudiates yoke-fellowship with the novelist of the Five Towns in a passage which gives us the key to Mr. Bennett's " philosophical " position. Mr. Bennett is there recorded as a " derelict," an " imperfectly developed," an " aborted " great man surviving from the old times : " Would have made a Great Victorian and had a crowd of satellite helpers. No one will ever treasure his old hats and pipes." This is both amusing and instructive. Mr. Wells does not call a man a Victorian without malice aforethought. If I may be pardoned a violent expression, Mr. Wells would like to slay all the Victorians ; better still, he would like to believe that they are all dead. What he objects to in that generation is not the " mere representation " of the novelist ; it is the accursed philosophy of life which underlies their representations. Mr. Bennett rises up to prove, alas, that this philosophy is not dead yet. His solid realistic novels protest against Mr. Wells's fairy tales. His vision of life protests against Mr. Wells's vision of life. *The Old Wives'*

Tale makes *The Research Magnificent* look like child's play. Put *These Twain* beside *Marriage*, and instantly the art of the latter seems flimsy and incondite, and its informing ideas fantastic. And one may perhaps just note in passing that beside any one of Mr. Bennett's novels, Mr. Dreiser's *Genius* instantly appears to be a barbaric yawp. An author whose work thus judges, so to speak, another work with which it is brought into contact, has a potent critical value meriting examination.

The popular impression that Mr. Bennett has no general ideas is easily explained by the fact that he does not attempt, as Mr. Wells does, to break down the boundaries between the literary genres, and to make the novel serve at the same time as a narrative of events and as a philosophical dissertation. Respecting the personalities of his *dramatis personae*, wishing to preserve the sharpness of their outlines in their own atmosphere, he does not obviously impute to them his ideas nor set them to discussing them. With a restraint unusual among English novelists, he refrains from elaborate " editorial " comment upon his " news." When he wishes to set forth his ideas explicitly, he writes a book of popular philosophy: *Mental Efficiency, The Feast of St. Friend, The Plain Man and His Wife.* If these books were as well known to the American public as the novels are, we should hear no more in this country about Mr. Bennett's lack of ideas. On the contrary, all our women's clubs would be debating, in their eager simple-hearted fashion, " The Philosophy of Arnold Bennett."

Mr. Darton, more sophisticated than our fellow coun-

trymen, says in effect that the philosophy in these
books is not worth discussing; and it does not seem to
occur to him that it can have any bearing upon Mr.
Bennett's fiction.   The works named above have been
advertised in England, he tells us, as containing " big,
strong, vital thinking."   But, he continues, " big,
strong, vital thinking is just what these remarkable
little books do not contain.   They contain the completest common-sense, expressed with astonishing simplicity and directness, and based upon unimpeachable
honesty of outlook.   They are a guide to efficiency, to
self-help, to practical idealism, to alertness of intelligence, to sinewy culture, to every high quality which
every crass Briton has always thought the crass Briton
does not show.   The United Kingdom is almost over-
stocked with agencies for the purpose, from the physical
energies of Mr. Sandow to the benevolent writing of the
late Lord Avebury. . . . They are quite perfect lay sermons.   But "—and these are the damning words—" they
are not original."   I perfectly agree that Mr. Bennett's
general ideas are not " original," and on the whole com-
mend his judgment in not tying up his art to anything
so transitory as a " new " philosophy.   I object to the
implication, in which Mr. Wells will rejoice, that because
they are old they are dead or deficient in strength and
vitality.   I will not stand upon the word " big," a term
which should be reserved for the use of advertizing man-
agers and radical reformers.   But I cannot reconcile
Mr. Darton's description of these books as guides to
every high quality needed by the crass Briton with his
assertion that there is no criticism in the Five Towns

novels, except on what seems to me the untenable assumption that Mr. Bennett, the popular novelist, and Mr. Bennett, the popular philosopher, are distinct and non-communicating beings.   I shall attempt to show that the novelist's treatises on conduct are related to his artistic representation of it.

The beginning of wisdom, according to this philosophy, which runs counter to our current naturalism, is the recognition of a fundamental duality in human experience.   Mr. Bennett presumes not God to scan.   He is as completely emancipated from religious metaphysics as any of his contemporaries.   Like a true child of his scientific age, he takes nothing on authority; he brings everything to the test of his experience.   But looking into himself as a microcosm, he sees and reports that the universe consists of a controlling power, which is the quintessence of man; and of a power to be controlled, which is nature.   The zest, the object, the compensation of existence lie in the possibility of extending the dominion of the human over the natural power, the voluntary over the involuntary impulses, the conscious over the unconscious agents.   " For me," he says, " spiritual content (I will not use the word ' happiness,' which implies too much) springs from no mental or physical facts.   It springs from the spiritual fact that there is something higher in man than the mind, and that something can control the mind.   Call that something the soul, or what you will.   My sense of security amid the collisions of existence lies in the firm consciousness that just as my body is the servant of my mind, so is my mind the servant of *me*.   An unruly servant, but a servant and pos-

sibly less unruly every day! Often have I said to that
restive brain: ' Now, O mind, sole means of communication between the *me* and all external phenomena, you
are not a free agent; you are subordinate; you are nothing but a piece of machinery; and obey me you *shall*."

The responsibility for extending the dominion of man
over his own nature and, indirectly, over his remoter
circumstances, Mr. Bennett, in opposition to our popular sociological doctors, places primarily upon the individual. While Mr. Wells, for example, urges us to cast
our burdens and our sins upon society, and goes about
beating up enthusiasm for schemes to improve the " mind
of the race " by leagues of Samurai and legislative enact-
ments, Mr. Bennett fixes his eye upon plain John Smith,
and says: " I am convinced that we have already too
many societies for the furtherance of our ends. To my
mind, most societies with a moral aim are merely clumsy
machines for doing simple jobs with a maximum of fric-
tion, expense, and inefficiency. I should define the
majority of these societies as a group of persons each
of whom expects the other to do something very wonderful. Why create a society in order to help you perform
some act which nobody can perform but yourself? "
Arnold Bennett says disappointingly little about that
" big " idea, " the mind of the race." And whenever he
contemplates that impressive and admired abstraction
" the backbone of the nation," it resolves itself under
his realistic gaze into the by-him-no-less-admired but
certainly less generally impressive spinal columns of
John Smith and other homely vertebrates.

In dealing with the relations of John Smith to Mrs.

Smith, the Victorian Bennett feels obliged to say, in opposition to those who hold out for these plain people the prospect of a life of freedom and sustained ecstasy to be attained by upsetting the established order, that most of our ideas of freedom and ecstasy are romantic will-o'-the wisps. In the recent " evolution " of society he perceives rapid changes for the better in living conditions and a gradual amelioration of manners and tastes, but no significant alteration in the elements of human nature. " Passionate love," he insists, " does not mean happiness; it means excitement, apprehension, and continually renewed desires." " Luxury," he adds, " according to the universal experience of those who have had it, has no connection whatever with happiness." " Happiness as it is dreamed of cannot possibly exist save for short periods of self-deception which are followed by terrible periods of reaction. Real practicable happiness is due primarily not to any kind of environment, but to an inward state of mind. Real happiness consists first in an acceptance of the facts that discontent is a condition of life, and, second, in an honest endeavor to adjust conduct to an ideal."

It must infuriate an advocate of moral revolution like Mr. Wells, to hear Mr. Bennett, bracketed with him as a leader of the new school, asserting that " the great principles, spiritual and moral, remain intact." It must perplex an apologist for moral anarchy and strident self-assertion like Mr. Dreiser to find a fellow realist declaring that " after all the shattering discoveries of science and conclusions of philosophy, mankind has still to live with dignity amid hostile nature," and that mankind can succeed in this tremendous feat only " by the exercise of faith and of that mutual good will which is based on sincerity and charity." But what must distress them beyond measure is this able craftsman's exposition of the relation of moral conventions to artistic form. " What form is in art, conventions are in life. . . . No art that is not planned in form is worth consideration, and no life that is not planned in conventions can ever be satisfactory. . . . The full beauty of an activity is never brought out until it is subjected to discipline and strict ordering and nice balancing. A life without petty artificiality would be the life of a tiger in the forest. . . . Laws and rules, forms and ceremonies are good in themselves, from a merely aesthetic point of view, apart from their social value and necessity."

These are the ideas of a man who has taken his stand against Mr. Wells's Utopia on the one hand and against Mr. Dreiser's jungle on the other. As old as civilized society, they have the conservative complexion of all traditional and enduring things. They are not worth discussing if they are not challenged. Like fire and water, they do not appear vital till they are denied. Ordinarily a novelist has not needed consciously to concern himself with them unless he has intended to trample them under foot. But in the face of the present naturalistic invasion, when humanistic ideas are in the trenches, under fire, fighting for existence, a novelist who paints men in preference to tigers, supermen, or scientific angels, has interestingly taken sides. His preference is an entirely discussable " criticism of life."

The general theme of Mr. Bennett's masterpieces,
determined by the central interest of his philosophy, is
the development of character in relation to a society
which is also developing. He has no foolishly simple
mechanical formula for the process. He has rather a
sense that this relationship involves an interplay of
forces of fascinating and inexplicable complexity.

His sense of the marvelous intricacy of his theme explains his elaborate presentation of the community life
in which his principal figures have their being. He is
bent upon bringing before the eye of the reader every
scrap of evidence that may be conceived of as relevant to the " case." The reader who believes that
character is determined mainly by inherited physiological traits finds in the Five Towns novels a physiological
account of three successive generations. The reader
who holds that education is the significant factor is
abundantly supplied with the educational history of
father and children and grandchildren. The reader who
lays stress upon a changing environment and the pressure of the hour sees how from decade to decade and
from year to year the hero or heroine is housed and
clothed and fed and occupied and amused; and wrought
upon by parents and children and relatives and friends
and servants and strangers; and subjected to the influences of social customs and business and politics and
religion and art and books and newspapers transmitting
to the thick local atmosphere the pressure of the world
outside. The reader who looks for the main currents of
the nineteenth century in the Five Towns discovers the
Clayhanger family and their neighbors developing in

relation to the democratic movement, the industrial revolution, the decay of dogmatic theology, the extension of scientific thought and invention, the organization of labor, and the diffusion of aesthetic consciousness. One's first impression before this spectacle is of admiration at the unrelenting artistic energy which keeps this presented community life whole and steady and yet perceptibly in motion through a long span of time.

One's second impression is of admiration at the force of composition which keeps the principal figures from being " swamped " in the life of the community. They are immersed in it and dyed in it and warped and battered and grooved by it; yet they are never made to appear as its impotent creatures; somehow they are made to emerge above their " environment " as its creators and preservers—its plain, grim, but enduring heroes. The secret of this " somehow " is that Mr. Bennett implicitly recognizes as an artist what he explicitly declares as a popular philosopher, namely, the existence in the individual of something deeper than the body, deeper than the mind—an ultimately responsible, independent, spiritual, self with the power to control, in some measure, its circumstances.

In his preface to *The Old Wives' Tale* he tells us that the originating impulse of that work was a conviction that a " heartrending novel " might be written to express " the extreme pathos in the fact that every stout aging woman was once a young girl with the unique charm of youth in her form and movements and in her mind." The theme as he states it is only the threadbare platitude of cavalier poetry—the deciduousness of physical beauty; and its pathos is only skin deep. But the theme as he develops it is the spiritual truth sung by George Herbert—" only a sweet and virtuous soul, like seasoned timber never gives "; and its pathos is indeed heartrending. Constance and Sophia, the two heroines of *The Old Wives' Tale,* appeal to tragic compassion not because they were young and have grown old and grotesque but because they hungered for life and love, yet quietly and proudly starved in their respectability rather than touch a morsel of forbidden food. After a considerable course of reading in the " temperamental " novels of the naturalistic school, one begins to feel that the resisting power of formed character has vanished from the earth. I shall not forget the sigh of relief that I uttered when I came upon a certain passage in the story of Sophia's resistance to the various invitations of Paris sensuality. The poor girl in her loneliness craving for sympathy and affection finds her physical and mental self responding involuntarily to the ardent wooing of the kindly Chirac. " ' My dear friend,' he urges with undaunted confidence, ' you must know that I love you.' She shook her head impatiently, all the time wondering what it was that prevented her from slipping into his arms." She does not slip into his arms; and one rejoices —not because one's moral sense is gratified, but simply because one is pleased to find occasionally a novelist who recognizes the inhibited impulse, in the sexual connection, as among the interesting facts of life. Mr. Bennett portrays persons with various powers of inhibition; but he does not give the place of hero or heroine to a slave of instinct. He paints an abundance of unlovely men and

women—hard, shrewd, smart, selfish, bigoted; but the
interest of his story centers in the deliberate acts of
rational beings, who are conscious, like Hilda Lessways,
of their miraculous power " to create all their future
by a single gesture," and who have or achieve some of
the substance and fixity of character. By the very
design of his novels Mr. Bennett reveals his admiration
for the prudent, foresighted, purposeful people. The
man who has himself in hand he makes, by his com-
positional emphasis, a measure of the subordinated
figures.

The Clayhanger trilogy, triumphantly completed by
the publication of *These Twain*, expresses with the moving force of dramatic representation the ideas more
simply exposed in *The Plain Man and His Wife*. The
first volume has for its theme the development of the
character of Edwin Clayhanger from the formlessness
of his boyhood to the steadiness, honesty, application,
efficiency, solidity, tolerance, justice, and self-control of
his manhood. The theme of the second volume is the
development of the characters of Hilda Lessways from
the innocent, ignorant rebelliousness and rapturousness
of girlhood through a brief ill-advised matrimonial adventure to the vibrant, hopeful, open-eyed egoism and
rather grim determination of early womanhood. The
theme of the third volume is the further development of
this " dynamic " and that " static " character through
the difficult and at times almost baffling process of adapt-
ing themselves to living together as man and wife.
Taken together the three novels constitute an impressive
dramatic criticism of Mr. Wells's theory of the life of

sustained ecstasy and, if you please, of Mr. Dreiser's theory of the life of ruthless animality.

It is clear that Mr. Bennett has attempted to present in the completed trilogy an adequate account of the fiery conflict, with typical antagonists, of the Eternal-Feminine and the Eternal-Masculine. If you are a man, you will writhe, or you ought to writhe, at the exposure in Edwin of your own obstinate conviction that you think straight and that your wife does not, and at the exposure of your hot fits of indignation at her shifty evasions of your flawless argument. If you are a woman, you will blush, or ought to blush, at the exposure in Hilda of your own illogicality and your willingness to gain ends—commendable no doubt—by perfectly unscrupulous means. Hilda respects and loves her husband deeply, but she is irritated by his colds, by his little set habits, by the deliberateness of his temper, and by the inarticulateness of his appreciation of her. Edwin loves his wife and feels the charm and force of her personality; but he distrusts her intellect and cannot entirely approve her morality. He is exasperated by her interference in his business. He keenly resents the injustice in which she involves him through acts inspired by her ambition for him and by her passionate and jealous devotion to the advancement of their own family interests. She develops social aspirations in which he does not share, and a desire for a style of living which promises him increased burdens with no added satisfaction. Their common effort seems to multiply luxuries and superficial refinements without in the least sweetening or deepening or strengthening their spir-

itual intercourse.   He tells himself in a moment of
intense self-commiseration that the great complex edifice
of his business " with its dirt, noise, crudity, strain, and
eternal effort " exists solely that Hilda may exist " in
her elegance, her disturbing femininity, her restricted
and deep affections, her irrational capriciousness, and
her strange, brusque commonsense."   He asks himself in
poignant self-pity: " Where do I come in? "   After
repeated scenes of domestic tension he walks out of his
house and home with hot brain and twitching nerves.
He mutters to himself: " She won't alter her ways—and
I shan't stand them."   In what he takes for ultimate
despair, he says to himself, " as millions of men and
women have said to themselves, with awestruck calm:
' My marriage was a mistake.' "

But as this plain, average man wanders aimlessly
through the streets of the Five Towns with tumult in
his breast, confronting the ruin of his private universe,
he has an experience comparable in character and in
significance to him with that of Thomas Carlyle when in
sultry Leith Walk he authentically took the Devil by
the nose.   When his brain cools and his nerves stop
twitching and his formed character returns to its equi-
librium, he has first a flashing intuition into a method
by which he can reconcile himself to his " universe."
" It was banal; it was commonplace; it was what every
one knew.   Yet it was the great discovery of all his
career.   If Hilda had not been unjust in the assertion of
her own individuality, there could be no merit in yielding
to her. . . . He was objecting to injustice as a child
objects to rain on a holiday.   Injustice was a tre-

mendous actuality! It had to be faced and accepted.
(He himself was unjust. At any rate he intellectually
conceived that he must be, though honestly he could
remember no instance of injustice on his part.) To
reconcile oneself to injustice was the master achievement. . . . He yielded on the canal-bridge. And in
yielding, it seemed to him that he was victorious." For,
and this is the second part of Edwin's spiritual experience, in the instant when he gains the wisdom he feels in
his innermost self the power to put it into effect. His
joyous sense that he is not going to be " downed " by
his circumstances, he expresses with a certain crudity—
perhaps with a certain vulgarity; but something may
be forgiven a man who has just solved the " problem of
marriage "—" I'm not going to be beaten by Hilda!
And I'm not goinf, to be beaten by marriage. Dashed
if I am! A nice thing if I had to admit that I wasn't
clever enough to be a husband! " Clayhanger does not
return to his home with a notion that his discovery will
" transform marriage into an everlasting Eden." He
anticipates further trouble and further sacrifices. But
he has found content by accepting discontent as a condition of life, and by honestly endeavoring to adapt his
conduct to an ideal. In his recognition of the need of
a more flexible intelligence and a stiffer backbone he
embodies at once the principle of progress and the principle of conservation. He is a hero of his generation,
not victorious but conquering. He cannot stand like
Benham in *The Research Magnificent*, and say, " I am a
Man. The Thought of the world." But he might
stand, if he had the habit of attitudinizing, and say,

" I am a man. A vertebral unit in the backbone of the nation."

One cannot plan a life in conventions without cutting out of it many wayward desires and " beautiful impulses." The young lions and lionesses of radicalism are forcing the question upon us whether one can plan a life in beautiful impulses and wayward desires without cutting out the plan. Mr. Bennett answers in the negative, and votes for preserving the plan. I do not undertake to speak critically of his philosophy. I only observe that it seems to support an altogether decent theory of human conduct. And this in turn underlies an artistic representation of life remarkable for its fullness, its energy, its gusto, its pathos, its play of tragic and comic lights, its dramatic clashes, its catastrophes, and its reconciliations—in short, for its adequacy. I fear that my reasoning will not make much impression upon the young, for the young, as Mr. Randolph Bourne tells us, the young are in love with life; and to accept conventions is to refuse life. The young will still turn to Mr. Wells, " for he," says Miss Rebecca West—" for he has inspired the young to demand clear thinking and intellectual passion from the governing classes, instead of the sexual regularity which was their one virtue and which he has hinted is merely part of a general slothfulness and disinclination for adventure." As I sadly take my place in the rear of the " cretinous butlers " who " do not like Mr. Wells," I summon my Christian charity to declare that much shall be forgiven a champion of Mr. Wells, whose critical arrows go singing, like this sentence of Rebecca West's, straight to the heart of laughter.

V

THE AESTHETIC NATURALISM OF GEORGE MOORE

It is now about forty years since George Moore, not content with the priestly auditor provided by his Church, abandoned the private confessional and began to pour along the town the secret flood of his ideas and emotions. How could he have done otherwise? Ireland taught his tongue not to cleave to the roof of his mouth; Roman Catholicism taught him to confess his sins; Jean Jacques, his Delphian Apollo, taught him to dulcify and ventilate them. He has been as beguilingly various in the moods and forms of his personal effusions as in the matter and manner of his ostensibly objective prose fiction. Like most born men of letters, he delivered his first message to the world in verse—*Flowers of Passion*, 1877. In *Confessions of a Young Man*, 1888, he adopts a glittering, paradoxical, impudent ruthless air befitting a young man who has lived in Paris and passed through all the illusions. With *Memoirs Of My Dead Life*, 1906, he lowers his pitch, softens his accents, introduces a note of pleased satiety and gloating languor proper to the sensuous reminiscences of later middle-age. In the three volumes of *Hail and Farewell*, 1911-14, he holds our attention still by subtler modulations of his malicious revery, by a studied alteration of nakedness

and filmy sophistication in his garb, by the dreamy
femininity of his gesture, by the lax almost unaccented
movement of his voice. In his alluring latest manner,
always dulcet, always fluent, he has laid bare a personality compact of nearly everything that is detestable
to the mind of a plain citizen going about his business in
the marketplace. He has confessed consuming egotism,
quivering sensibility, fastidiousness, vanity, timidity,
calculating shamelessness, sensuality, a streak of feline
cruelty, and absolute spiritual incontinence. Manet's
portrait of him, the weird, wide-eyed face veiled in wispy
hair, corresponds to his own unflattering self-por-
traiture: an elderly Irish satyr fluting among the reeds
to a decadent Irish naiad, and, in the pauses of the
fluting, mingling reminiscences of his adventures, artistic and amatory, with the notes of the impressions made
by the fading sunlight upon his soul.

Though this personality possesses a certain acrid
bouquet of its own, it challenges our attention less by
its uniqueness than by its representativeness. Clearly
enough he was cast—if anything so essentially fluid
can be said to have been cast—in that temperamental
mold which Rousseau idly intimated was broken up
after his own creation. That temperament at work
in contemporary art and morals, persisting unaltered
under many manifestations, he represents with remarkable consistency and completeness. Purely intellectual
initiative he has none: but he has been swiftly respon-
sive to every new influence in art and literature. All
his life he has lurked in the purlieus of schools and
insinuated himself into movements, soliciting, like the

barren Calpurnia, the fructifying touch of some fleet clear-eyed runner. His literary *liaisons* have been as facile and as frequent as the infatuations of George Sand. He has succumbed in turn, not to enter into particulars, to three movements, very different on the surface but impelled by the same general undercurrent: he has been wooed, won, and lost by " aesthetism," naturalism, and the symbolism of the Irish Renaissance. Let us trace here the course of this interesting " evolution."

The first step in the aesthetic novitiate is the preparation of the self for its own independent activity by detaching it from the complex organic network of domestic, social, racial, national, and religious relationships in which it has been placed by the irrelevant accident of birth. In the *Confessions of a Young Man* Mr. Moore dismissed in a page or two the Ireland of his childhood. The reason was obvious: it had nothing to do with the first phase of his literary career. From the day when he read the *Sensitive Plant* of Shelley " by the shores of a pale green Irish lake," he was destined to shake from his feet the dust of Ireland, he was devoted to art and letters, and dedicated to the continuation of Shelley's terrible mission—the " emancipation " of the human spirit.

An impressionable Irishman who had severed all natural ties could easily enough in the early 'seventies of the last century, have become a perfect aesthete in England. The spring had come slowly up that way, but at last it had definitely announced itself. Rossetti, having struck the note of intensity in painting and poetry, had gone on to the collection of blue china and

Japanese bric-a-brac. In 1870 William Morris completed *The Earthly Paradise*. Ruskin in the same year began to lecture on art at Oxford, teaching—to be sure, from his own high ethical standpoint—the pregnant doctrine that taste is morality. In 1873 Pater put forth his seductive studies in the art and poetry of the Renaissance, setting up the aesthetic ideal in Mona Lisa, committing to posterity the aesthetic testament in the famous Conclusion. Before the end of the decade Moore's fellow-countryman Wilde was delighting his circle, shocking the burgesses, and achieving notoriety by brilliant paradoxes and the hard gem-like beauties of strange verse. In ten years the aesthetic movement had run its swift course through beauty to intensity and thence to perverseness; and it had produced an effective school for the transformation of English youths into sun-flowered Corinthian dandies.

Of this Oxford aestheticism Mr. Moore felt the influence in due season, but he somewhat anticipated its effects by crossing the Channel to France, and at once immersing his divested soul in the Lethe of an alien art. There he was gradually born again in the Ptolemaic world of the Latin Quarter, in the free society of the temporarily and permanently untied, in an atmosphere of smoke bounded by an horizon of canvas. There the deracinated Irishman assumed the language and the pleasures of the Parisian without assuming his responsibilities, lived in bachelor apartments surrounded with rare books, old furniture, and fantastic curios; rose at noon and retired at daybreak, and maintained a model and a python—the latter daily propitiated with guinea-

pigs. Mistresses and pythons, cameos and sphinxes—
these were the themes of his favorite poets and ro-
mancers, representatives of an older than the English
aestheticism and potent contributors to it—Gautier and
Baudelaire, Banville and Verlaine. In the unreal world
of the studios which he haunted, Bohemian dreamers
were painting dancing girls borrowed from the unreal
world of the stage, Aphrodites rising from the sea,
Harlequins and Columbines. In this little eccentric
planet where the problems of good and evil resolved
themselves into questions of green and gold, light and
shadow, line and mass, pleasure and pain, Mr. Moore
seems to have learned all the morality that he has ever
practiced or advocated.

After a sojourn in Paris so long that he almost forgot
the idiomatic use of English, he returned to England,
an appetent and ambitious ego, in time to catch the
aesthetic movement of the late 'seventies. In 1877,
synchronizing with Oscar Wilde's arrival as a poet, he
published his first book, of which the title, *Flowers of
Passion,* sufficiently indicates the character and the
literary inspiration. He followed this up in 1881 with
Pagan Poems, and for several years to come diverted
himself as a journalist, critic of art, realistic novelist,
and fop. The experiences and the spirit of the aesthetic period are adequately represented in *Confessions
of a Young Man.* As there was nothing novel in the
processes by which Mr. Moore was turned out an
aesthete, so there was nothing novel in the product.
The compact gospel of aesthetic egotism unfolded by
his Young Man in 1888, France had received from

Gautier and Baudelaire twenty to fifty years earlier. Mr. Moore's originality consisted merely in carrying Parisian " aestheticism "—the corrupt leavings of the Romantic Movement—across the Channel, and offering it to the Anglo-Saxon world. Let us have a few jewels from the monument which he raised to eternalize his youth:

My father's death freed me, and I sprang like a loosened bough up to the light. His death gave me power to create myself, that is to say, to create a complete and absolute self out of the partial self which was all the restraint of home had permitted; this future self, this ideal George Moore, beckoned me, lured me like a ghost; and as I followed the funeral the question, Would I sacrifice this ghostly self, if by so doing I should bring my father back? presented itself without intermission, and I shrank horrified at the answer which I could not crush out of mind.

Art was not for us then as it is now,—a mere emotion, right or wrong only in proportion to its intensity.

I am feminine, morbid, perverse. But above all perverse, almost everything perverse interests me, fascinates me.

I could not understand how anybody could bring himself to acknowledge the vulgar details of our vulgar age. The fiery glory of José de Heredia, on the contrary, filled me with enthusiasm—ruins and sand, shadow and silhouette of palms and pillars, negroes, crimson, swords, silence, and arabesques.

Two dominant notes in my character—an original hatred of my native country, and a brutal loathing of the religion I was brought up in.

A little bourgeois comfort, a little bourgeois sense of right, cry the moderns. Hither the world has been drifting since the coming of the pale socialist of Galilee: and this is why I hate Him, and deny His divinity. . . . I, who hold nought else pitiful, pity Thee, Thy bleeding face and hands and feet, Thy hanging body; Thou at least art picturesque. . . .

The healthy school is played out in England: all that could be said has been said.

What care I that some millions of wretched Israelites died under Pharaoh's lash or Egypt's sun? It was well that they died that I might have the pyramids to look on, or to fill a musing hour with wonderment.

I am ashamed of nothing I have done, especially my sins, and I boldly confess that I have desired notoriety.

Humanity is a pigsty, where liars, hypocrites, and the obscene in spirit congregate: and it has been so since the great Jew conceived it, and it will be so till the end. Far better the blithe modern pagan in his white tie and evening clothes, and his facile philosophy. He says: " I don't care how the poor live; my only regret is that they live at all," and he gives the beggar a shilling.

In this year of grace these glowing Neronics no longer make us shudder; they are happily beginning to make us yawn. The sickly little poetasters in America who have attempted in recent years to dish this decayed pottage up again are even from a merely aesthetic point of view beneath mention and beneath contempt. If anything is dead, the aesthetic movement that took shape in the 'seventies is dead. The sphinxes and the green carnations, the flowers of passion and the ballads in blue china, already associate themselves in memory with the stucco and the stuffed birds of an elder decorative scheme. To burn always with a hard, gem-like flame before a masterpiece of the Italian Renaissance no longer epitomizes for the younger generation " success in life." Where are the aesthetes of yesteryear? Where are our Oscar Wildes and Ernest Dowsons and Aubrey Beardsleys? Where are the authors and illustrators of the *Yellow Book* and the *Savoy?* Early death made havoc in their ranks, Socialism distracted the younger generation, fresh pastures invited them. They have left the banks of their Dead Sea desolate. Somewhat in advance of the general exodus, Mr. Moore's prescient nostrils perceived a fetid odor rising from the waters, and he took refuge among the " naturalists," or, as he called them in those days, the " realists."

It may appear at first thought a far cry from feeding guinea-pigs to pythons, and indulging in Neronic musings on the Egyptian pyramids, to writing a realistic novel of life in the slums of London. As aesthete, Mr. Moore had declared that he did not care how the poor lived. In 1894, as realistic novelist, he brought out *Esther Waters,* the intimate life history of an illiterate servant-girl who in the course of her squalid existence spent some time in the poor-house. If the author's confession did not belie the suggestion, we might infer that a great change had come over him. Knowing him as we do, we are not permitted to conjecture that his contempt for the lower classes has dissolved in compassion for the poor. We must seek for the point of view from which an English scullery maid can be made to yield artistic satisfaction equivalent to that formerly yielded by the perfumed lady of romance.

We may approach the question by remarking that this point of view had been discovered by several of Mr. Moore's masters in fiction—by Balzac, Maupassant, and, notably, Flaubert. That relentless lover of *le mot*

unique occupies in French literature a position closely
corresponding to that occupied by Mr. Moore in English: he is the link between the romanticists and the
realists.   Frenchman and Irishman were temperamentally akin; open the *Education Sentimentale,* and through
page after page you will feel as if you were in the pres-
cnce of an earlier version of Mr. Moore's memoirs.
Formed in the intensely aesthetic school of Gautier and
Baudelaire, Flaubert, like the Young Man, held that the
only virtue is perfection of form.   Fundamentally engrossed in sex, he, too, craved refinement in the seduction of the senses—the intoxication of perfumes, the
allurement of lace, religious veilings, Oriental coloring,
barbaric splendors.   Finally, he, too, abhorred and despised the Philistine and all his virtues.   *Salammbô, La
Tentation de Saint Antoine, Hérodias*—such are the
works one should expect from a man of his romantic
origins.   Why, then, does this great romantic artist
bend all his talents to the portrayal of the bourgeois life
of Madame Bovary, depraved wife of a stupid country
doctor?   Why, then, does this despiser of the vulgar
herd cause to be bound up in the same volume with
Hérodias, the tale of an ignorant, sensual, long-suffering
servant-girl *(Un Coeur Simple),* obviously related to
Esther Waters?

Upon this peculiar transition from romanticism to
realism Mr. Moore throws a luminous beam in several
passages of his works commenting upon an artistic inno-
vation of Dégas.   To this original painter, a man of
penetrating intellect, belongs, according to our author,
the credit for discovering that the nude was becoming

well-nigh incapable of artistic treatment. To him belongs also the credit for the discovery of a method for
rehabilitating the nude. The formula is novelty through
cynicism. Having asked the rhetorical question, " Who
in sheer beauty has a new word to say? " Dégas sent for
a butcher's fat wife, and requested her to pose for him.
Following the clue of ugliness, Dégas escaped from the
tedious palace of romantic art into a new world of vivid
sensations. Mr. Moore's delight with the results he
has expressed in *Confessions of a Young Man*, in *Impressions and Opinions*, 1891, and again in the first volume of *Hail and Farewell*, 1911. The following passage
is from *Impressions and Opinions:*

> Three coarse women, middle-aged and deformed by toil,
> are perhaps the most wonderful. One sponges herself in a
> tin bath: another passes a rough nightdress over her lumpy
> shoulders, and the touching ugliness of this poor human
> creature goes straight to the heart. A woman who has
> stepped out of a bath examines her arm. Dégas says, *La
> bête humaine qui s'occupe d'elle-même; une chatte qui se
> lèche.* Yes, it is the portrayal of the animal life of the
> human being, the animal conscious of nothing but itself.

How superbly these figures stand forth in the hard
clear light of contempt! George Eliot digressed in a
familiar passage in *Adam Bede* to protest against the
exclusion from art of Dutch subjects—" old women
scraping carrots with their work-worn hands . . .
rounded backs and stupid, weather-beaten faces that
have bent over the spade and done the rough work of the
world." But George Eliot did not find it necessary to
strip her old women or peep at them through a keyhole;

it was not their essential animality but their essential
humanity that attracted her; and the kindly light which
fills her pictures is that light of moral sympathy and
love which irradiates the bowed head of Wordsworth's
leech-gatherer.   A man detached from his species like
Mr. Moore defends the ugly in art on entirely different
grounds.   Aesthetically very piquant indeed!   As " picturesque," when your eyes have been opened to it,
as the crucifixion of Christ!   That, so far as he is concerned, is a sufficient justification of naturalism.

Mr. Moore has profited by the lessons of Dégas.
How he probed into the animal life of his laundress when
he was writing *Esther Waters* he has related with gusto.
How in that novel he opened the door upon the physical
terrors of childbirth the reader may determine for himself, if he is not already satiated with the innumerable
morbid and hysterical representations of later writers.
Moore's aesthetic zest in the repulsive he has carried
over into the sentimentalities of his memoirs, employing
quite habitually a dash of the disgusting as a *sauce
piquante* to intensify the sweetness of his reveries.   If it
were possible for him to make a perfectly straightfor-
ward explanation of his use of the nauseous, he would
tell us just this: It is an aesthetic novelty.   But when
an aesthete introduces an indecency in the Anglo-Saxon
world, he still hesitates a little to admit that it is introduced merely to furnish a new sensation.   He assumes
for the moment the air of the veracious and dispassionate historian; he says with a false appearance of candor:
It is a fact of civilization.   A good illustration of this
pseudo-scientific pose of the artist may be seen in this

record of his observation of a house-maid in *Confessions of a Young Man:*

Emma, I remember you—you are not to be forgotten—up at five o'clock every morning, scouring, washing, cooking, dressing those infamous children; seventeen hours at least out of the twenty-four at the beck and call of landlady, lodgers, and quarreling children; seventeen hours at least cut of the twenty-four drudging in that horrible kitchen, running upstairs with coals and breakfasts and cans of hot water; down on your knees before a grate, pulling out the cinders with those hands—can I call them hands? The lodgers sometimes threw you a kind word, but never one that recognized that you were akin to us, only the pity that might be extended to a dog. And I used to ask you all sorts of cruel questions; I was curious to know the depth of animalism you had sunk to, or rather out of which you had been raised. And generally you answered innocently and naïvely enough. But sometimes my words were too crude, and they struck through the thick hide into the quick, into the human, and you winced a little; but this was rarely, for you were nearly, oh, very nearly an animal; your temperament and intelligence were just those of a dog that has picked up a master, not a real master, but a makeshift master who may turn it out any moment. Dickens would sentimentalize or laugh over you; I do neither. I merely recognize you as one of the facts of civilization.

The last sentence, being interpreted, means, " I merely *aestheticize* over you." The kinship with Dégas extends below the surface. Mr. Moore's work is conceived and produced in a cynical contempt for humanity—a contempt which he had fed and fattened from every available source. From Baudelaire, Dégas, and Zola he derived his conception of the aesthetic possibilities of the human beast; and Zola gave him the formula, *naturalisme, la vérité, la science*. These direct literary and artistic influences were reinforced in the 'eighties by some acquaintance with the pessimistic philosophy of Schopenhauer and of Eduard von Hartmann, which in this same period was shaping the cynical spirit of Samuel Butler. A Teutonic-Oriental nihilism was about the most perverse and blighting spirit then abroad in the land; accordingly Mr. Moore embraced it, and did what he could to propagate it. " That I may die childless," exclaims his Young Man, " that when my hour comes I may turn my face to the wall saying, I have not increased the great evil of human life—then, though I were a murderer, fornicator, thief, and liar, my sins shall melt even as a cloud. But he who dies with children about him, though his life were in all else an excellent deed, shall be held accursed by the truly wise, and the stain upon him shall endure forever." His conviction that existence is an evil is modified by a conviction that existence may be made fairly savory by an artist with plenty of money who rids himself of Christianity, his conscience, and his humanitarian sympathies, and with nicely calculating selfishness gratifies his natural impulses.

Mr. Moore is an accomplished literary artist: that is to say, he is a master of the means necessary to produce the effects which he preconceives. Lewis Seymour in *A Modern Lover*, Mr. Moore's first novel published in 1883, is an eloquently cynical representation of the successful Victorian artist, flowering in the studios, boudoirs, and ball-rooms of the late 'seventies. " Lewis," says the historian with a grimace, " believed in passion, eternal devotion, and, above all, fidelity; he could not understand the sin of unfaithfulness, in any shape or form; without truth, there could not be love, and how any man could make love to his friend's wife, passed his comprehension." So much for the Victorian ideality. Lewis, like the hero of Maupassant's *Bel Ami,* lives mentally and physically at the expense of the numerous women whom he captivates; he flirts with his models; he goes up the aisle of the church in which he is married past pews full of the ladies with whom he has been intimate; in the days of his honeymoon his bride discovers upon his finger a diamond ring sent to him by a married mistress; he prospers exceedingly, and is elected to the Academy. So much for the Victorian reality. If you exclaim, " This is mere caricature," Mr. Moore replies in the *Confessions* that " the whole " of his own " moral nature is reflected in Lewis Seymour."

As a foil to Lewis as artist, he introduces a group of " realist " painters who are sick of sentiment and the " conventional prettiness of things." They can put up with the sentiment of Swinburne's leper, because the subject is fresh and unhackneyed. Instead of occupying themselves, like Sir Frederick Leighton, for example, with " graceful nymphs languishing on green banks, either nude or in classical draperies," they paint " housemaids in print dresses, leaning out of windows, or bar-girls serving drinks to beery-looking clerks." This they declare is the " positivism of art," and they rejoice that they have achieved an art in accord with the philosophy of the age. Mr. Moore's entire picture of society in

A Modern Lover is a contribution to the new " realism."
It is an exhibit offered in support of the thesis of the
Restoration dramatists, that every man is a sensualist
and every woman a rake.   The thesis is proved by the
simple Restoration device of representing every professed allegiance to ideal standards as a hollow sham.

His second novel, *A Mummer's Wife*, 1884, " reeks "
more powerfully of actuality than any other of his works
before *Esther Waters*; but its special interest is still
more or less " theoretical."   It is an exhibit offered in
support of a thesis selected from Duruy's *L'Introduction Générale a l'Histoire de France:* " Change the surroundings in which a man lives, and in two or three generations, you will have changed his physical constitution, his habits of life, and a goodly number of his
ideas."   The novel is a kind of English " transposition "
of *Madame Bovary*, flavored with a handful of something
of Zola's.   Kate Ede, the soft, good-natured, respectable
wife of a horribly asthmatic shopkeeper whose physical
agonies are rendered with disgusting closeness, escapes
mentally from the humdrum of her shop and sewing-
room by reading sentimental poetry and cheap romantic
novels.   It never occurs to her to make any attempt to
realize her romantic dreams till a traveling theatrical
company visits the town, and a gross but amiable actor
is lodged in her house.   She brings him hot water in the
morning and serves him his breakfasts; they chat at odd
moments and surreptitiously visit a crockery factory;
after a few meetings and facile embraces in dark hall-
ways, she runs away with him and travels with the
troupe.   Her good-humored fat-legged companion—the

fat legs and good humor are about the only notes of his character—treats her kindly, and obligingly marries her; but under the new Bohemian influences Kate's respectability disintegrates, she begins to tipple, she becomes morbidly jealous and furiously quarrelsome, and she dies in squalid and nauseating dipsomania. As a study in mental and physical dissolution *A Mummer's Wife* is wonderfully impressive. The analysis and the representation of drunken female rage are beyond praise. The total emotional effect upon the reader resembles that of an intense sea-sickness—a somewhat novel asethetic effect. With notable self-restraint, Mr. Moore in this case strives for a hard, clear, dry objectivity. He offers no moral conclusion; so that the orthodox moralist is at liberty to say, Here is a stinging illustration of the consequences of drink and adultery. But if there is any sincerity in Mr. Moore's personal writings, we may be sure that, if called upon, he would moralize the tale in some such fashion as this: Don't go in for the fast life if you haven't the stamina to stand the pace.

To introduce such a moral as this into the book would spoil Mr. Moore's aesthetic effect. He does not intend here to present his gospel of enlightened egotism. He desires only to convey to the reader his sense of the dull pathos of things—his contemptuous pity for humanity; and he marvellously well understands how to do it. There is page after page as poignant as this description of Kate in her rapid decline:

She had a box in which she kept her souvenirs. They

were a curious collection. A withered flower, a broken cigarette-holder, two or three old buttons that had fallen from his clothes, and a lock of hair. But it was underneath these that lay the prize of prizes—a string of false pearls. Never did she see this precious relic without trembling, and to put it round her neck for a few minutes after her lonely dinner when she was waiting for him to come home, charmed and softened her as nothing else did. It was a necklace she had to wear in a comedietta they had both played in, *The Lover's Knot*. Well did she remember the day they had gone to buy it together; it had been one of the happiest in her life. But it was precisely the reaction caused by these moments of tenderness that was terrible to witness. Gradually from looks of dreamy happiness the face would become clouded, and as bitter thoughts of wrongs done her surged up in her mind, the tiny nostril would dilate and the upper lip contract, until the white canine tooth was visible. For ten minutes more she would remain, her hands grasping nervously at the arms of her chair: by that time the paroxysm would have obtained complete mastery over her, and with her brain deaf and cold as stone she would walk across the room to where the liquor was kept, and moodily sipping gin-and-water, she would form plans as to how she would attack him when he arrived home.

In *A Drama in Muslin*, 1886, Mr. Moore sets himself a more complex task than he undertakes in *A Mummer's Wife*, and his treatment of this theme is intensely personal. He paints here on a fairly wide canvas Irish social life in town and country in the days of the Land League. His central characters are four or five girls belonging to various country families, who have just completed their education in a convent and are now to be provided with husbands and careers. The spirit in which Mr. Moore approaches his subject I have already indicated by a quotation from his nearly contemporaneous *Confessions:* " Two dominant notes in my character—an original hatred of my native country, and a brutal loathing of the religion I was brought up in." Let us supplement this with another passage from the same source, indicating his attitude toward the popular discontent in Ireland which threatened to cut off his revenues and forced his return from Paris—a passage breathing the spirit of the Nietzschean *Herrenmoral* and the German invasion of Belgium:

That some wretched farmers should refuse to starve, that I may not be deprived of my *demi-tasse* at *Tortoni's,* that I may not be forced to leave this beautiful retreat, my cat and my python—monstrous. And these wretched creatures will find moral support in England; they will find pity! Pity, that most vile of all virtues, has never been known to me. The great pagan world I love knew it not. Now the world proposes to interrupt the terrible austere laws of nature which ordain that the weak shall be trampled upon, shall be ground into death and dust, that the strong shall be really strong,—that the strong shall be glorious, sublime.

Mr. Moore's problem, then, is to make his picture of Irish society express adequately his contempt for it— and, incidentally, for humanity in general. I will enumerate and illustrate some of the means by which he accomplishes his end.

In the first place he makes his characters creatures of heredity and environment, according to the naturalistic formula; and he insists with brutal emphasis upon physiological structure as the determining element in

their behavior. How explicit his shallow pseudo-science.
becomes may be illustrated by the following paragraph:

Alice Barton's power to judge between right and wrong,
her love of sentiment, her collectedness, yes, I will say her
reasoned collectedness were, as has been partially shown,
*the consequence of the passivity of the life and nature of
her grandfather (the historian);* her power of will, and her
clear, concise intelligence were inherited from her mother,
and these qualities being placed in a perfectly healthy subject, a subject in whom every organ functioned admirably,
the result was a mind that turned instinctively from mystic-
ism and its adjuncts. . . . And Cecilia's dark and illogical
mind can also be accounted for, her hatred of all that concerned sexual passion was *consequent on her father's age
and her mother's loathing for him during conception and
pregnancy;* and then, if it be considered that this transmitted hatred was planted and left to germinate in a mis-
shapen body, it will be understood how a weird love of the
spiritual, of the mystical, was the almost inevitable psychical
characteristic that a human being born under such circumstances would possess.

The conduct of each of the young girls is deduced
from the shape of her limbs, the color of her eyes and
hair, her complexion, and other carefully enumerated
physical marks. From Alice Barton's " thin arms and
straight hips and shoulders " Mr. Moore proves her
" *natural powerlessness* to do aught but live up to the
practical rectitudes of life, as she conceived them to
exist "; and accordingly Alice is married to a prosaic
doctor, and lives a life of dull British respectability.
The " amorous plenitude " of arm and bosom in her
sister Olive and her extremities flowing into " chaste

slendernesses " mark her out for a vapid and futile pursuit of a titled husband.   May Gould is a round, soft-limbed girl: " the soft, the melting, the almost fluid eyes, the bosom large and just a little falling, the full lips, the absence of any marked point or line, the rolling roundness of every part of the body announced a want of fixed principle, and a somewhat gross and sensual temperament."   May gives and takes pleasure as opportunity offers, and fares as prosperously as any of her friends.   Cecilia, having a deformed body, necessarily conceives of life as " a libidinous monster crouching in a cave, with red jaws dripping with foul spume."   She abhors equally Alice's honest marriage and May's *liaisons:* " It is the same thing; one seeks a husband, another gratifies herself with a lover.   It is the same thing.   Where's the difference?   It is animal passion all the same."

Mr. Moore himself takes essentially Cecilia's position. For him animal passion is the reality underlying all the mummeries of marriage, society, fashion, and religion. He finds his " fun," as Henry James would say, in stripping off the masks.   Here, for example, is his not altogether sympathetic account of the celebration of the Mass in the presence of an elegantly hypocritical gentry and a brutal and superstitious peasantry:

The mumbled Latin, the by-play of the wine and water, the mumming of the uplifted hands, were so appallingly trivial, and, worse still, all realisation of the idea seemed impossible to the mind of the congregation.   Passing by, without scorn, the belief that the white wafer the priest held above his head, in this lonely Irish chapel, was the Creator of the twenty millions of suns in the Milky Way, she (Alice) mused on the faith as exhibited by those who came to worship, and that which would have, which must have, inspired them, were Christianity now, as it once was, a burning, a vital force in the world.   Looking round, what did she see? Here, at her elbow, were the gentry.   How elegantly they prayed, with what refinement!   Their social position was as manifest in their religion as in their homes, their language, their food.   The delicate eyelids were closed from time to time; the long slim fingers held the gilt missals with the same well-bred grace as they would a fan; their thoughts would have passed from one to the other without embarrassment.   Clearly they considered one the complement of the other.   At the Elevation, the delicate necks were bowed, and, had lovers been whispering in their ears, greater modesty could not have been shown.

They had come to be in the absolute presence of God, the Distributor of Eternal rewards and punishments—and yet they had taken advantage of this stupendous mystery to meet for the purpose of arranging the details of a ball.

The peasantry filled the body of the church.   They prayed coarsely, ignorantly, with the same brutality as they lived.   Just behind Alice a man groaned.   He cleared his throat with loud guffaws: she listened to hear the saliva fall: it splashed on the earthen floor.   Further away a circle of dried and yellowing faces bespoke centuries of damp cabins, brutalising toil, occasional starvation.   They moaned and sighed, a prey to the gross superstition of the moment.   One man, bent double, beat a ragged shirt with a clenched fist; the women of forty, with cloaks drawn over their foreheads and trailing on the ground in long black folds, crouched until only the lean hard-worked hands that held the rosary were seen over the bench rail.   The young men stared arrogantly, wearied by the length of the service.

They, too, had come to be in the absolute presence of God—the Distributor of Eternal rewards and punishments —and yet they had taken advantage of the occasion of this stupendous mystery for the purpose of arranging a land meeting.

One can readily enough understand why a " blithe pagan " like Mr. Moore finds little to enlist his sympathies in witnessing a celebration of the Mass in a little Irish chapel. It is not so easy to explain why he sustains his air of disgust in describing such eminently " worldly " scenes as the great ball at Dublin Castle. The fact is that he is a pretty poor " pagan," and not very " blithe." He is a nineteenth century " naturalist " who has read Schopenhauer's essay on women and has seen an opportunity for a novel aesthetic effect in a sneeringly anti-romantic representation of the relations between men and women. He describes this brilliant event of the social season very much as a hunter of literary turn might describe the behavior of a herd of elk in mating time—a hunter who should take his stand with the females of the herd, and try to interpret their emotions of nervous expectation and their efforts to make themselves attractive to the ranging males. In Mr. Moore's opinion the women novelists—George Eliot, George Sand, and the rest—have failed to utilize the opportunities of their sex; they have written like men; they have left unpictured the mating encounter as seen from the feminine point of view. Mr. Moore with his feminine intuitions has stepped into the breach, has familiarized himself with the mysteries of petticoats and lingerie, and has shown just how the despicable man-hunt looks to intriguing mammas and rosy compliant daughters and to the hysterical feminist

of 1885. His picture reminds one very faintly of
Jane Austen; but she dissipates romance with eighteenth century common sense, and he with the cynicism
of a nineteenth century naturalist. His contempt for
the whole social exhibition is curiously emphasized by
the interjection of an occasional highly-wrought paragraph in the manner of Huysmans, descriptive of the
silks and shoulders and odors, which, for the sniffing
aesthetic observer, constitute the high points of the
occasion. Has any English novelist written a more exquisite appreciation of dress goods than this?

With words of compliment and solicitation, the black-
dressed assistant displayed the armouries of Venus—armouries filled with the deep blue of midnight, with the
faint tints of dawn, with strange flowers and birds, with
moths, and moons, and stars. Lengths of white silk clear
as the notes of violins playing in a minor key; white poplin
falling into folds statuesque as the bass of a fugue by Bach;
yards of ruby velvet, rich as an air from Verdi played on
the piano; tender green velvet, pastoral as hautboys heard
beneath trees in a fair Arcadian vale; blue turquoise faille
Française fanciful as the twinkling of a guitar twanged
by a Watteau shepherd; . . . white faille, soft draperies
of tulle, garlands of white lilac, sprays of white heather,
delicate and resonant as the treble voices of children singing carols in dewy English woods; berthas, flounces, plumes,
stomachers, lappets, veils frivolous as the strains of a
German waltz played on Liddell's band.

Has any one ever exhibited greater connoiseurship
in shoulders than appears in the following?—

There heat and fatigue soon put an end to all coquetting

between the sexes. The beautiful silks were hidden by the crowd; only the shoulders remained, and, to appease their terrible ennui, the men gazed down the backs of the women's dresses stupidly. Shoulders were there, of all tints and shapes. Indeed, it was like a vast rosary, alive with white, pink, and cream-colored flowers: of Maréchal Niels, Souvenir de Malmaisons, Mademoiselle Eugène Verdiers, Aimée Vibert Scandens. Sweetly turned adolescent shoulders, blush white, smooth and even as the petals of a Marquise Mortemarle; the strong commonly turned shoulders, abundant and free as the fresh rosy pink of the Anna Alinuff; the drooping white shoulders full of falling contours as pale as a Madame Lacharme; the chlorotic shoulders, deadly white, of the almost greenish shade that is found in a Princess Clementine . . . and, just in front of me, under my eyes, the flowery, the voluptuous, the statuesque shoulders of a tall blonde woman of thirty whose flesh is full of the exquisite peach-like tones of a Mademoiselle Eugène Verdier, blooming in all its pride of summer loveliness.

Finally, has any writer in English ever given to the odors of the human herd more lyrical expression than this?—

Momentarily the air grew hotter and more silicious; the brain ached with the dusty odor of poudre de ris, and the many acidities of evaporating perfumes; the sugary sweetness of the blondes, the salt flavours of the brunettes, and this allegro movement of odors was interrupted suddenly by the garlicky andante, deep as the pedal notes of an organ, that the perspiring arms of a fat chaperone slowly exhaled.

What is the artistic intention of these purple paragraphs? They are designed to intensify the curious dull emotion of revulsion which a healthy human being feels in the presence of a subtly derisive representation of his kind—a representation of human weakness and folly and sensuality unrelieved by the admission of anything sacred, anything noble, anything morally sound and sweet. A novelist who cares a rap about representing life whole feels bound to establish somewhere in his picture of the human scene " reflectors " of the light of his own ideals or of his common sense, if he has no ideals. This light may be reflected by some of the characters in the action; it may be irradiated over them all by the author's comments upon the characters; it may even flash out with adequate illumination from the course of the action itself. At the points in Mr. Moore's narrative where one looks for light, what does one find? Well, when one turns from the petty and sordid " souls " of his presented characters, one is invited by the author to fix one's mind upon the sounds of their dress goods, the tones of their skins, and the tastes of their odors!

Does Mr. Moore sympathize with any of the characters in *A Muslin Drama?* Yes, at certain points of the story he sympathizes with the intellectual position of Alice Barton. This young woman has at least partly emancipated herself from religious and conventional modes of thought. She has half-formulated for herself George Moore's own naturalistic philosophy. She believes that " the most feasible mode of life is to try to live up to the ordinary simple laws of nature of which we are but a part." " In an obscure and formless way," he says, " she had divined the doctrines of Eduard von

Hartmann, the entire and unconditional resignation of personal existence into the arms of the cosmic process." Her solution beautifully makes an end of the moral conflict of the ages—the struggle of man to subject his lower to his higher nature, to make his conduct conform to an ideal of conduct: she would make " the ends of nature also the ends of what we call conscience "—just as the other animals do. Virtue under this principle consists in frankly yielding to one's instincts. The misery of life comes from resisting them. If you resist them it is because you are a hypocrite, or a coward, or a fool.

It is not necessary to examine in detail all Mr. Moore's later " realistic " representation of man as animal. Novels like *Spring Days*, for example, which was published in 1888, and *Vain Fortune*, published in 1890, are comparatively insipid performances, and they add nothing to our previous impression of his methods and purposes. Nor need we tarry long over his realistic masterpiece *Esther Waters*, 1894. It is the most elaborate and learned study in literature of the English housemaid and barmaid and her environment. When Mr. Moore was a youth, before Shelley had kindled his imagination, he acquired an intimate knowledge of certain aspects of life in his father's racing stables; and to this fund of special information he has added from time to time by intimate studies of charwomen and chambermaids. Drawing upon these rich resources, he has recreated with amazing verisimilitude all the smells and sights and voices amid which Esther's stubborn " will-to-live " shaped her inconspicuous career: jockeys and stable-talk, kitchen wenches and kitchen talk, the lying-in hospital, the nursery where unwelcome children are killed off at £5 " per," the bedroom in the garret, the tavern, the drunkards, the race-track, the betting-man, the street-walkers, and only so much of the life above stairs as an English " slavey " sees. Esther has an illegitimate child by a man in livery at her first place of employment. The man in livery is dismissed because he is courted by a young lady who is a guest upstairs. Later Esther also loses a position through the amorous approaches of a young gentleman in the house to whose advances she has not responded. After her first slip she is kept straight by a dogged, instinctive, passionate fidelity to her child—by the necessity of keeping in her employer's graces so that she and her child may live. In the course of eight or ten years she meets again and marries the man who abandoned her; but presently he loses all he has in the races, and dies of consumption. The widowed Esther returns to her first mistress, now a widow also; and the two lonely women in the lonely decaying house live on together in an almost sisterly relationship. Her son becomes a soldier, and she is very proud and happy when she sees him in his red uniform. The story has a certain dull gray pathos, for which it has been much admired. Esther is only a strong igno-rant drudge, innately stupid—she cannot be taught to read; yet she is the most appealing figure in all Mr. Moore's fictitious world. Her patient endurance of the world, her heroic toil for her offspring, and her all-absorbing maternal passion would awaken elementary and profound sympathies, if one were a little less con-

scious of her rôle as demonstrator of the thesis that the
blind instincts of reproduction and self-preservation
account for everything that is significant in human
destiny.

If you accept this thesis, you will not judge people
as of " good " or of " bad " character. You will only
mark in them the strength or the weakness of the " vital
force " which impels them to act as they do and not
otherwise. If the vital force in them is a powerful
driving stream of energy, you will envy and admire
them. If it is fluctuating and feeble, you will despise
them. The desire to sing, to paint, to pray—all these
you will recognize as but allotropic phases of sexual
emotion. When Mr. Moore had thoroughly grasped
this thought, his spirit was cheered and comforted.
He had long lacked a hero. He had perhaps grown a
little weary of sneering at all things. Some inappeas-
able instinct in him demanded some object for his allegiance. He found his hero, his object of allegiance, in
the " cosmic processes." When one compares his novels
written in the 'nineties with those written in the
'eighties, one perceives a certain shifting in emphasis
from the external to the internal factors in character—a
shifting from a " mechanistic " to a " vitalistic "
formula. There is, for example, this distinction between
A Mummer's Wife and *Esther Waters:* the first is a
study of the victorious force of environment; the second
is a study of the victorious force of the " will-to-live "
and to perpetuate one's kind.

As a champion of the cosmic processes, Mr. Moore
feels a growing interest in artistic sterility and religious

celibacy and their physiological connections. There is something of his new note, the pathos of sterility, in *A Muslin Drama:* there is much more of it in *Vain Fortune:* and it is plangent in *Celibates*, 1895. Celibates, according to his interpretation, are persons in whom the vital force is feeble, or has been checked and thwarted by some perversity of doctrine or by some hostility of environment. Mildred Lawson in *Celibates* is a study of unchaste chastity. The vital force in her is represented as just strong enough to make her lascivious and just feeble enough to keep her " chaste." She has a queasy appetite for artistic expression and a life of passion: she toys with art and abandons it to toy with and torment a series of lovers; not virtue but timidity and impotence inhibit her desires. One suspects that she, like many of Mr. Moore's women, is in considerable measure an " autobiographical revelation." She is a Vestal vampire—one of the most noxious and noisome creatures in English literature. But mark how artfully Mr. Moore avails himself of her low value, or rather, let us say, of her worthlessness, to raise the " price " of a common commodity. The mouthpiece of the " cosmic processes " in this story is an artist's model who has also served in another capacity one of Mildred's lovers, killed by Mildred's unkindness. Between Mildred and the model this clarification of the moral issues takes place:

' I did not know of your existence till the other day. I heard that——'

' That I was his mistress. Well, so I was. It appears that you were not. But, I should like to know which of us two is the most virtuous, which has done the least harm. I made him happy, you killed him.'

In " John Norton," a second story in *Celibates*, Mr. Moore occupies himself with tracing to a kind of faintness of sexual impulse his hero's taste for the marmoreal and virginal type of woman, his taste for monastic severity in his material surroundings, and, finally, his taste for the cloister and an ascetic God. The story is written with aesthetic intensity; and the *aesthetically* exquisite appreciations of the vernal beauty of Kitty, alive and dead, are calculated to make the casual reader unmindful of the anti-religious innuendo, the insidious malice, which lurks in every page. John Norton is presented a little in the manner of Anatole France, as this passage will perhaps suggest to readers of *Thaïs*:

He rose from the table, and looked round the room. The room seemed to him a symbol—the voluptuous bed, the corpulent arm-chair, the toilet-table shapeless with muslin—of the hideous laws of the world and the flesh, ever at variance and at war, and ever defeating the indomitable aspirations of the soul. John ordered his room to be changed; and in the face of much opposition from his mother, who declared that he would never be able to sleep there, and would lose his health, he selected a narrow room at the end of the passage. He would have no carpet. He placed a small iron bed against the wall; two plair chairs, a screen to keep off the draft from the door, a small basin-stand, such as you might find in a ship's cabin, and a *prie-dieu* were all the furniture he permitted himself.

'Oh, what a relief!' he murmured. 'Now there is line, there is definite shape. That formless upholstery frets my eye as false notes grate on my ear': and, becoming suddenly conscious of the presence of God, he fell on his knees and prayed.

In *Evelyn Innes*, 1898, and its sequel *Sister Teresa*, 1901, Mr. Moore presents a heroine of genuine artistic temperament and artistic power. She yields with perfect abandon to the vital forces within her which crave expression in sensual passion and sensuous music. When she has realized all her possibilities as lover and as artist she is impelled to realize with similar completeness all the possibilities of the religious life. All phases of her career—the sexual, the musical, and the religious—are represented as consequences and manifestation of a profound *élan vital* over which she has no more control than a rose has over its thorns or the sap in its stem or the vermeil tints in its petals. The notion of a rational self-determination, of an intelligible object guiding a man like a star to ideal ends—this we are to believe is an illusion. We—that is the housemaids and artists with whom Mr. Moore is familiar—can do nothing but what is predetermined by the blind push in the darkness below and behind us of the unconscious energy which animates the flowers and the beasts of the field. To surrender wholly to the current of our natural impulses, to relish the undirected streaming of our sensations, to ask not whither we are drifting—this is the way to make the most of ourselves. This is Mr. Moore's philosophy of naturalism.

We must return now to record Mr. Moore's *liaison* with his native land. In 1894, three years after the date which Lady Gregory regards as the definitive awak-

ening of the Irish imagination, he still thought of Ireland as a wretched realm by him happily abandoned,
where no one did anything " except bring turf from the
bogs and say prayers." He was still writing realistic
English novels, explaining Ingres and Manet to the
British public, and enriching his midnights by the exchange of impressions and sensations with Mr. Arthur
Symons in the Temple. He had begun, however, to hear
with increasing interest rumors that a mysterious angel
was troubling the waters of the pale green Irish lake.
In Kiltartan Lady Gregory was collecting folklore and
by humble hearthsides learning the quaint old songs of
the peasants. In Dublin a pale, thin poet, William
Butler Yeats, was dreaming his way backward into the
dim legendary days of Cuchullin and Diarmuid. One
momentous night his fellow Templar, Edward Martyn,
Roman Catholic, celibate, amateur in letters, hinted in
his presence a desire for the ability to compose his plays
in Irish. Piquant suggestion! As at the touch of an
enchanted wand the closed cavern of Mr. Moore's youth
opened, and through his consciousness drifted vague
Irish memories faintly pungent like the smoke of a peat
fire trailing over a low roof of thatch. Along his nerves
he felt a premonitory tingling prophetic of a literary
movement. He recalled an ancient saw of Turgénieff's,
" Russia can do without any of us, but none of us can
do without Russia." What if he should go to Ireland
and look into the matter.

Behold him now in Dublin with bosom bared to every
wanton breeze, whiffing and sniffing the exciting air, and
eagerly wooing to be wooed. A little chilled by the want

of salvos greeting the return of the distinguished prodi-
gal and literary elder brother, he duly casts a superior
eye over the undertakings of the Celtic enthusiasts,
inspects the theatre, revises plays, passes judgment on
poems, and even delivers an occasional speech at a meeting of the Gaelic League. But something present in
them or lacking in him prevented their working in perfect unity of spirit. Lady Gregory feared that he
would break up the mold of Yeats's mind. He feared
that Yeats would break up the mold of his. A suspicion
on their side that he was not quite one of them and a
tinge of jealousy on his side, reinforced by a conviction
that they were " subalterns," widened the rift between
them. The fact is that in their divers fashions they
loved Ireland as their venerable mother. He, an international philanderer, despised Ireland, hoped that she
would make love to him, tell him her secrets, " enwomb "
his thoughts, and let him go. It were tedious to detail
the long-drawn-out aesthetic coquetry which terminated
in his final rupture with England and the formation of
the Irish *liaison.*

Perhaps the most interesting first fruits of this amour
were the volume of sketches entitled *The Untilled Field*
and the symbolistic novel called *The Lake;* I have frequently tried to read two of his plays but quite without
success. The first of these books is comparable in many
ways with the justly celebrated work which seems to have
inspired it, Turgénieff's *Memoirs of a Sportsman.* The
second is Mr. Moore's own very contemporaneous version of the unbinding of Prometheus—a piece of symbolism which summarizes whatever there has been of

" Messianic " character in the author's career.   The
protagonist of this strange fiction is Father Oliver, a
Roman Catholic priest, who dwells in a little cottage by
a pale green Irish lake.   He is fettered there by accident, custom, tradition; the vulture that consumes his
liver is the ordinary routine of life.   Through more
than three hundred pages Father Oliver hovers about
this lake, as vague, indeterminate, and purposeless as
the mist that gathers and dissolves upon its bosom.   At
last an imperative instinct quickens in his blood like that
which directs the mating and seasonal migrations of wild
geese; he steals down to the bank, strips to the skin,
hesitates for a moment, then plunges into the deep,
swims to the other shore, and flees away.   Thus the
naturalistic philosophy of *Esther Waters, Evelyn Innes,*
and *Sister Teresa* is " enwombed " in Ireland.   Father
Oliver is the spirit of man in modern times; he is the
spirit of the Irish Renaissance; he is, in short, the perfectly emancipated spirit of George Moore.

The first volume of *Hail and Farewell* sets forth in
full the considerations and reconsiderations which led
Mr. Moore in the days of the Boer War to make his
reconnoitering expedition into Ireland and to take counsel with the literary chiefs in Dublin concerning the
future of art.   The second volume treats of the trans-
ference from London to Dublin of his bag and baggage,
his Manets and his Monets, of his long and earnest
endeavor to become a concordant note in the Irish
Renaissance, and of his final tragic conviction that
Roman Catholicism is hostile to art, and that dogma
and literature are incompatible.   The anti-Roman thesis

gives a certain tenuous continuity, but it appears to be only incidental to the main purpose of the work. The third volume is a mélange of reminiscences, musings, and informal criticism.

The main purpose of *Hail and Farewell* may best be explained by reference to the nearest French equivalent. In the preface to the great *Journal des Goncourt,* brother Edmond says: " We have tried to make our contemporaries live again among posterity in life-like guise, to make them live again by the spirited stenography of a conversation, by the physiological surprise of a gesture, by those flashes of passion in which a personality is revealed, by that *je ne sais quoi* which renders the intensity of life—by noting, in short, a little of that fever which is peculiar to the heady life of Paris." On the 28th of May, 1857, the Goncourt firm entered this thought in their journal: *Un joli titre pour des souvenirs publiés de son vivant:* SOUVENIRS DE MA VIE MORTE. In 1906 Mr. Moore carried out the hint with his *Memoirs of My Dead Life.* Add to this his earlier *Confessions of a Young Man* and the Irish trilogy, and the scope of his design becomes apparent: he aspires to be the Goncourt of the English decadence—the Boswell of a literary generation.

It is hardly necessary to remark that the matter of his epos is distinctly inferior. In the French work we are confronted with the real leaders of the generation, the peers of France who received their inheritance from Hugo and Balzac: Flaubert with his life poisoned by remorse for once having coupled two genitives, Gautier exploding in reckless paradox, Sainte-Beuve adorned with earrings of cherries and overflowing in fine malicious chat, Taine disputatious, Scherer coldly circumspect, Renan silent but curious like a respectable woman at a supper of courtesans, Zola comparing notes with Edmond on the pain in his intestines—and much more of less and greater import. This gossip at the lowest is still, so to speak, gossip from the tents of the heroes encamped before Troy. When we turn to Mr. Moore's journals, we are not turning to the Goncourt of a corresponding literary generation in England. We are no longer at the center of the engagement. We are rather regaled with gossip from the camp-followers of the French movement. It is Symons, and Yeats, and Moore against Sainte-Beuve, and Flaubert, and Zola. On the whole, it is an English " Epigoniad " against a French " Iliad."

Yet as the Goncourt of English " side-issues " Mr. Moore has no rival. He deserves the credit for introducing into English a vivid personal narrative of literary contemporaries, which is almost a new literary form: what though all his heresies were long since anticipated by the guests at the Magny dinners. His work, furthermore, so far as the manner is concerned, possesses both the merits and defects of his French predecessors. He says apparently everything that he pleases without regard to the pleasure of living sensibilities. He mingles delightful bits of reverie with passages of studied grossness, pages of piquant dialogue, epigrams, criticisms of music, art, poetry, characters of the living and the dead. Most of his Irish fellow-workers he sketches with the detachment of a whimsical contempt.

Of " dear old " Edward Martyn, one of the lesser dramatists, he writes, with his usual felicity of suggestion:

> A great psychologist might have predicted his solitary
> life in two musty rooms above a tobacconist's shop, and his
> last habits, such as pouring his tea into a saucer, balancing
> the saucer on three fingers like an old woman in the country.
> Edward is all right if he gets his mass in the morning and
> his pipe in the evening. A great bulk of peasantry with a
> delicious strain of Palestrina running through it.

He never lets slip an opportunity to add a comic
stroke to his delineation of the character of Mr. Yeats:

> When the hooker that was taking Yeats over to Aran, or
> taking him back to Galway, was caught in a storm, Yeats fell
> upon his knees and tried to say a prayer; but the nearest
> thing to one he could think of was, " Of man's first dis-
> obedience and the fruit," and he spoke as much of " Para-
> dise Lost " as he could remember.

As usual, Mr. Moore writes with most particularity
and interest of himself. He makes it perfectly clear that
Ireland could never be anything to him but an exquisite
place to dream in: " Oh, how beautiful is the world of
vagrancy lost to us forever, AE.! " There is nothing
finer in all Moore's works than some of these occasional
passages of vague and drifting reverie:

> A numbness stole upon my eyelids, and I began to see the
> strange folk plainer, coming in procession to the altar,
> headed by the Druids. Ireland was wonderful then, . . .
> and, opening my eyes, Ireland seemed wonderful in the blue
> morning that hung above her, unfolding like a flower—a
> great blue convolvulus hanging above the green land, swell-

ing like the sea. My eyes closed again. It seemed to me
that I could dream for ever of the gods, and the mysteries
of Time, and the changes in the life of Man, of the listless
beauty of the sky above, fading imperceptibly as the hours
went by.

After a succession of these fine swan flights, it is
amusing to find Mr. Moore comparing himself with
Catholic Martyn, and wondering whether it would be
wise for him to exchange, " were it possible, a wine-
glass of intelligence for a rummer of temperament."
More to the point is the passage in which he seems to
reveal an awareness that his quarrel is not with Catholic
Ireland nor with Protestant England, but with the whole
spirit of Western civilization. His final words of self-
justification will remind the reader of Dowden's defence
of Shelley:

> The right of property holds good in all society; but in
> the West ethics invade the personal life in a manner un-
> known to the East, so much so that the Oriental stands
> agape at our folly, knowing well that every man brings
> different instincts and ideas into the world with them. The
> East says to the West, " You prate incessantly about
> monogamy—" A sudden thought darting across my mind
> left my sentence unfinished, and I asked myself what man-
> ner of man I was. . . . An extraordinarily clear and in-
> flexible moral sense rose up and confronted me, and looking
> down my past life, I was astonished to see how dependent
> my deeds had always been upon my ideas. *I had never been
> able to do anything that I thought wrong, and my conscience
> had inspired my books.*

However ill Mr. Moore has prospered in his endeavor
to domesticate in England this Franco-Turkish latitude

of conscience, it must be very satisfactory to him for his own part to look back over a perfectly impeccable past. We Occidentals know little of this inflexible rectitude of conduct.   It is at odds with the genius of our morals and of our literature.   Even our priests and holy men have not professed it; they have acknowledged their bad days of backsliding and shameful defeat.   For we of English race know ourselves to be men of blood and sin, emerging from the welter and conflict with blotted 'scutcheons to partial triumphs; and, at our final retrospect, the best of us are of Henry Fifth's mood:

> More will I do;
> Though all that I can do is nothing worth,
> Since that my penitence comes after all,
> Imploring pardon.

To put the whole matter on merely literary grounds, we resist Moore—though he is a pretty writer—to save Shakespeare, whom, on the whole, year in and year out, we prefer.   East is East, and West is West; and when Mr. Moore has drained that wine-glass of intelligence, he may have another flash of insight, in which he may perceive that it is not dogma and literature that are incompatible, but George Moore and an English tradition of a thousand years.

If one writes well enough, one may say anything one pleases.   A man who takes great pains with his style is likely in the long run to have a devoted following, and to get a hearing, even for his indiscretions and ineptitudes.   If he unites with his talent for dulcet utterance a certain instinct for " sex " and salacity and shocking middle-class sensibilities, he is pretty sure to become a celebrity, and he has a fair chance of becoming a classic, in his own lifetime. There is at present a strong demand for the sanction given to the discussion of questionable subjects by an unquestionable style. Mr. Moore knows how to meet that demand. Some people read him for his style, and some people read him for his subjects. And so one was not surprised to hear him hailed, not long ago, as the greatest master of English since Thackeray. His latest book, *The Brook Kerith*, is said by his admirers to exhibit him at his best. The best work of the " greatest master of English since Thackeray " should be an event of first-rate literary importance. It should, at least, bear " looking into."

It does. I have looked into it rather carefully and with curiosity sharpened by the fine things that have been said about it. An honest and benevolent critic ought, however, to indicate clearly from what point of view it will bear inspection. It will be a kindness to readers who wish to keep in touch with the really " great " living writers to say frankly what sort of readers will not be able to bear looking into it. The first sort are those who accept the traditional view of the Bible and the life of Jesus: to them *The Brook Kerith* can be nothing but an impudent and detestable profanation of the sanctuary. The second sort are those who, without accepting all the traditional views of the Bible and the life of Jesus, preserve a profound admiration and reverence for the founders of Christianity and for the poetic truth and beauty of the Scripture: to them *The Brook Kerith* can hardly fail to appear a licentious and ignoble travesty. There remain George Moore's followers, to whom every line of his is precious; and there remain those who can, in the case of a " great " living writer, put aside their own religious and literary predilections, and yield to their quite unholy curiosity to know what a man like George Moore can have to say about Jesus.

The book leaves no doubt that Mr. Moore has for many years done a good deal of—I will not say, of thinking. Mr. Moore does not think; he muses. That, for persons of musing temperament, is the charm of his later manner. He has then, I say, done a great deal of musing about his subject. For some reason, Jesus is a phenomenon that has disturbed his equanimity. The Beatitudes, the Crucifixion, the Resurrection have been obstacles to the equable flow of his naturalistic revery. The " cross," the " crown," " renunciation," " self-sacrifice," " redemption "—all these knotty ideas and symbols of our need of a spiritual life and of the means of attaining it have puzzled George Moore, have annoyed him, have almost forced him to think. But Mr. Moore does not like to think; it is contrary to the stream of his tendency. And why, he " mutters " to himself, should one do what one does not like? Why, he muses, should one go against the stream of one's tendency? Have not all great artists found themselves by following their tendency? There was Dégas, for example. . . . Christian tradition, however dwindled, runs counter to, and thwarts, one's instincts. Clearly, one cannot muse in comfort till one gets this Jesus out of one's system!

Novelists and dramatists of this generation have tried

various means to get the spiritual Jesus of the gospels
out of their systems.   Oscar Wilde exorcised the spiritual Jesus by repeating to himself that it was an exquisite Pre-Raphaelitish aesthete who walked in the Garden
of Gethsemane.   Others have accomplished the same end
by repeating to themselves that it was an anarchist, a
socialist, a humanitarian enthusiast.   George Moore
must have mused on these modern literary exorcisms till
be became aware that all methods have one common element ; any one who desires to rid himself of the obsession
of the spiritual Jesus has but to put his own natural
instinctive self in the place of Jesus.   The substitution
brings instant relief from the pressure upon the consciousness of an exacting alien force.   Thus, when Mr.
Moore has performed this substitution and has converted
Jesus of Nazareth into a sentimental Irish naturalist of
our own day, he is no longer troubled by the hallucina-
tion of a voice calling: " Follow me."   The voice says
now: " Follow your inclinations "—which, of course, is
precisely what he was " getting at."

Mr. Moore creates the Moore-ish Jesus of this curious
fiction untrammelled by the spirit or the letter of the
gospel narratives.   His Jesus does not die on the cross,
but is removed from it alive, and is slowly nursed back
to health in the house of Joseph of Arimathæa.   It is
shortly after the descent from the cross and during the
convalescence that the following conversation takes
place:

Joseph asked, not because he was interested in dog breed-
ing, but to make talk, if the puppies were mongrels.   Mon-

grels, Jesus repeated overlooking them; not altogether mongrels, three-quarter bred; the dog that begot them was a mongrel, half Syrian, half Thracian. I've seen worse dogs highly prized. Send the bitch to a dog of pure Thracian stock and thou'lt get some puppies that will be the sort that I used to seek.

This is not the most nor the least quotable of the innumerable passages by which our ingenious author gives to his narration a kind of sex-interest in which the gospel story is quite deficient. When the continuance of Jesus in Jerusalem becomes dangerous, Joseph sends him into the hills by the brook Kerith. There, among the ascetic Essenes, with whom he had lived before he went out to preach, he dwells as a shepherd for some twenty years, busily occupied in improving the stock by a judicious selection of rams, but finding occasion to muse from time to time on the events of the past—composing, so to speak, his *Memoirs of My Dead Life*. In these pastoral musings among the hills, he exhibits all George Moore's mental manners or mannerisms—picks up a definite theme, toys with it, strays from it, loses the thread, drifts off on the stream of revery, and perhaps eventually drifts back again. It is not to be wondered at that this somewhat languid form of mental activity brings him ultimately around to Mr. Moore's own " intellectual position." Here is a selection of his sayings and musings on pages 365 and 366:

Repentance changes nothing, it brings nothing unless grief peradventure. . . . I used, he said, to despise the air I breathed, and long for the airs of paradise, but what did these longings bring me?—grief. God bade us live on earth and we bring unhappiness upon ourselves by desiring heaven. Jesus stopped, and looking through the blue air of evening, he could see the shepherds eating their bread and garlic on the hillside. . . . His thoughts began again, flowing like a wind. . . . In the desert he had looked for God in the flowers that the sun called forth and in the clouds that the wind shepherded, and he had learnt to prize the earth and live content among his sheep, all things being the gift of God and his holy will. *He had not placed himself above the flowers and grasses of the earth, nor the sheep that fed upon them, nor above the men that fed upon the sheep.* . . . Rites and observances, all that comes under the name of religion, estranges us from God, he repeated. God is not here, nor there, but everywhere: in the flower, and in the star, and in the earth under foot. . . . But shall we gather the universal will into an image and call it God?—for by doing this do we not drift back to the starting place of all our misery? We again become the dupes of illusion and desire; God and his heaven are our old enemies in disguise. He who yields himself to God goes forth to persuade others to love God, and very soon his love of God impels him to violent ends and cruel deeds. It cannot be else, for *God is but desire;* and whosoever yields to desire falls into sin. To be without sin we must be without God. . . . Jesus stood before the door of the cenoby, . . . asking himself if any man had dared to ask himself *if God were not indeed the last uncleanliness of the mind.* (My italics: the "daring" of the question reminds one rather less of Jesus than of the talented poet-editor of the *Vaterland*.)

The foregoing passage gives us the positive or " constructive " message of the book. This soft, sentimental, pseudo-pantheism is no doubt really Mr. Moore's. When he expresses it, he speaks with as much sincerity as the chary gods have vouchsafed to him. It is when

he is steeped to the lips in a vague sweet sense that there
is no difference between him and a flower—it is in such
moments that he writes the " delicious " half-pages that
persuade even *schöne Seelen* that he is the greatest
master of English since Thackeray. It is when he is in
the grip of a vague sense that there is no difference between him and a sheep or, let us say, one of the Essene
rams which so much solicit his attention—it is in such
moments that he writes the sly half-pages which persuade some of us that he is not far from right: that
there is probably no very great difference between his
religion and that of the sheep. And so one comes back
to a sense that a religion which helps a man make the
distinction between himself and a flower has a certain
usefulness yet.

  Revenons à nos—let us return to Mr. Moore's Jesus.
His musing by the brook Kerith has a destructive tendency along with its benevolent sentimentality. He muses
slowly to the conclusion that his great mission was a
mistake; that a large part of his teaching was fanatical;
that his renunciation of the earthly life was perverse;
that his presentation of himself as the Messiah was im-
posture. Finally, in the assembly of the Essenes, he
confesses his sins. Conducted by a master-confessor,
the recital is rather prolix. Here is part of the confession:

  I fear to speak of the things I said at that time, but I
must speak of them. One man asked me before he left all
things to follow me if he might not bury his father first. I
answered, leave the dead to bury their dead, and to another
who said, my hand is at the plough, may I not drive it to the

headland, I answered: leave all things and follow me. My teaching grew more and more violent. It is not peace, I said, that I bring you, but a sword, and I come as a brand wherewith to set the world in flame. . . . It seems to me that in telling the story, brethren, I am doing but the work of God: *no man strays very far from the work that God has decreed to him.* But in the time I am telling I was so exalted by the many miracles which I had performed by the power of God or the power of a demon, I know not which, that I encouraged my disciples to speak of me as the son of David, though I knew myself to be the son of Joseph the carpenter; and when I rode into Jerusalem and the people strewed palms before me and called out, the son of David, and Joseph said to me, let them not call thee the son of David, I answered in my pride, if they did not call it forth the stones themselves would. . . . A day passed in great exaltation and hope, and one evening I took bread and broke it, saying that I was the bread of life that came down from heaven and that whosoever ate of it had everlasting life given to him. After saying these words a great disquiet fell upon me, and calling my disciples together I asked them to come to the garden of olives with me. And it was while asking God's forgiveness for my blasphemies that the emissaries and agents of the Priests came and took me prisoner.

The " great situation " in the book is the confrontation of Jesus with the apostle Paul. He staggers into the cenoby of the Essenes one night, full of the " glad tidings of the resurrection " which he has been preaching from Damascus to Jerusalem. He is present through part of the confession of Jesus, but imagines that he is listening to a madman, and is himself seized with a fit in the midst of the disclosure. Jesus makes several efforts later to persuade Paul that he is indeed the crucified Nazarene; but Paul departs utterly incredulous and unmoved, and goes on his way, proclaiming the risen Lord. Jesus had intended to return to Jerusalem, and to destroy his following by exploding his " legend." But having seen how Paul has set his heart on the resurrection idea, he hates to do it; he does not do it; he simply disappears, leaving Paul uncontradicted to preach his colossal error throughout the earth—" because," as one admiring reviewer has put it, " because in his gentleness he cannot give so much pain "!

I can think of but one passage in literature which equals this in its special quality. That is the passage in *Tristram Shandy* where Uncle Toby picks up the fly which has tormented him cruelly all dinnertime: " I'll not hurt thee, says my Uncle Toby, rising from his chair, and going across the room with the fly in his hand—I'll not hurt a hair of thy head:—go—says he, lifting up the sash, and opening his hand as he spoke to let it escape;—go, poor devil, get thee gone, why should I hurt thee?—This world surely is wide enough to hold both thee and me." If Jesus were the sentimentalist that Mr. Moore depicts him, one could imagine him tossing his Irish " apologist " out the window with the remark that Uncle Toby addressed to the fly.

We owe the same debt of attention to Mr. Moore that we should owe to a man who should push his boat into the river above Niagara Falls, ship his oars, and submit to the will of the waters; he would demonstrate the force and consequences of the current. Mr. Moore has shot the falls of naturalism. We were acquainted with its clear spring in the high mountain home, where Words-

worth, drinking, vowed himself " well pleased to recognize in nature and the language of the sense, the author
of his purest thoughts, the nurse, the guide, the
guardian of his heart, and soul of all his moral being."
We had seen Wordsworth's pleasant faith in the concurrence of nature with the moral ends of man elab-
orately clothed in the fiction of George Meredith's
Richard Feverel, specifically in the chapter entitled
" Nature Speaks."   We had seen in the work of
Thomas Hardy the sweet pantheistic illusion give way
to tragic insight into the actual relationship existing
between nature and society.   He, too, recognized in
nature a power that molds the characters and destinies
of men.   But it was not clear to him that an impulse
from a vernal wood would always send a Peter Bell to
church or an errant father to his child; it seemed quite
as likely that it would send a Jude to an Arabella or a
Tess to an Alec.   It appeared, in brief, to his vision
that this blind power which moves through all things,
though occasionally coinciding with human law, urges
men on to the fulfilment of its own tendencies, irrespective of the disasters which may consequently befall them
in that social order established and regulated by reason
and foresight.   Because, however, he is fully aware of
the resolute power perpetually conflicting with the incessant pressure of instinct, naturalism attains in him
to tragedy.   His grim symbol of nature and the morality
of society is Tess of the D'Urbervilles swinging on the
gallows.   After Hardy, to speak of the concurrence of
nature in the moral ends of man becomes impossible.
We have reached the fork in the road; we must turn to

the right with reason to guide us into the walled and steepled cities and the civil life of our kind, or turn to the left and trust to instinct.

Mr. Moore turned to the left. In a few strides he passed beyond good and evil into that wilderness where birds and cantatrices sing, where wild creatures conceive and aesthetes confess, where every creeping thing brings forth its young, and the simple servant girl, having given to the world a natural son, lives happy ever after in the consciousness that she has accomplished that whereunto she was sent. In this Arcadian world there is neither comedy nor tragedy; for there is neither passion nor joy, conflict nor climax, reconciliation nor catastrophe: there are only the flush and fading of sensual excitement, the vicissitudes of wind and weather, the progress of the seasons, and the cyclic changes of birth and death. Mr. Moore is right in regarding his life as more significant than any of his works. When a man of great talent has made his mind a courtesan to nature, the only tragedy that he can write is his confession. When a man has shaken off the bonds that united him with civil society, the only confession that he can make of significance to civil readers is that such emancipation is exile. What, then, does George Moore mean by telling us that beneath his frivolous mask is concealed a tragic actor?

VI

THE SKEPTICISM OF ANATOLE FRANCE

JULES LEMAÎTRE, one of the most delicately appreciative of French critics, thus defined for himself the charm
of Anatole France: " I feel the saturation of his work
with all its antecedents; I find in it the latest state of
the human consciousness."

His work thus accomplishes what Mona Lisa, according to Pater, accomplishes in art—" the summing up in
itself all modes of thought and life." One escapes in
his books from the shallow and savorless modernity of
contemporary literature. He is a cosmopolitan not
merely of the present year of grace; he was a citizen of
the world before the Christian era. A leisurely aristocrat, polished, imperturbable, he has strolled with ironic
smile among the neglected ruins of antiquity, and has
reanimated their fallen splendor. He has walked under
the plane trees without the city wall conversing with
Socrates and the Sophists on the reality of our ideas.
He has discussed Greek philosophy in the Tusculan
villa with Cicero, has sauntered over the Aventine chat-
ting with Horace, and has listened with bowed head
while Virgil read to the grief-stricken household his
divine praise of the young Marcellus. He observed the
strange star in the East, heard the stories of Lazarus
and Magdalen, and dined with Pilate, Procurator of

Judea. In the Egyptian desert he occupied a cell with
the Christian cenobites; in Alexandria he tasted the
last luxuries of the pagan world. He caught from the
catacombs the fervent murmur of prayer and the mysterious hymns of the martyrs. He saw with a regret-
ful smile nymphs and dryads and fauns at twilight
scurrying through country woodlands in terror of the
cathedral bell. A lover of masquerade, he has crept
into the cassock of mediæval monks, and gravely announced the performance of miracles, or discoursed
upon the lusts of the flesh and the pride of life, or whiled
away long hours on a settle in the cloister splitting theological hairs with the church fathers. Especially, has
he haunted the steps of the Brides of Christ, irresistibly
drawn by the allurement of their celestial roses, hoping,
perhaps, to catch a drop of the spilled milk of Paradise. And all this he has told, not as one passing fever-
ishly through successive stages of intellectual intoxication, but as one sitting at ease and leaning indolently
out from a casement in Elysium.

More fascinating than all this selected world-experi-
ence is the point of view of the narrator. He keeps us
wondering where he is. The detachment of M. France
is not that of Flaubert or of Maupassant. The realist
withdraws a little from his object to gain the proper
focus for his microscope. He is nevertheless savagely
absorbed in it. He means to bring it home to us, to
make us enter into it and feel it tingling in our five
senses. M. France, on the other hand, seeks in general
to tranquilize the senses. When I say this, I do not
forget the vein of cold salacity which runs through his

works. In presenting the simian proclivities of man he
maintains an air of smiling aloofness. He contemplates
the troubled face of the world through serene leagues of
motionless ether. He will report mundane affairs not
to the prurient ears of mortals, but to the gods of Epicurus who inhabit the quiet above the clouds and winds,
and feel from time to time a mild amusement in the
human spectacle. Passing beyond the flaming ramparts
of the world, he would enter the celestial hall where the
blithe Immortals revel, crying: O Shining Ones, let me,
a mortal, share your feast. I have withdrawn my heart
and hope from the miserable race of men. For they
come out of the darkness and struggle like beasts in the
brief light and go into the darkness again. All their
achievements are but as the excellencies of worms differing among one another. They are rent with a love more
cruel than the grave. They are burnt in the fire of their
own flesh. They are terrified by the shadows which they
cast upon eternity. But I—I have learned the secret
of your immortal calm. I have found that there is
peace for those who are content to perceive and not to
possess the world. I have learned to look upon the
labors of Hercules without an impulse to lift a finger,
upon the temptations of St. Anthony with no stirring
of the flesh, upon the crucifixion of the martyrs with
scarcely a throb of sympathetic pain. To the ego wisely
isolated from the contagious fevers of existence all these
things are but as the fierce vexation of a dream. Make
me, therefore, a place beside you, and I will tell you
tales of men, provoking supernal mirth.

If one rereads the works of M. France in the English

translation, one unconsciously associates each successive volume with the bland and laurelled old Epicurean stamped in gold upon the cover.   Even with the translator's note reminding us that the volume entitled *Jocasta and the Famished Cat* was his first venture in fiction, originally published in 1879, it is difficult to think of the author as a young writer, for already he is surveying his contemporaries in their keenest self-absorption with the cool detachment of an old resident in the ivory tower.   *Jocasta* appeared in the heyday of naturalism two years after *L'Assommoir*, and in its elements it is an ugly piece of bourgeois tragedy with a sentimental heroine hanging herself in a bathhouse with her nephew's necktie, loved by a young surgeon who analyzes his sensations and dissects the nervous system of frogs.   In the hands of almost any other writer of his generation this material would have taken shape as a depressing " human document " illustrative of a mechanical theory of life.   But M. France has never grimly adopted the mechanical theory of life; he has only played with it and amused himself with the spectacle of those who were in the grip of it.   " A delightfully novel basi. for composition," he seems to murmur to himself, " in this notion of scientifically dissecting the nervous system of frogs and heroines.   Let us see what can be made of it."   The air of artifice, of technical experimentation, removes, for my sense, the sting of actuality; so that the suicide of the modern heroine affects me less than a knife thrust in an old tale of Boccaccio.   It affects me rather like a demonstration in geometry or the last move in a game of chess.

Still, if this somber matter has left a bad taste in the mouth, one has only to turn the page and forget the sordid sorrows of Philistines in a gorgeous chronicle of the picturesque denizens of the Latin Quarter who foregathered at the sign of the Famished Cat. " No one who is sane affords me much amusement," quotes M. France with approval; and, as he sees it, all Bohemia wears motley. From the windows of the ivory tower he looks down upon the poetical enthusiast in his garret no less than upon the scientific enthusiast in his laboratory. Yet though he preserves here his attitude of aloofness, he portrays his troop of intoxicated originals with an incomparable zest in their idiosyncrasies, and with a mellowness of mirth that suggest an only half-extinguished sympathy. Labanne, the sculptor, who thinks he must read fifteen hundred volumes on the *pigmentum* of the black races and the geological formation of the Antilles before he can touch clay for his statue of Black Liberty, must occupy a warm place in his creator's learned heart. Indeed, the door of Labanne's studio, with its strange conflict of inscriptions carved and chalked by " various people," will seem to some readers almost to epitomize M. France's bewildering " criticism of life." These are some of the inscriptions:

" Woman is more bitter than death."
" Academicians are all bourgeois, Cabanel is a hairdresser's assistant."
" Laud we the womanly form, which still, as of old, uplifts
  Chants hieratic, in praise of the greatest of beauty's gifts.
                                        —Paul Dion."

" I have brought back the clean linen. Monday I will call for the dirty at the porter's lodge."

" Athens, ever venerable city, if thou hadst not existed, the world would not yet know the meaning of beauty."

" Labanne is a rat.   I don't care a damn for him.
                                        —Maria."

And there were many others on the door.

The career of Thaïs, a fair Alexandrian courtesan of the fourth century, offered unusual attractions to the feasting eye of the philosophic angel. No other writer has realized so completely—so *deliciously*, as a disciple of Renan would say—certain artistic possibilities in ecclesiastical history and the legends of saints and martyrs. With few exceptions, romances in English concerned with the lives of the early Christians are to any but juvenile readers extremely insipid. It must be admitted that an ulterior religious purpose seldom seems entirely favorable to the art of fiction. Cardinal Newman wrote his pallid and long-forgotten romances in a religious ascetic's revulsion from paganism and with an eye to furthering the cause of Rome. Kingsley, with a more virile art, wrote with a keen detestation of asceticism and with a special pleasure in barking at Newman. Anatole France, perhaps knowing as much about certain aspects of the saints as Newman, and certainly knowing as much about sinners as Kingsley, aspires to write of both like a philosophical angel, hovering a little above the earth, spectator of everything, participator in nothing. The belief and the unbelief of Gentile and Jew concern him not at all save as they offer to the aesthetic sense some new note of intensity, some unexploited

mingling of strangeness with beauty. It is difficult to
say whether he enters with more penetrating and illuminating curiosity into the life of the Alexandrian beauty
and her favorites set in the dazzling luxury of the wicked
city, or into the gaunt soul and body of the stylite
Paphnutius ringed by the tombs and the desert. The
picturesque qualities of both engage him, but from both
he preserves a complete spiritual detachment. In the end,
however, the mask slips a little from the observant angel,
and reveals the smile of the lurking cynic. It is made
perfectly clear that Thaïs turned toward heaven merely
from satiety of the flesh, and that Paphnutius turned
toward hell merely from satiety of the spirit—a conclusion sufficiently devoid of edification. There is not
one breath of genuine holiness in the book. Yet for
piquancy of attack, for malicious insight into the psychology of the anchorite, and for sheer brilliancy of representation there is nothing like this in English.

M. France is one of the innumerable champions of
intellectual emancipation who have compromised the
cause of liberty by their libertinism. He will pay his
penalty in the inevitable reaction. Inspired by a quite
righteous indignation against his subtle voluptuousness
and his moral impotence, various French critics [1] have
in recent years attempted to damage or to destroy his
reputation as a creative artist. His work, they tell us,
is deficient in originality; it is but a superlatively bril-

[1] See. for example, Giraud's *Maîtres de l'Heure*, Michaut's
Anatole France, and compare Guérard's *Five Masters of French
Romance*. An interesting review of recent critical literature
appears in an article by D. S. Blondheim in *Modern Philology*,
July, 1916.

liant *pastiche*. A writer whose work is saturated, as
M. Lemaître says, with everything that has preceded
it lays himself open to that sort of attack; and it must
be admitted that many of his volumes are very loosely
composed. Some of his books, nevertheless, will last as
long as men continue to read Lucian, Boccaccio, Rabe-
lais, Voltaire. *Sylvestre Bonnard* has already established itself as a student's classic. *At the Sign of the
Reine Pédauque* will probably never attain that honor—
and for " good and sufficient " reasons; but it is likely
to live without that aid. When you have turned the
last page, you will recognize that the work belongs on
the Index, you may think that it should be supplied with
an appendix like Don Juan's classics, you may pitch it
into the fire, chuckling like the delighted monastic
censors in the painting. But you know very well that
you cannot put an end to the abounding life that is in
Monsieur l'Abbé Jérôme Coignard and his reverent
pupil Tournebroche. With all their gross imperfec-
tions on their heads they are marked, like Tom Jones
and Falstaff, for immortality. The English parallels
are very inadequate. Tom Jones is only a spirited
young animal. Falstaff resembles the abbé in his girth,
his geniality, his drunkenness, his larceny, his carnality,
and his sentimentality; and yet, after all, Falstaff is
but an amiable brutal Englishman without culture or
philosophy other than that which we attribute nowadays to the man in the street. Jérôme Coignard par-
takes heartily of the common sinful humanity of Sir
John, but he includes, besides, within his ample sphere,
nearly everything that his creator finds to love, pity,

and deride in the civilization of the ancients, the Latin
Christianity filtered through the Middle Ages, and the
rationalism of the early eighteenth century. He is one
of the richly endowed rogues of whom one says, " Of
course he is an unspeakable rascal, yet you can't resist
him."

Ex-priest, ex-professor of eloquence in the college of
Beauvais, ex-librarian to the bishop of Séez, author of
a translation of Zozimus the Panipolitan, this wine-
drinking, wenching, mellow-hearted debauchee is, like
M. France himself, a follower at the same time of Epicurus and Saint Francis of Assisi. A child of the " en-
lightenment " before the Encyclopædists and a disciple
of Descartes, he keeps his religion and his philosophy in
water-tight compartments : " Jacques Tournebroche, my
son, be mindful never to put faith in absurdities, but to
bring everything to the test of reason save in the matter
of our holy religion." A student of theology, he is
deeply read in the Fathers, and when he is in the vein,
can be unctuous, devout, and seriously concerned for the
salvation of his soul. He is also a classical scholar
versed in the most recondite Grecian and Roman authors,
and his rich table-talk is redolent of a charming erudi-
tion ; but, when he is buried in a library and weary of
labor and devotion, he does not hesitate to indulge his
powerful sensuality in fare fitter for Trimalchio's feast
than for the provender of a man of God. Escaping
with stolen diamonds and some bottles of white wine
from a drunken brawl in which he has stabbed a man,
the good abbé is delayed on the Lyons road by the wreck-
ing of his coach, overtaken by his pursuers at nightfall,

and mortally wounded. Yet he lives long enough to make a beautiful repentance, obtaining salvation in the moment of death, and he expires in a pleasant odor of sanctity, not a little consoled by the fact that, as he had been struck down by a Jew, he " perished a victim to a descendant of the executioners of Christ."

M. France has given us his personal commentary on the abbé in a pleasant study of thirty-five pages prefixed to the companion volume, *Les Opinions de M. Jérôme Coignard*, published in the same year, 1893, with the *Reine Pédauque*. In 1909 he returned to the theme with *Les Contes de Jacques Tournebroche*. I mention these facts because, in the two or three pages of general appreciation with which Mr. W. J. Locke introduces the English translation, he does not mention them. After due reflection I cannot guess why Mr. Locke was asked to write this preface, unless it was because he is the author of a popular book called *The Beloved Vagabond*. If my conjecture is correct, he has neglected a very pretty opportunity to acknowledge a debt and to discourse on the differences between the spirit of English and French fiction. The relation between *At the Sign of the Reine Pédauque* and *The Beloved Vagabond* is interesting. That Mr. Locke has borrowed in some fashion the happy invention of Coignard and Tournebroche—*cela saute aux yeux*. He sets out, just as M. France does, with the adoption of a clever boy, engaged in a menial occupation, by a very learned, very dirty, very benevolent vagabond of philosophical habit; and the boy in each case writes the memoirs of the alliance. But the two authors walk only a short way together.

Mr. Locke's tale is conceived in English sentiment; his philosopher conceals beneath his soiled shirt a deathless romantic passion. M. France's tale is conceived in philosophical irony and Gallic cynicism; beneath all his classical and Christian culture, M. Jérôme Coignard is a sensualist, pure and simple—or, more strictly speaking, impure and complex. Mr. Locke would persuade us that man is a flower that at heart smells sweet though it blossoms in the dust. M. France, on the contrary, would have us believe that man is an " obscure and evil fly " remarkably imprisoned in the amber of his ideals.

When M. France, after forty years of philosophical romancing in the garden of Epicurus, published his *Vie de Jeanne d'Arc*, the professional historians were shocked and the Epicureans were perplexed. It did not seem quite respectful to the Muse of History, for the author of *Le Lys Rouge* to present her with the life of the virgin of Domrémy. On the other hand, it appeared out of character for the author of M. Jérôme Coignard to take the scholarly ideal so seriously. To most of his followers his perilous charm had been that he always seemed to say—Mr. George Santayana has said it, too, in three lines of a seductive sonnet:

> The crown of olive let another wear;
> It is my crown to mock the runner's heat
> With gentle wonder and with laughter sweet.

Nor was it clear what garland a novice of over threescore could hope to win in the trite and well-gleaned field of history where he made his début. To be sure, some critics tried to show that this work did not really represent a new departure in M. France's development; for, they said, even in his romances he had been an historian, as even in his history he had been a romancer. Both views are partly right; the history of Jeanne d'Arc was, in a sense, only the latest in a long series of naturalistic and iconoclastic saints' lives. But there was a difference. How explain the lengthy preface discussing predecessors, theories of history, original documents? M. France had sent his fine Ariel often enough among ancient libraries, but had never allowed him to appear in the sunlight with dust on his wings. What conviction, slowly formulating, had brought this volant, elusive spirit, this mocking beguiler of an empty day into step with his sober contemporaries? Let us not attempt to discover, said M. Achille Luchaire, reviewing the first volume of the work, *ne cherchons pas à pénétrer le mystère de cette évolution.*

M. France has something of Prosper Mérimée's repugnance to being divined. On the heels of Jeanne d'Arc, as if anxious to complicate the chart of his evolution, he sends a satirical afterpiece, *L'Ile des Pingouins,* which dissipates in peals of derisive laughter any notion that its author has joined the modern historians. This, too, is a history prefaced by a critical account of sources; but, though shorter, it is much more comprehensive than its forerunner. It is an abridgment of all history that has been or shall be, under the form of a veiled comic history of France. " In spite of the apparent diversity of the amusements which seem to attract me," begins the preface in the old ironical vein, " my life has only one object. It is wholly bent toward the

accomplishment of one great design. I am writing the
history of the Penguins." In the search for the buried
monuments of this people, continues the author, " I have
excavated by the seashore an unviolated tumulus; I
found in it, *according to custom,* stone axes, swords of
bronze, Roman coins, and a twenty-sous piece with the
head of Louis-Philippe I, King of the French."

Embarrassed by difficulties attendant on the interpretation of conflicting evidence, the historian called in
counsel several eminent archaeologists and palaeograph-
ers:—" They looked at me with a smile of pity which
seemed to say: ' Do we write history? Do we attempt
to extract from a text, from a document the least scrap
of life or truth? We publish texts pure and simple.
We stick to the letter. The letter alone is appreciable
and definite. The spirit is not; ideas are crotchets.
One must be very presumptuous to write history; one
must have imagination.' " A surviving historian of the
old school was more encouraging—" Why take the
trouble to compose a history when you have only to
copy the standard works, as every one does. . . . One
word more. If you wish your book to be welcomed, neglect no opportunity to extol the virtues upon which
societies are based: devotion to riches, pious sentiments,
and especially the resignation of the poor, which is the
foundation of order. Assert, sir, that the origins of
property, nobility, and gendarmery will be treated in
your history with all the respect which these institutions
merit. Have it understood that you admit the supernatural when it appears. On that condition you will
succeed in good company."—" I have meditated these

judicious observations," says M. France demurely, " and
have paid good heed to them."

The narrative accordingly begins with the apostolic
calling of Saint Maël, and his wonderful conversions, his
wide wanderings, and finally his voyage in a miraculous
stone trough over the turbulent Northern Sea to an
undiscovered island. After a detour of the place, the
holy man, somewhat advanced in age and understanding,
comes upon a circle of penguins. Mistaking them for
a primitive heathen people, Saint Maël explains to them
successively Adoption, Rebirth, Regeneration, and Illumination, and then in three days and three nights bap-
tizes them all. " When the baptism of the penguins was
known in Heaven," proceeds the historian with the suave
gravity which heightens the effect of his daring, " it
caused there neither joy nor sorrow, but extreme surprise. The Lord himself was embarrassed. He called
an assembly of scholars and theologians and asked them
if they considered the baptism valid." As a result of a
long, hot debate, participated in by St. Patrick and
Saint Catherine, Saint Augustine and Saint Antony,
Tertullian, Orosius, and Saint Gregory of Nazianzen,
with interposed questions and objections by the Lord, it
was decided that the penguins must be changed into men.
And it was done.

Thus does M. France admit the supernatural, when
it appears! Since Lucian set the infernal gods to quarreling over the ferry hire in Hades, dramatized the loves
of the Olympians, and represented Zeus, when Timon
began to rail, as inquiring casually of Hermes what
dirty fellow was bawling from Attica beside Hymettus,

no one, perhaps, has dealt so unabashedly with the reigning dynasty of the Heavenly Ones.   A late unpersecuted Voltaire—tolerance has made a long march since the eighteenth century—he would gently laugh Jehovah out of Paradise. *Rien n'est plus lâche,* says Pascal, *que de faire le brave contre Dieu.*   True, one can fancy Anatole France replying, but see: The walls of chrysoprase, the solemn temples of the twelve-gated city are fast dissolving like an insubstantial pageant of the air.   Is it not better to smile than to weep?

With similar fidelity to the instructions of his adviser against disparaging sacred institutions, M. France describes the origins of " property, nobility, and gendarmery."   Shortly after the baptism and transformation of the penguins, they begin to clothe themselves, inclose land, and fight.   One brains his neighbor with a club; another furious fellow fixes his teeth in the nose of his prostrate adversary; a third brays the head of a woman under an enormous stone.   Saint Maël is horrified, but he is assured by a religious brother of wider experience that the penguins are accomplishing the most august of functions—" they are creating law; they are founding property; they are establishing the principles of civilization."   All this reminds one of the *Social Contract* and the famous *Discourses* of Rousseau, but it is to be remembered that in the state of nature the penguins are feathered bipeds.   No golden age glimmers for Anatole France behind the age of blood.   Indeed, in *Jérôme Coignard* he has subjected the revolutionary illusions to the most penetrating criticism: " If one is going to take a hand in governing men," he declares,

" one must not forget that they are bad monkeys." The history of the penguin nation is the history of half-intelligent beasts—the history of Yahoos and Houyhnhnms.   At this point, I cannot forbear quoting the brief, mordant sketch of " Draco the Great," a hero of the Middle Ages :

> He carried fire indifferently over the territory of the enemy and his own domain.   And he was wont to say, to explain his conduct: " War without burning is like tripe without mustard; it is insipid."   His justice was rigorous. When the peasants whom he had taken prisoners could not pay their ransom, he had them hanged on a tree, and if any unfortunate woman came to beg mercy on her penniless husband, he dragged her by the hair at the tail of his horse. He lived like a soldier, free from all effeminacy *(Il vêcut en soldat, sans molesse)*.   It is a pleasure to acknowledge that his morals were pure.

Something in that reminds one at the same time of Swift and of Tacitus.   If the style is indeed the man himself, there is a tincture of iron in the blood of this Epicure.

There is much piquancy in the contemptuous account of *Les Temps Modernes*, but one feels the author's point most sharply in the exultant pessimism of his vision of the future.   The notion that there is a grim limit set to the evolution of life on our planet has long been dear to the heart of M. France.   Long ago he prophetically buried the last desperate relic of our race in the frozen rind of the sunless world.   But here he has worked out more fully the stages by which the human tragedy is to decline to the ultimate catastrophe.

Before the somewhat remote Last Day there are to be
a number of false or temporary endings precipitated by
forces at work within the social organism.   M. France
seems now to have turned his back upon the socialistic
hope which he courted a few years ago.   To the central-
izing tendency of wealth no effective check can be imposed; in the long run, it is as irresistible as gravitation,
the rising of sap in forests, the swing of planets in their
orbits.   But at certain periods when the remorseless
oppression of capitalists brings the lower orders to the
verge of extinction, they will gain for themselves a
dreary breathing space with dynamite.   They will level
all populous cities to the dust and incinerate the painfully acquired material and intellectual riches of civilization.   For a little while the exhausted survivors will
rest, and gasping in dismal anarchy recover their animal
strength.   Then the old blind urge of life will begin
anew; step by step poor posterity will fight its way up
the long ascent again; once more the many-storied cities
will hum, and lean anaemic millionaires, Pharoahs half-
mummified, lord it over the Egyptian millions laying the
bricks for their mausoleums.   And so the old wheel of
life will turn round and round in concentric circles, ever
shortening its diameter, till, at last it vanishes in a
point, and the barren globe freed of its feverish animal-
cules journeys on through the void!

   " It is the duty of every thinker who has formed an
idea of the world," said M. France in one of his essays
on contemporary literature, " to express that idea,
whatever it may be." If the last chapters of *L'Ile des
Pingouins* were a faithful transcript of his sense of the

facts of life crowding in upon the sensitive consciousness, we should have deeply to commiserate the author.
But the pessimism of M. France is partly polemical.
" The spiritualist," Emerson tells us, " finds himself
driven to express his faith in a series of skepticisms."
M. France began life as a devout humanist, forming his
taste and his style on the noblest literature of Greece
and Rome. In early manhood, however, he felt powerfully the new hope and enthusiasm of the early followers
of Darwin. To the young men of his generation, it was
a fresh, firmly-founded revolutionary gospel. But as the
century wore on, the scientific millennium receded into
the infinitely remote future. To believe in it demanded
as pure an exercise of faith as to believe in the New
Jerusalem. M. France's faith was unequal to the task.
What faith remained in him reverted to his early humanism. Meantime the unreflecting mass of humanity had
caught the fanatic fervor of the scientific dream, and
had left humanism far in the rear. When M. France
returned to the temples of his gods he found them empty
of worshipers. And so, like most humanists to-day, he
is a disheartened humanist. He would, perhaps, have
spoken seriously of his faith if he could have found
serious listeners. It is rather dreary to praise Pallas
Athene in perfect solitude. It is more diverting to steal
into the camp of the victors, and mock their cause and
insinuate horrible doubt into every heart. Yet by a
happy law of the universe only the potential philanthro-
pist can be misanthropic. The Olympian detachment
of M. France is illusory. Without a place to stand on,
a man can no more despise his fellows than Archimedes

could lift the world. So long as M. France despises us, we need not despair; the earth beneath his scornful feet is a part of the common heritage.

I find a still more serious flaw in the would-be seamless garment of M. France's skepticism. He has often assured us that the skeptic is a good citizen, because, uncertain of all things, he is the least radical of men. But the salt of the right skeptic is the love of truth. Whatever enters his head he reports freely, as one holding a commission to act as the disinterested intelligence of mankind, surveying the past and present and spying out the future. That salt was in the virile fiber of Montaigne sitting in his tower in Perigord, cupboarding the choice viands of the ancients and portraying with unflinching hand the manners and mind of the man he knew best. But Anatole France—does he candidly attempt to represent the world as it appears? Does he love the truth and search for the truth above all else? As it seems to me he loves above all else the luxury of philosophic despair. He is a kind of refined, philosophical sentimentalist. With the assiduity of the Graveyard Poets, he cultivates and cherishes those truths, or seeming truths, which make for melancholy. We hear every day: This is the truth; we must face it. The fact is we may usually turn our backs upon it, and it is often the part of wisdom to do so. There may be a more wholesome truth at the opposite point of the compass. It is true that when a good man dies he rots like a rascal. It is also true that he lives a fragrant life in the memory of his friends. To embrace the latter truth strengthens the heart; but a certain kind of sentimentalist always embraces the worm that inherits the shroud. It is the truth; we must face it. But no man can face all truth. We judge a man's wisdom by his power of making intimates of those truths which give channel and speed to the languid, diffusive drift of his days. M. France has sought through all the world for the truths inducing in the perceiver a pensive and helpless sadness. M. France is too much concerned about the misery of the last man. If the good die young, as there is some warrant for believing, the last man will deserve hanging.

The skepticism of M. France is largely a literary pose. It is his justification for making capital of unspeakable things. It is his justification for unlimited intellectual self-indulgence. For a good skeptic he knows altogether too much about the future. When a man's philosophy has carried him to the point where several million years of civilization are as to-morrow, are as nothing, to him, it is a pity that it should not go a step further to the point where space vanishes and time expires and the illusive ages evaporate into the eternity of the everlasting Now. For a good skeptic he is altogether too sure that the world has exhausted its possibilities. He holds, indeed, that we live in a bright-flowing mist of days and nights, of sleeping and waking dreams. But he does not hold this belief with strength enough to be dumb and astonished at thought of the germs of new orders of ideas now forming in society or slumbering as yet unstirred in the unused mind of the world. He does not recognize as frankly as a skeptic should how plastic is the eternal flux under the creative energy of the desire of man, who had only

to say, " Let the flux be peopled with demons and with
seraphim," and it was.   Only the new-born babe enjoys,
however, that purity of uncertainty to which M. France
pretends.   And as soon as the babe first sniffs the vital
air, it is a judge as well as an observer.   It discovers at
once that for the present at least some things are good
and beautiful, and others terrible and necessary.

VII

THE EXOTICISM OF JOHN SYNGE

John Synge was dead before he was celebrated, and even his posthumous fame was curiously impersonal. If you asked any man that you met what he thought of the *Playboy of the Western World*, the chances were in favor of an interested response on the freshness of the Irish actors, the stupidity of the noisy objectors in the audience, or the hilarious and unexpected beauty of the piece. But if in your encounter with the ordinary play-goer you led out with the question, " What do you think of John Synge? ", the chances were even that you would be met with the query, " Who is he? " Even to many who have written about his plays, his personality seems to be as indistinct as that of the author of *The Book of the Dun Cow;* and the inferences which they have drawn from his words recall Mr. Archer's preconception of the invalid Stevenson as a happy athlete. From a half-dozen reviews, English and American, one gathers the impression that *The Playboy* is an " intensely national Irish play," that the author is notable for " freshness of outlook and spontaneity of expression," " depth of ardent sympathy " and " tender charity," that he has " experienced the rich joy found only in what is superb and wild in reality," and, finally, that in his presence " somehow criticism becomes meaningless; it is enough

to share his vision and his joy." All these phrases
indicate what some one has called a positive genius for
hitting the wrong nail on the head. All this reminds
one of what the curate in the Aran Islands said to Synge
on finding him one Sunday morning loafing outside his
cottage door. "Tell me," inquired the curate, "did
you read your Bible this morning?" Synge replied in
the negative. "Well, begob, Mr. Synge," said the
good man, "if you ever go to heaven, you'll have a good
laugh at us."

This misconception of the man is closely related to
the still persistent misconception of the literary movement with which he was associated. Apparently the
"vulgar error" will not down, which holds that the
so-called Irish Renaissance is essentially a folk movement—that the new literature is a spontaneous burgeon-
ing of the ancient and wellnigh extinct Celtic crabtree,
stirred at his roots by Mr. Douglas Hyde and a generation of peasant children reading popular poetry in the
original Gaelic. The more deeply one looks into the
matter the more firmly one is convinced that the historical, Catholic, England-hating Ireland, which finds
voice in a number of the lesser playwrights of the Dublin
group, is producing little of consequence to the outside
world. Wherever new blossoms have appeared and fruit
has prospered there have been cross-fertilization and the
skilful grafting of exotics in the hands of a little band
of learned experimenters held together by the fine tact
of Lady Gregory and the unflagging enthusiasm of Mr.
W. B. Yeats. The informing spirit and quickening
power have drifted in on all the winds of heaven—from

England, Norway, Germany, Russia, and France, and
there have been innumerable insets from the plantations
of Blake and Ibsen and Hauptman and Tolstoy and
Maeterlinck. As any disciple of D'Arbois de Jubainville
or of Kuno Meyer will tell you with some disdain, the
animating spirit of this new poetry that walks the world
is not the spirit of the ancient Irish bards. As any
intelligent observer should be able to perceive, it is the
spirit of an entirely contemporary, an entirely modern
romanticism, which happens, to borrow Mr. George
Moore's word, to have "enwombed itself" in Ireland,
but which might with almost equal facility enwomb itself
in China or Persia; just as the eighteenth century melancholy and unrest which enwombed itself in Macpherson's Ossian later reappeared in the Werther of Goethe
and the René of Chateaubriand.

Now though the relation of men like Mr. Yeats and
Mr. Moore to general European romanticism and naturalism is for the most part obvious and unconcealed,
Synge seems at first glance to stand apart from them
and from every one else. For special reasons those
who knew him best have not been unwilling to maintain
him   his isolation. He was the man that Mr. Yeats
had prophesied in the beginning, the proof of all his
theories, the realization of his dreams—the indigenous
Irish poet inspired by close contact with the ancient
peasantry to utter the deep passion of the people in
the strong fresh speech of the folk. He was like the
author of the Cuchulin story; he was like Homer. For,
as Mr. Yeats said, the idea of the Irish Renaissance is:
" the epic interpreted through the peasant, the peasant

interpreted through the epic." He cared nothing for
recent books; he had no relation to the decadent writers
of France; " if he was influenced by the French writers,
they were of the pre-Molière period ":—thus Mr. Yeats.
And Mr. Moore tells us with his customary malice that
when Yeats first heard *The Shadow of the Glen*, he cried,
" Euripides! "; and when he heard the *Riders to the Sea,*
he cried, " Aeschylus! " Very similar to Mr. Yeats's
was the critical feeling of the young Werther when he
carried in one pocket the songs of the divine Homer
and in the other the songs of the divine Macpherson—
equally divine and, in the fall of the year, far more sympathetic. Voltaire malignantly pointed out that these
ancient Celtic lays contained certain plagiarisms from
Solomon and Milton, and unfortunately those who have
insisted on the French antecedents of Synge have not
always been free from a malicious desire to damage his
reputation as a poet and especially as a representative
of Ireland. In consequence of various non-literary
forces there has been rather a partisan than a critical
division of opinion. On the one hand, we are told that
he owes everything to the French decadents; on the
other, that his work came straight from the heart of
Erin. On the one hand it is argued that he was only a
clever craftsman; on the other, that he stands by his
absolute achievement only a little lower than Shakespeare. While these parties are reconciling their differences, it may be worth while to inquire in an entirely
dispassionate way, with Synge's collected works before
us, what manner of man he was.

There are before me five portraits of Synge, each one

of which suggests under scrutiny one aspect of his somewhat elusive character. One, a grotesque sketch by
Mr. J. B. Yeats, shows us a hatted figure with back
turned and shoulders hunched. If you look closely, you
will see that it is " Synge at rehearsal." But if you
trust your first impression, you will say that it is a
dilapidated tramp gazing at the stars. A second portrait in the collective edition has a strikingly elvish or
faunish look—half timidity and half mischief. A third
presents the likeness of the literary Bohemian—mous-
tache, chin-tuft, and general effect call up a favorite
pose of R. L. Stevenson. The fourth, a set piece in
profile against a curtain, faintly reminds one of a similar
study of Walter Pater with eyes fixed in aesthetic contemplation. The impressive features of the physiog-
nomy exhibited in Mr. Howe's book are the brooding
impenetrable eyes—eyes filled with dreams and shadowed with pain and sadness. Now what we know of
Synge's life makes it not wholly fanciful to read in these
faces a brief abstract of his personality with his vagrant
yearnings, his homeless laughter, his facility in disguises,
his love of the picturesque and strange, and his deep-
seated melancholy and despair.

If a tramp be defined as a man with an obscure past,
without home or family or visible means of support,
drifting unaccountably from place to place, Synge was
for a considerable period of his life—and that the formative period—a tramp. We know that he was born at
Rathfarnham, near Dublin, in 1871, and that he passed
through Trinity College. Then the door is almost
closed upon his occupations till 1898–9, when he was

called from abroad to take part in the new movement in
Ireland.   Yet we are permitted to catch one significant
glimpse of a poverty-stricken, silent, rather morose
young man in ill health, who has left his native land and
is apparently seeking to escape from his memories in
aimless wanderings among alien people and alien modes
of thought.   His first wayfaring was in Germany, where
Heine was perhaps the will-o'-the-wisp to his feet; but
all roads lead the literary vagabond ultimately to Paris,
and when he had made his pilgrimages, he brought up
in the Latin Quarter. ' Before I met him,' says Mr.
Yeats, ' he had wandered over much of Europe, listening
to stories in the Black Forest, making friends with
servants and with poor people, and this from no aesthetic interest, for he had gathered no statistics, had
no money to give, and *cared nothing for the wrongs* of
the poor, being content to pay for the pleasure of eye
and ear with a tune upon the fiddle.'

Synge's transformation from a tramp into an Irishman of letters his sponsors represent to us as a kind of
modern miracle.   But they can preserve this air of
mystery only by insisting that the return to Ireland
meant an abrupt break and a fresh beginning rather
than the natural evolution of his career—only, in short,
by maintaining that what is clearly illuminating is wholly
irrelevant.   Now about 1895 Synge installed himself
in solitary lodgings in Paris and undertook to prepare
himself to be a ' critic of French literature from the
French point of view.'   At this point our authorities
diverge, and Mr. Yeats executes a bit of skilful and
characteristic legerdemain.   He lifts the curtain in

the garret of the Latin Quarter some four years later and discovers the author of two or three poor poems studying the works of Racine. George Moore, on the other hand, says explicitly that Synge was writing indifferent impressionistic criticisms of Lemaître and Anatole France. There is no necessary conflict between these two reports, but there is a noticeable difference of emphasis. Between Synge and Racine I should never attempt to establish any affinity. But between Anatole France and Synge?—that is quite another matter. For the discreet discoverer of the new poet admits that he found Synge ' full of that kind of morbidity that has its root in too much brooding over methods of expression, and ways of looking upon life which come, not out of life but out of literature.' Was that Mr. Yeats's covert way of confessing that Synge was steeped in Anatole France? This, at any rate, can be established: Synge's point of view in comedy is almost identical with that of Anatole France. Despite the Frenchman's vastly greater range of culture, the two men are absolutely at one in their aloof, pyrrhonic irony and their homeless laughter—the laughter of men who have wandered all the highways of the world and have found no abiding city.

Mr. Yeats, who is crammed with convictions and constitutionally incapable of understanding this desperate and smiling skepticism—no one, I think, asserts that Synge acquired his humor from the Dublin singers—Mr. Yeats gives a puzzled account of Synge's ideas which unintentionally confirms our conjecture. Synge had, he tells us, ' no obvious ideal '; he seemed ' unfitted to think

a political thought '; he looked on Catholic and Protestant alike with amused indifference; all that comes
down to us from education, and all the earnest conten-
tions of the day excited his irony; ' so far as casual eye
could see,' he had ' little personal will.' This description of moral and volitional prostration could be applied
with hardly an alteration to Anatole France. And it
should help put to rest the legend of the joyous Synge,
bounding over the hills with the glad, wild life of the
unspoiled barbarian. The creators of the legend of the
joyous Synge have made much of one or two pages in his
island notebook which reveal high nervous excitement
induced by wild storms. I am impressed by the equally
frequent and important symptoms of weariness and low
vitality. His attitude toward death is too friendly. He
cannot make a dangerous passage over rough seas without hinting at his readiness to sink out of sight beneath
the gray waters. He undergoes a surgical operation and
describes his sensations in a gruesome little narrative
called *Under Ether.* While his nurses suppose him to
be making ready for the ordeal, he slips quietly down
into the operating room and examines the instruments.
The consternation of the attendants when they come
upon him there alone is as if they had discovered a condemned man on the morning of his execution secretly
fingering the ax. In the grim humor of this recital there
is something more than manly resolution in the face of
death.

Synge's verse is what we should expect of a rather
despondent young Bohemian, unsure of himself, and
seeking among other poets food and forms for his mel-

ancholy. I wish to tarry for a moment upon his small collection of poems and translations, partly because, though little known, it is intrinsically interesting, and partly because it reveals so clearly on a small scale the nature of his literary talent. The poems are due to the influence of various masters—to Burns, Wordsworth, Swinburne, and notably, to that fascinating outlaw, Maistre François Villon. In about one-third of them he sings of death, and in nearly all of them there is a distinguishable echo of some earlier singer.

In " Queene," for example, one hears an echo of Villon's " Ballade of Dead Ladies ":

> Seven dog-days we let pass
> Naming queens in Glenmacnass,
> All the rare and royal names
> Wormy sheepskin yet retains:
> Etain, Helen, Maeve, and Fand,
> Golden Deirdre's tender hand.
>
> .   .   .   .
>
> These are rotten, so you're the Queen
> Of all are living, or have been

In the poem, " To the Oaks of Glencree," again, we notice how Maistre Villon helps him shape and round out the first pure impulse of lyric exultation:

> My arms are round you, and I lean
>   Against you, while the lark
> Sings over us, and golden lights and green
>   Shadows are on your bark.
> There'll come a season when you'll stretch
>   Black boards to cover me;
> Then in Mount Jerome I will lie, poor wretch,
>   With worms eternally.

The startling and paradoxical fact about this collection is that the original poems constantly remind us of some one else; the translations alone seem unmistakably Synge's. The original poems have the merits of skilful literary imitation. They might have been written, however, by Stevenson or Lang or by Mr. Edmund Gosse, or by half a dozen other cultivators of old French verse. But neither Mr. Gosse nor Lang nor Stevenson could have written a line of the poem that follows:

Are you bearing in mind that time when there was a fine look out of your eyes, and yourself, pleased and thoughtful, were going up the boundaries that are set to childhood? That time the quiet rooms, and the lanes about the house, would be noisy with your songs that were never tired out; the time you'd be sitting down with some work that is right for women, and well pleased with the hazy coming times you were looking out at in your own mind.

May was sweet that year, and it was pleasantly you'd pass the day.

Then I'd leave my pleasant studies, and the paper I had smudged with ink where I would be spending the better part of the day, and cock my ears from the sill of my father's house, till I'd hear the sound of your voice, or of your loom when your hands moved quickly. It's then I would set store of the quiet sky and the lanes and little places, and the sea was far away in one place and the high hills in another.

There is no tongue will tell till the judgment what I feel in myself those times.

Here are all the peculiar marks of Synge himself—the irresistibly quaint idiom, the drifting rhythm, the loose sentence structure, thought thrown out after thought, as it were, without premeditation, and blos-

soming from phrase to phrase, the window opened upon
a mist of vague and limitless emotion, the poignant and
adorable Celtic wistfulness; while, as a matter of fact,
these lines are a tolerably close translation of Leopardi's
" Silva." We are here in the presence of a pure miracle
of that style which is Synge's special creation, and
which distinguishes him not merely from Leopardi, but
also from all his Anglo-Irish contemporaries. With all
its apparent spontaneity, his style is as patiently and
cunningly wrought out as the style of Walter Pater—
wrought of a scrupulously select vocabulary, idiom, and
images, with an exacting ear controlling the cadence
and shepherding the roving and dreamy phrases. With
the aid of this perfected instrument he is able to appropriate and seal as his own poem from authors as diverse
as Petrarch and Walter von der Vogelweide, Leopardi
and Villon. This fact, taken together with his depend-
ence in the original poems, tends to justify a search
beneath the surface of his other work for alien forces
secretly shaping his emotions and determining his
forms.

The orthodox method of " explaining " Synge is to
ignore the poems and translations and point to the
volume on the Aran Islands. This is the record, we are
told, of Synge's literary salvation; here lies the key to
the dramas. In other words, we are asked to believe
that Mr. Yeats's theory of poetry has been demonstrated. A stranded Irishman living gloomily in Paris
without ideal and almost without ideas is sent to a little
group of lonely islands to the southwest of Galway,
inhabited by stolid fisher-folk in a very backward state

of culture.   He spends part of every year there—we
pass over the fact that the other part is spent in Paris—
wearing the rawhide shoes of the natives, warming his
blood with their fires and their poteen, living in their
kitchens, hearing their legends, and sharing in their
noble primitive customs till the folk passion streams
through him and makes him a genius.   If any one is
skeptical, we point to the fact that something like the
" germ " of two or three of Synge's plays is actually
present here in the form of jottings on folk story and
belief.   Now, this is a delightfully simple recipe for
making a genius.   If this were the whole truth, one
might agree without reservation with one of the reviewers who declares that the *Aran Islands* is of " vast
importance as throwing light on this curious development," and who adds that it " is like no other book we
have ever read."

When I first read the *Aran Islands*, I thought of that
much-experienced vagabond and subtle exploiter of
exotic and primitive cultures, Pierre Loti; and I have
learned recently with some satisfaction from a foot-
note in Mr. Howe's book, that Synge thought Pierre
Loti " the best living writer of prose."   And when I
found Synge comparing conditions in the Aran Islands
to a disadvantage with what he had seen in his rambles
in Brittany, I thought of Anatole le Braz and all his
charming studies of the songs and superstitions and customs and characters of that other Celtic people.   And
then there drifted into my remembrance the pensive face
of another wanderer and exile, half-Irish and half-Greek,
known in the Orient as Koizumi Yakumo, and in the

western world as Lafcadio Hearn. As I turned once more the pages of his book on Japan and ran through the *Life and Letters,* glancing at his Eastern costume and at the almond eyes of his sons, I reflected that he, at any rate, had possessed the courage to realize the dreams of his favorite author, Théophile Gautier, and the Oriental reveries of Victor Hugo. Finally I opened the book of Chateaubriand, great father of them all, and read: 'When he arrived among the Natchez, René had been obliged, in order to conform to the customs of the Indians, to take a wife, but he did not live with her. A melancholy disposition drew him to the depths of the forest; there he passed whole days alone, and seemed a savage among the savages.'

The attitude, the point of view—that is the question about this Irishman and his book on the Aran Islands. *Que diable allait-il faire dans cette galère?* Now, it is an essential error to imagine that when Synge passed from the Latin Quarter to the Aran Islands he was returning to his own people. He never desired to return to his own people. He went to this group of islands, and then to the most remote and backward of them, because he wished to escape into a perfectly strange and virgin environment.

The peculiar charm of the *Aran Islands* and other books of its class consists not in the identification of the narrator with the life of the people whom he describes, but rather in accentuating the contrast between the sophisticated son of the cities and the simple barbarian. It is the aesthetic charm of looking upon illusions through the eyes of the disillusioned. In the

earlier examples of this *genre* the sense of the sundering
gulf is emphasized by bringing the weary heir of all the
ages into sentimental relations with a ' noble ' female
savage—an unspoiled daughter of the wilderness.   But
the sentiment now smacks of the romanticism of the
old school.   In the various books in which Pierre Loti
pictures his exotic amours, you may trace the declension
of the lovely and beloved barbarian into a mere transitory symbol of the ' soul ' of the land in which she is
found.   In the *Mariage de Loti,* for example, there is
still a breath of strange passion for the poor Poly-
nesian girl, yet the lover comments as follows: ' In truth
we were children of two natures, widely sundered and
diverse, and the union of our souls could only be transitory, incomplete, and troubled.'   But in that most
heartlessly beautiful book in contemporary literature,
Madame Chrysanthème, the breath of passion has given
way to sheer nervous disgust.   With the little yellow
poupée, Loti has nothing in common, not even an emotion.   As he takes pains to point out in the dedication
to the Duchesse de Richelieu, though Madame Chrysanthème seems to have the longest rôle, it is certain that
the three principal personages are: *Moi, le Japon et
l'Effet que ce pays m'a produit,* ' Myself, Japan and
the Effect which that country produces in me '—the
bitter perfume which a crushed chrysanthemum of
Nagasaki exhales for the nostrils of a disillusioned
Academician.

Essentially Synge was seeking the same thing—the
perfume which the Aran Islands could yield to the disillusioned Irish-Parisian.   He, too, has transferred the

sentiment, which was formerly attached to the fair savage, to the land itself. Despite his apparent solicitude for realistic detail, it is the subjective soul of the islands that he is striving to capture. His book, like Loti's, is pieced together of short impressionistic sketches which are related to one another only through the mood of the author. 'It is only in the intonation of a few sentences,' he writes, 'or some fragment of melody that I catch the real spirit of the island, for in general the men sit together and talk of the tides and the fish, and the price of kelp in Connemara.' The traditional lovely savage has here suffered a further declension into a peasant girl in her teens toward whom only a friendly attachment exists. Yet this girl, like her famous predecessors, becomes the symbol of what he has come to seek: ' At one moment she is a simple peasant, at another she seems to be looking out at the world with a sense of prehistoric disillusion and to sum up in the expression of her gray-blue eyes the whole external despondency of the clouds and sea.' And after he has talked to her of the ' men who live alone in Paris,' he notes that ' below the sympathy we feel there is still a chasm between us.' I do not wish to push this parallelism farther than it goes. In the *Aran Islands* the *Moi*, as well as the maiden, is subdued almost beyond comparison. But both men, like all the children of Chateaubriand, avail themselves of picturesque exotic scenes to enlarge and reverberate the lyric cry of their own weariness in civilized life and their loneliness out of it.

Synge's dramas are all sad, tragedies and comedies

alike, because they are all based upon a radical and
hopeless disillusion. In them the native lyrical impulse,
which in the poems we found checked by the cynicism
of Villon, and which in the Aran Islands expanded under
the influence of Loti, is again checked and controlled by
the irony of Anatole France. This is no doubt a bald
and over-emphatic way of putting the case, but it may
serve to indicate the general modes in which foreign
forces determined his talent. Synge has been praised
by many critics on the ground that he has reconciled
poetry with life. In the sense that he has broken
through the old 'poetic diction' and invented a new
poetic dialect with a fresh savor of earth in it, this is
doubtless true. But in a profounder sense it is nearer
the truth to say that he has widened the rift that was
between them. For the drift of all his work is to empha-
size the eternal hostility between a harsh and repugnant world of facts controlled by law, and the inviting
realm of lawless imagination. In one of the long_st
of his plays, *The Well of the Saints*, this idea becomes
perfectly explicit. Two blind beggars who have long
pleased themselves with thinking of each other's beauty
are, through a miracle, restored to sight. But the vision
of 'things as they are' is so hideous that they fall into
a violent hatred of each other. And they are both so
thankful when they go blind again that they reject
with scorn the holy man's offer to repeat the miracle.
This is perhaps the most elaborate expression of an idea
in all Synge's works, and one is not surprised to learn
that four years before *The Well of the Saints* there
was performed and printed in Paris a 'Chinese' play

by M. George Clemenceau, called the *Voile du Bonheur,* which contains identically the same idea, and which, as Mr. Howe concedes, it is ' perfectly probable ' that Synge knew.

For us *The Well of the Saints* is significant only as illustrating with especial clearness that profound sense of disillusion which underlies all Synge's eccentric comedies, and constitutes, as I have said, his point of contact with Anatole France.   The most France-like comedy that he ever conceived was never written, but the scenario is reported to us by Mr. Yeats. ' Two women, a Protestant and a Catholic, take refuge in a cave, and there quarrel about religion, abusing the Pope or Henry VIII, but in low voices, for the one fears to be ravished by the soldiers, the other by the rebels.   At last one woman goes out because she would sooner meet any fate than such wicked company.'   Now it is just this homeless elfishness of his mirth that distinguishes Synge from Jonson and Molière and Congreve, with whose names his has been so fearlessly coupled.   In all the classical comedy of the world one is made aware of the seat whence the laughing spirit sallies forth to scourge the vices or sport with the follies and affectations of men.   When the play is over, something has been accomplished toward the clarification of one's feelings and ideas; after the comic catharsis, illusions dissolve and give way to a fresh vision of what is true and permanent and reasonable.   Synge's comedies end in a kind of ironical bewilderment.   His, indeed, is outlaw comedy with gypsy laughter coming from somewhere in the shrubbery by the roadside, pealing out against church and state, and man and wife, and all the ordinances of civil life.

It is not that many of the *dramatis personæ* are vagrants, but that the dramatist himself is in secret heart a vagrant, and his inmost vision of felicity is purposeless vagabondage. What are the passages in these plays that all the critics delight to quote, and that the playgoer carries home from the theatre—fragments of them—singing in his memory? They are the passages in which some queen or beggar, touched with the lyric ecstasy, expresses a longing to go roaming down the open road or into the wilderness. You will find this gypsy call in every one of Synge's dramas except *The Riders to the Sea*. In the *Shadow in the Glen* it is a peasant housewife who loathes her little cottage and her dry and oldish husband, and follows a shabby tramp out into the hills where " you'll be hearing the herons crying out over the black lakes, and you'll be hearing the grouse and the owls with them, and the larks and the big thrushes when the days are warm." In the *Well of the Saints* it is the blind beggars fleeing from the light and reality and preferring to sit in darkness and illusion by the highway, " hearing a soft wind turning round the little leaves of the spring, and feeling the sun, and we not tormenting our souls with the sight of the gray days, and the holy men, and the dirty feet is trampling the world." In the *Tinker's Wedding* it is a trio of itinerant peddlers who after a brief skirmish with the Holy Church, gag the priest and scurry off with the gold originally intended as a wedding fee, " to have a good time drinking that bit with the trampers

on the green of Clash." In the *Playboy* it is Christy
Mahon dreaming of the time when he and Pegeen will
be " pacing Neifin in the dews of night, the time sweet
smells do be rising, and you'd see a little shiny new
moon, maybe, sinking on the hills." Even to that piece
built of the heroic stuff of the bards, *Deirdre of the
Sorrows*, he gives the same turn : here it is a wondrously
fair woman scorning a share in sovereignty and the high
king of Ulster to go salmon-spearing and vagabonding
with the sons of Naisi. To this man in whose vision of
joy we are invited to participate, life presents itself in
its comic aspects as a juxtaposition and irreconcilable
opposition of hideous realities and hopeless dreams,
dreams like the glens of Neifin in the dews of night,
realities like Old Mahon in the potato field—' He was a
dirty man, God forgive him.'

What, then, shall we say of his tragedy? Those who
are sealed of the tribe of Synge speak high praise of
The Riders to the Sea, that picture of the drear old
woman who has lost all her sons. As Mr. Edward
O'Brien declares in the preface printed in the collective
edition, this drama is set in the atmosphere of universal
action ; it holds the " ' timeless peace ' that passeth all
understanding." This is rare vision, indeed. It is a
noble phrase, this ' timeless peace.' It connotes in my
imagination the serene enduring forever of victorious
heroes and saints who have passed out of tribulation.
It is not, at any rate, an empty euphemism for annihilation, but a state in which even those of the living dwell
who, like the Stoic emperor, have caught a vision of a
central beauty and abiding harmony in all the works

of God. It is the mood in which all high tragedy leaves
us; the still elation into which we rise when blind
Œdipus answers the call of the god; the ' calm of mind,
all passions spent ' with which we are dismissed by that
superb last chorus in *Samson Agonistes*, beginning:

> All is best, though oft we doubt
> What the unsearchable dispose
> Of Highest Wisdom brings about.

Such, they tell us, is the atmosphere of *Riders to the
Sea*. It is like *Lear*, it is like Greek tragedy; it is not,
as they hasten to say—it is not like Maeterlinck's *Home*
or *The Intruder*. Synge certainly does differ from
Maeterlinck in two striking respects. While the Belgian
' mystic ' deprives his persons of personality and local-
ity and confers a kind of demonic personality upon
death, the naturalistic Irishman steeps his lines in personality and the reek of the gray sky and the smell of
the sea, and he represents death, in spite of the premo-
nitions of Maurya, as only the old dark way of nature.
But so far as what the Germans call the ' inner form '
is concerned, Synge gives us simply an Irish transposition of Maeterlinck. Strictly speaking, *Riders to the
Sea* is not a tragedy at all, because it is not a drama.
It might with more propriety be called a tragic idyl—a
somber picture, impressive enough in its kind, with the
fearful whispering of the young girls, whose necks have
not yet bowed beneath the ancient burden, and the gray
broken old mother, who looks before and after and has
passed through all illusions, sitting there patiently,
passively, receiving the tidings of disaster. Protagonist

in the proper sense of the word there is none; no act of the will turning against destiny as a token of human participation in that divine energy into which death resumes us all. It is this turning of the will that makes just the difference between what is drama and what is not; and between the mood with which Samson in Gaza affects us when he says, ' And I shall shortly be with them that rest,' and the mood with which Maurya affects us when she says, ' No man at all can be living forever, and we must be satisfied.' It is the difference between Milton looking into the timeless peace and Synge looking into the noisome grave. We heard him before crying aloud under the golden lights of the oaks of Glencree that in the end black boards would cover him and he should lie with worms eternally. Just that is the tragic vision and significance of *The Riders to the Sea.*

VIII

THE COMPLACENT TORYISM OF ALFRED AUSTIN

In a day when ancient manuscripts are opened and made to yield up misprized and forgotten genuises, it is singular that no one seems to have discovered Mr. Alfred Austin. Fortune, who deals inscrutably with the reputation of poets, has apportioned him a unique destiny. To some she has given merit without fame; to others, fame without merit; to him alone, fame without being read. Both before and after he entered upon the laureateship, his works were considered inessential to salvation. But upon his assumption of the singing robes of Lord Tennyson, he stepped at one conspicuous stride into the hot sunlight of journalistic derision. His own long participation in conservative journalism as leader writer for the *Standard* contributed to the acrimonious hilarity of his reception. Liberal knives hitherto exercised against his politics were now for the first time fleshed in his poetry. Little Englanders, become for the nonce literary critics, collected all the hasty and unfiled lines in the lays of the " hysterical Helot of Imperialism." The merciless cartoonist elevated him to the ancient throne of Dulness and twined the Parnassian laurels about his girdle. The wits of the press undertook to commit him with his peers, sagely debating whether to lodge him by copious Southey or elegant James Pye, or whether to bid Shadwell lie a shade nearer Flecknoe and make room for the newcomer by Colley Cibber. His name has thus become a household allusion; his works—who has read them? Here was surely a porridge to have killed a stouter poet than the Quarterly's martyr.

Mr. Austin is different; at seventy-six, still apparently as hale, happy, and industrious as ever, he published his memoirs [1] in two volumes comprising some six hundred pages written with unflagging zest and genuine power in self-revelation. Those familiar with him only through floating rumor may surmise that he erected this memorial to anticipate a neglectful and prejudiced posterity—lest, if he set not hand to the task, there should be a lacuna in the Lives of the British Poets. All the evidence, however, indicates that Mr. Austin became his own biographer, as he became his own poet, on the principle that if one would have a thing done well one should do it one's self; and he has left little to the hands of subsequent biographers or critics. Certainly in this happy work there is not the slightest trace of a head beneath the critical bludgeonings "bloody but unbowed." There is no trace of blood or echo of bludgeon. Throughout the book, which is not approached in interest by any of the author's previous writings, there is only smiling self-complacency and the mild afterglow of a long and successful experience in— to quote his own summary—" Literature, in verse and prose; Politics, internal and international; Journalism,

[1] The Autobiography of Alfred Austin, 1835-1910; New York.

War, Law, Religion, Art, Travel, Society, Town and
Country Life."

This self-complacency appears in the record of his
influence with political leaders; in the glimpse that he
offers us of Parliamentary honors proffered him but
thrust aside for higher rewards; in his words to young
writers on the secrets of style; in his hints for future
pilgrims to Italian shrines consecrated by his verse;
and, above all, in the account—since Wordsworth's
Prelude, unequalled in minuteness and self-reverence—of
his own poetical development. His early satirical poem
entitled *The Season* contains, he tells us, in spite of the
faults of irresponsible youth, " the germ of what Matthew Arnold called ' the criticism of life ' to be gathered
from *one's* works in their entirety." (A peculiar substitution of " *one* " for " *I* " is a " note " of Mr. Austin's
style.) From this germ, he traces with retrospective,
brooding, and affectionate finger the movement—ofttimes
unconscious—of his poetical powers toward that far-off,
divine event, his masterpiece, *The Human Tragedy*.
Pointing out that Italy cradled, though England bore,
his poetry, he declares that his Italian sojournings
" stripped him " of that insularity of familiar knowledge that marks so much of English literature. Recall-
ing early days in Rome, he speaks with wonder of his
unawareness of the divine things then a-brewing: " I
little knew that *The Human Tragedy*, not to come fully
and finally to the birth till more than ten years later,
was already germinating, and was waiting only for the
simultaneous occurrence of the mighty European events
between the years 1866 and 1871 and the much-needed

expansion of my own mind." This sense of cosmic gestation, then carried so blithely, but almost oppressive in the retrospect, reminds us of Eckermann and Goethe marveling together over the genesis of *Faust*. And sure enough, a few lines later Mr. Austin adds in the benevolent tone which he adopts toward his period of poetic adolescence: " But, as Goethe said, ' No youth can be a master,' and *one* was young." As he dwells on what he now sees were the high points of his experience, the phrase comes in like a refrain: " I did not then know or suspect "; " without any consciousness that *one's* poetic education was being promoted by it "; " I now can retrospectively see that *one's* education and the storing of *one's* mental, moral and emotional capacity were going forward. Had I known it at the time, what pain it would have spared me (? *one*) ! " This Little-did-I-wot runs like a silver thread throughout the autobiography: Mr. Austin is the most spontaneous of poets. His appreciation of his own poetry—nowhere deficient in delicacy—reaches its tenderest expression in his comment on certain villages in northern Italy once visited by him: " Suppressing their less attractive features, imaginative memory transfigured them later in the grave, sad journey of Godfrid and Olympia to Milan from the little chapel in Spiaggiscura, that closes with the melancholy line,

Ah! life is sad, and scarcely worth the pain."

This is indeed a melancholy line, but though it illustrates Mr. Austin's sympathetic imagination and his power over the sententious poetic phrase, it by no means represents his criticism of life. As I have already intimated, a divine satisfaction with his own position, a bland unconsciousness of contemporary feeling and opinion—these are precisely the startling and notable traits of the Laureate's character. They are startling because at first view one cannot see what supports them. They are notable because, as one considers the pages of this autoboigraphy, one sees exactly what supports them. One perceives that these traits are not mere personal idiosyncracies but the traditional and distinguishing marks of a diminishing but dogged literary, social, and political group. Mr. Austin, though he wots it not, is the last minstrel of Toryism. As he writes, he feels himself soothed, sustained, and magnified by the support of the landed gentlemen of England. He is not, he fancies, dipping his pen into the shallow well of egotism but into the inexhaustible springs of English sentiment. The genial and versatile figure that he portrays full length before us he conceives as no mere longaminous minor poet but as a typical, if somewhat superior, gentleman of Albion to whom some celestial beneficence has accorded, besides the common excellencies of his class, the sacred gift of song. He has consecrated the sacred gift of song to the celebration of the common excellencies of his class. We can make no sound valuation of his poetry without some consideration of the origin and nature of his ideas.

Like Sir Walter Scott of Abbotford, who first made him conscious that he was a poet, and like Lord Byron of Newstead Abbey, whose verse and romantic pilgrimage he has imitated in *The Human Tragedy*—though without passion, rebellion, wit, or *diablerie*—Mr. Austin is a great respecter of family. On the basis of his trivial mention of literary contemporaries and his ample enlargement upon his intimacy with baronets and lords, we can easily credit his declaration that " no one admires honourable descent and the easy gradations of English society, from class to class, more than I do." This feeling, eminently becoming in an official singer to the royal household, is apparent in his treatment of his own lineage. Born of Roman Catholic parents in this best possible of worlds six years after the Catholic Emancipation Act, Mr. Austin is derived from what every American would regard as comfortable aristocratic stock, his family for three generations before him having dealt in wool. And yet with a peculiarly Victorian instinct for adorning whatever he touches, he contrives to cast an additional glamour over his family-tree. Though he does not attempt to follow his physical ancestry beyond his great-grandfather, he shows at any rate—with the aid of Chambers's Encyclopædia—that the " honourable trade of wool-stapling " flourished as early as the time of Edward III; and he has himself seen houses of " striking architectural beauty " which belonged to wool-staplers " in the days of the Plantagenets."

Since he traces his forebears only to satisfy legitimate curiosity as to the antecedents of his literary talent, it is no less essential than interesting to exhibit the close relationship existing between the manufacture of wool and verse; so that we may not think it anomalous but entirely natural to find the same stock which through three generations put forth wool-staplers in the next putting forth a poet. History is on Mr. Austin's side. As he playfully reminds us, Shakespeare's father was a wool-stapler; Dante belonged to the Guild of the Woolcombers. " Such mental ancestry," says the autobiographer with perhaps a touch of modesty, " may inoffensively be recalled, since none can hope "—Mr. Austin has an old-world grace and facility in classical allusion—" to approach the supreme greatness of these poetic *Dioscuri.*" So much for his main inheritance in the paternal line. The blood of the Austins, conspiring with Shakespeare, Dante, and the Guild of the Woolcombers, determined that he should be a poet.

The special field of his poetry, however, appears to have been strongly influenced by the Hutton strain which came to him through his grandmother. Close attention will be required here, for heredity is a slippery matter at the best, and the argument runs at this point through a narrow defile: Mr. Austin " seems to remember that there existed a floating tradition that the Huttons had at one time been among *the landed gentry.*" Skeptical biologists may cry out that land is an acquired non-transmissible characteristic. Socialists—of which sect there were none in the England of the elder Huttons, merry England, the real England, the England of Mr. Austin—socialists are said to hold similar views.

The incontestable fact remains that Mr. Austin received from the Huttons, or from somewhere, an impulse inclining him affectionately toward land, and land in large parcels. From childhood, he tells us, he has experienced " a passionate clinging to the country, a keen admiration of territorial homes, with their deer-parks and wide-stretching woodlands, and an unconquerable antipathy, of a most prejudiced character, to towns, mills, and manufactures." At first thought the unwary reader may suspect a conflict between the hereditary Austin instinct for commerce and the Hutton impulse toward the serene life of the landed gentry. But wool-stapling as well as the business of owning land, we are assured, was in the time of the poet's childhood " a singularly light occupation " with ample margins for a nine o'clock breakfast and a half hour's lingering before business among " the flowers, the poultry, and the pigeons."

In such a mold heredity cast him. " *Qualis ab incepto*—" says Mr. Austin; as he was in the beginning, so essentially he has remained, except that he has relinquished the Roman faith which was not quite English. He came into the world with a few strong innate ideas, and has neither discarded nor added many since. Pigeons, poultry, and flowers surrounding a territorial home with background and foreground of deer-park and wide-spreading woodland—these constitute his central conception of nature. These things the Laureate has sung with sweetness and sincerity both in prose and in verse—in *Veronica's Garden, Haunts of Ancient Peace,* and in many a lyric, vernal, aestival, autumnal, and hibernal. None but a resolutely incredulous critic would question his knowledge of English seasons; and, in spite of his deprecatory " such gardening knowledge as I may later have acquired," there is no reason for doubting his intimate acquaintance with English flowers. If poetry avails at all in these evil days, his songs must have done something toward keeping alive a love of territorial homes in the hearts of their owners. Nor has Mr. Austin confined himself to groves and gardens. He has sung also of man and especially of woman—the occupants of territorial homes, and of all the prejudices and sentiments that uphold and beautify them.

Though not a poet of wide-ranging passion, he has given their due to English love, courtship, and marriage. Summing up at the close of his first chapter the forces that most moved his childhood, he mentions " a dim sense of the magnetic difference of the sexes." This sense became with advancing years steadily keener without losing any of its pristine quality. In witness whereof read the naïve but attractive incident of the beautiful chambermaid of Megara, who—fleetingly beheld in the evening—the poet hoped might wait upon him at breakfast. " That excusable love of what is beautiful," says the Laureate, silently distinguishing himself from an earlier Grecian pilgrim, " was disappointed." But tarry! As Mr. Austin and his party, after the morning meal, were setting forth on their journey, the fair one appeared for a moment in the doorway. They doffed their hats. She inclined her head. They drove away to Eleusis, never to see her more. Mr. Austin exclaims in another prose work of his containing certain strictures on Shelley: " What a fortunate circumstance it has been for the English people, that they can respect as well as admire their greatest writers. . . . Chaucer, Spenser, Shakespeare, Milton, Wordsworth, Tennyson, all good reputable citizens, all pillars of the Commonwealth, strengthening England by their conduct as much as by their genius."

The maturer phase of this sense of the " magnetic difference " and its important place in Mr. Austin's work are symbolically adumbrated in the poem called *In the Heart of the Forest*. The poet, accosting the shrilling missel-thrush, inquires the meaning of his music:

> Then louder, still louder he shrilled: I sing
>   For the pleasure and pride of shrilling,
> For the sheen and the sap and the showers of spring
>   That fill me to overfilling.
>
> Yet a something deeper than Springtime, though
>   It is Spring-like, my throat keeps flooding:
> Peep soft at my mate,—she is there below,—
>   Where the bramble trails are budding.
>
> She sits on the nest and she never stirs;
>   She is true to the trust I gave her;
> And what were my love if I cheered not hers
>   As long as my throat can quaver.

In this shy lyric, Mr. Austin hints darkly at the true solution of the vexed woman question. Fortunately I am able to illuminate this matter by a gloss extracted from the series of articles which he contributed to the *Spectator* in 1894, reporting his researches through England for " haunts of ancient peace." One of these haunts was the household of the fourth Countess of Leicester. "In the church at Penhurst, where we abode that night," says our author, "there is a monument to the fourth Countess of Leicester, and on it is recorded, *presumably in obedience to her own wish* (my italics), that ' Her sole desire was to make a good wife and good mother.' Could there be a nobler ambition? And shall I be forgiven if I add that when the little ' emancipating ' hubbub of our day has subsided, the ineradicable instinct of women will re-echo that devout and humble vow? "

In the seventeen years since these lines were written the " little ' emancipating ' hubbub " does not seem to have subsided much. While Mr. Austin was penning the pages of his autobiography, young women wearing a bandeau inscribed with the motto " Votes for Women " were parading in Picadilly. The tumult, however, has not reached the Laureate among the primroses and lady-smocks of Swinford Old Manor. While we who do not live in territorial homes have been asking, *Où sont les neiges d'antan?*—" where are the wives who sit on the nest and never stir? ", he has sung on imperturbably, celebrating the Lucille, the Dora, the Maud of the mid-Victorian dream—the fair and lissome English maiden blushing and trembling toward her lover and her lord with the reverence implanted in her unsunned bosom by God and Nature.

The remote charm that invests Mr. Austin's conception of the eternal-feminine pervades also his picture of man in family relations—a picture which helps us, since the family is a little image of the State, to understand his political ideals. For men of the modern democratic way of thinking, marriage exists in order to give representation to the Opposition. When a man marries, as we view the matter, he grants voice and vote to his sharpest and most remorseless critic. And this concession, most of us are agreed, whatever difficulties may attend it, is good for the government. To Mr. Austin, on the other hand, ideal marriage means a man's quiet and unchallenged assumption of the domestic throne of his fathers and his mild paternal reign over devoted and adoring subjects. But why blunder toward this lofty idea in prose when the Laureate has already embodied it in poetry of inimitable clearness and simplicity? In quoting from his lines on " Wordsworth at Dove Cottage " I shall be following his own practice in dealing with matters ineffable in the baser medium. Recurring to the figure of the missel-thrush, he declares that Fame's sweetest minister is " she who broods upon one's name, but calls it not aloud "; then addressing Wordsworth:

> And this at least, in full, you had,
>   From sister, and from wife:
> They made your gravest moments glad,
>   They havened you from strife;
> Hallowed your verse, revered your tread,
> Maintained a nimbus round your head
>   And deified your life.

Now the nimbus as a domestic ornament is no more hopelessly out of date than the whole social and political order which Mr. Austin has celebrated. In 1790 Burke saw it already in the last ditch; because it was no more,

Carlyle declared that the nations were hurtling pell-mell
into the Pit; Ruskin loved it still with a passionate regret as an exile in a strange land. It remained for Mr.
Austin to declare that it has not been and never shall
be shaken. His present attitude toward internal affairs
may be suggested by the postscript to a letter of his in
The Times, which he has deemed worthy a place near the
close of his autobiography. The sentiment, indorsed by
Mr. Austin, was originally uttered by the Comte
d'Haussonville, nephew of the Duc de Broglie, and friend
of the Duc d'Aumale, " and whose reception by the
Académie Française I had the good fortune to attend,
taken there by the late Lord Lytton when English
Ambassador in Paris—" etc. Here is the sentiment:
" The speeches of members of the House of Lords during the Election, so superior, even as platform oratory,
to those delivered by the members of the House of Com-
mons with one or two exceptions, would alone suffice to
save from successful attack any assault upon its
existence."

With democracy long since triumphant, with socialism
on foot, while dynamite is laid in broad daylight under
the House of Lords, Mr. Austin still confronts the times
with comfortable mien and inquires whether we shall
exchange for a modern democracy without a throne,
with no towers, with " mean plots without a tree "
(small holding cultivated by the owners?), a " herd of
hinds too equal to be free," dwelling together in " greed,
jealousy, envy, hate, and all uncharity "—shall the
gentlemen of England barter for this, he asks, " our
ancient, unaltered Motherland," " where sweet Order

now breathes cadenced tone," with its " hamlets meek,"
its lambs going " safe to the ewes " and its " calves to
the udder," its yearlings fattening, its heifers browsing,
its " whistling yokels " guiding the " gleaming share "
hard by the home where " gentle lordship dwells," in
country-seats with their " woodland amenity," where
" comely domain marches with comely domain," and the
plumped pheasant peeps through the boskage over " pastoral downs, as little changed since the time of Egbert
as the sea itself "?   " Shall this exchange be made? ",
cries the Laureate in feigned and rhetorical consternation.   " Banish the fear! ", he replies in his poem called
" Why England is Conservative," " Look Seaward, Sen-
tinel," and in many another patriotic lay of unique and
incomparable insolence.   While the " wild-beast mob "
of the nations whine with envy at her peace and prosperity, or roaring and sweating under their armor,
menace her across the " bastions of the brine," she
towers and shall forever tower supreme, " victor without
a blow," " smilingly leaning " on her " undrawn
sword "——

I have made this review of Mr. Austin's leading ideas
because it has been falsely rumored that he has none.   It
should now be apparent that, far from being content
with the fame of an idle pastoralist, he challenges recognition as a poetical representative of the conservative
spirit.   It should also be clear that the value of his representation is impaired by his complete identification of
conservatism with Toryism—a confusion due to his
obliviousness to the flight of time.   I suppose it is more
or less of the essence of genuine Toryism to confound

the amenity and stability of one's own fireside with the welfare of the country; in so far as that is true Mr. Austin seems to be a good Tory. In his system of ideas, furthermore, I can detect little that would have been repugnant to the sense of a country gentleman in the reign of Farmer George. But the possible historical value of his expression of Toryism is destroyed by a serious anachronism: the foundation on which his Georgian ideas rest, the sentiment which suffuses them, and the artistic coloring which invests them are mid-Victorian. Mr. Austin upholds the House of Lords, the territorial homes, and the whistling yokel not like a true blue Tory—because they were ordained by God, nor like the later philosophical Tory—because they were ordained by nature, but like the unphilosophical, atheistical, pseudo-Catholic Pre-Raphaelites—because they are aesthetically gratifying. That explains his " unconquerable antipathy " to towns, mills, and manufactures, and at the same time his fondness for depicting Brittannia leaning smilingly on her undrawn sword. That is why he hates and fears liberalism, and at the same time makes conservatism ridiculous by representing it as invincible. That is why his poems, if read, and his picture of happy England might loosen all the bricks in the pavements of Manchester and Liverpool. For the sentimental romantic Toryism of Mr. Austin is not so much dull as false; false and at the same time obsolete; obsolete but not yet old enough to have acquired an antiquarian interest.

IX

THE AESTHETIC IDEALISM OF
HENRY JAMES

" No one has the faintest conception of what I am trying for," says the celebrated novelist in *The Death of the Lion*, " and not many have read three pages that I've written; but I must dine with them first—they'll find out when they've time." These words are tinged with Henry James's own disdain of the fashionable world which wears, and wears out, a man of genius like a spangle on its robe. They are tinged too with the mixed regret and satisfaction of an author who knew what it was to grow too fine for one's public. Born in 1843, James established in the seventies and eighties of the last century the kind of reputation that calls for French and German translations. He lived to hear the wits of the late nineties and the following decade calling for the translation of his maturest works into English. Perhaps twenty years ago every one had read, or had attempted to read, a recent novel of his; but there has come up a generation of young people who have been permitted, with the connivance of critics, to concede the excellence of his earlier productions and the " impossibility " of his later ones without looking into either. Shortly before his death in 1916 he emerged for the general public from his obscure memoir-writing, and

226

stood for a moment conspicuous on the sky-line—a dark august figure bowed in devout allegiance beneath the English flag; then with a thunder of ordnance not made for *his* passing he slipped below the horizon. In the hour of trial he had given to England a beautiful gesture, which derived much of its interest from his life-long refusal to commit himself to any cause but art. Though the adoption of English citizenship by an American would have excited in ordinary circumstances the profane wit of our paragraph-writers, the gravity of this occasion chastened them; and when, a few months later, his death called for comment, many of them clutched at this transferral of allegiance as the last, if not the only, intelligible performance of his that was known to them. Some of them, to be sure, remembered, or said they remembered, *Daisy Miller* as a " perfect little thing of its kind," or professed a not unpleasant acquaintance with the *Portrait of a Lady*, or even exhibited a vague consciousness that the novelist had treated extensively the " international situation," but in general they betrayed their " unpreparedness " for defining his talent and valuing his accomplishment.

Criticism should have declared by this time, and should have declared with emphasis and authority, what Henry James was " trying for." It should also have declared whether, when he slipped below the horizon, he sank into the deepening shadows of literary history, or whether he passed on into a widening world of light— the Great Good Place of a grateful and enlightened posterity which will not dine with him but which will read him. May we securely let him pass while we go on to something better; or shall we find, if we go on, that he is the something better to which we come at last? There are wide differences of opinion in the critical jury. Mr. Brownell, who has said a multitude of penetrating things about his mind and his art, and who is, one should suppose, the critic in America best qualified to enjoy and to value him, does not conceal his quiet hope and expectation that among the novelists of the future we shall not meet his like again. Professor Pattee, who is " out " for American local colors and big native American ideas, declares in so many words that Henry James's novels " really accomplish nothing." Recent English criticism strikes up in another key. Mr. Ford Maddox Hueffer promises him immortality, if there is any immortality for extraordinarily fine work—a point about which he is doubtful; but he struggles to this handsome conclusion through such fantastic arguments, with such explosions of temper and erratic judgment, through such a stream of " Godforbids " and " Thankgods " and " Godknowses," with such a display of the new literary bad manners, that one wonders how he ever came to occupy himself with an author so dedicated to refinement. The little book of Miss Rebecca West, an acutely positive and intensely glowing young " intellectual," has delightful merits: its adverse criticism is cuttingly phrased if not always precisely keen, its appreciative passages are full of fresh ardor and luminous if not always illuminating imagery; it holds up a candle and swings a censer in the principal niches and chapels of the wide-arching cathedral upon which the builder toiled for half a century; but it rather evades the task of presenting a final and comprehensive view—of explaining, in short, in the honor of what deity the whole edifice was constructed.

Let us cut an avenue to the inner shrine by removing from consideration some of the objects for which most of his American and English compatriots profess a pious veneration. Henry James has insulted all the popular gods of democratic society—for example, the three persons of the French revolutionary trinity and the " sovereign people " collectively. Captain Sholto, almost unique among his characters in uttering a political thought, must express pretty nearly his creator's position when he says, " I believe those that are on top the heap are better than those that are under it, that they mean to stay there, and that if they are not a pack of poltroons they will." It would be difficult to name an American author more perfectly devoid of emotional interest in the general mass of humanity. His attitude toward the " submerged tenth " is chiefly established by his silence with regard to it. In *The Princess Casamassima*, one of the rare places in which he permits a view of the dark Netherward of society to fall upon the eye of a sensitive observer, this is the reported reaction: " Some of the women and girls, in particular, were appalling—saturated with alcohol and vice, brutal, bedraggled, obscene. ' What remedy but another deluge, what alchemy but annihilation? ' he asked himself as he went his way ; and he wondered what fate there could be, in the great scheme of things, for a planet overgrown with such vermin, what redemption but to be hurled against a ball of consuming fire." The passage is a little deficient, is it not? in warm fraternal feeling. Let us round out this impression with the reported reaction of a sensitive observer in *The Madonna of the Future* to a little glimpse of free life in Rome: " Cats and monkeys, monkeys and cats; all human life is there! "

These sensitive observers doubtless had cause for a shudder of revulsion, and dramatic reason as well. Their behavior becomes interesting when one compares it with James's personal account in *London Notes* of his own attitude toward a very different scene—the preparations for the Victoria Jubilee. " The foremost, the immense impression is of course the constant, the permanent, the ever-supreme—the impression of that greatest glory of our race, its passionate feeling for trade. . . . London has found in this particular chapter of the career of its aged sovereign only an enormous advertisement." Later he reports that he has been taking refuge from the Jubilee in novel-reading. The great thing to be said for the novelists, he adds, is " that at any given moment they offer us another world, another consciousness, an experience that, *as effective as the dentist's ether, muffles the ache of the actual* and, by helping us to an interval, tides us over and makes us face, in the return to the inevitable, a combination that may at least have changed." Was it a pose to speak of fiction as an ethereal pause in the midst of the perpetual toothache of the actual—and of a great patriotic demonstration as a peculiarly sharp toothache? Or was it " American humor "? The pose, if pose it was, is curiously of a piece with his saying to John Hay, who had been received with an " ovation " on his arrival in Southampton, " What impression does it make in your mind

to have these insects creeping about you and saying
things to you? "

A partial explanation of this disgust and this detachment from the major interests of the majority of men
may be found in a half-dozen familiar facts of his
biographical record: the peculiar genius of his Sweden-
borgian father, his early induction in old New York,
his birthplace, into " the religion of foreign things," his
foreign language teachers, his early perusal of the
London *Punch* and his devotion, a little later, to the
Revue de Deux Mondes, his glimpses in childhood of
London and the Continent, his artistic apprenticeship
under John de la Farge, his trifling contact with the
Harvard Law School, his serious contact as reviewer
with the New York *Nation* and with the *Atlantic
Monthly*, his discovery of a fine vein of fiction, and the
permanent settlement of his residence abroad.   The
leading idea in the elder James's plan for his son's life
seems to have been to rescue him from the typical democratic process in order to open to him some finer destiny:
to provide him with comfortable means and ample leisure, to save him from every exacting pressure, to preserve him from the stamp of any definite educational
system, by perpetual migrations to snap the root of
local attachments, to postpone for him as long as possible the choice of a career, so that at last the young
man should be whatever he was and do whatever he did
by the free impulse of his own spirit.   The perfect
working of this plan was probably marred by a physical
accident at the time of the Civil War, which as Henry
James circuitously explains, assigned him to the rôle

of an engrossed spectator. Whatever the significance
of this incident, the result of the plan of tasting life in
New York, Boston, Geneva, London, Paris, Rome, Florence, and Venice was to set up an endless process of
observation, comparison, discrimination, selection, and
appreciation—a process which for this highly civilized,
highly sensitized young spirit, became all-absorbing,
and made of him a fastidious connoisseur of experience,
an artistic celibate to whose finer sense promiscuous
mixing in the gross welter of the world was wearisome
and unprofitable.

There is no getting round the fact that he was as pro-
digiously " superior " inside as he was outside the field
of art. In his recent much quoted essay on the New
Novel he has the air of a conscious old master conde-
scending for the nonce to notice " the rough and tumble
' output ' " of the young vulgar democratic herd. A
false note in Miss West's treatment of his character is
her remark that he lacked " that necessary attribute of
the good critic, the power to bid bad authors to go to
the devil." Mr. Brownell, on the other hand, puts some
of his work at the head of American criticism. His
Hawthorne, his *Partial Portraits*, his *Essays in London
and Elsewhere*, his *Notes on Novelists*, his various " portraits " of cities and " scenes," including The American
Scene, and his introductions to his own novels constitute
certainly an impressive body of literary and social criticism of unique quality and high interest. As for the
" necessary attribute," he sent authors to their appropriate places so civilly and suavely that they probably
failed frequently to notice where they were sent; but no

critic ever more remorselessly sent to the devil bad authors, mediocre authors, and even very distinguished authors. In his later years, he very blandly, very courteously, sent the whole general public to the devil. He was mortally weary of the general public's obtuseness; he despaired of the general public, and despised it. At the same time he reiterated in his stories, his critical articles, and in the prefaces to the New York edition of his work challenges and entreaties to the critical few to come and find him.

In that fascinating work *The Figure in the Carpet* he depicts, for criticism, what he would have called his own " case." He presents there, amid various intensifications of interest, Hugh Vereker, a master-novelist, head and shoulders above his contemporaries; so that even his devoutest admirers and his most studious critics miss the thing that he has written his books " most *for*." " Isn't there," he says to one of them, " for every writer a particular thing of that sort, the thing that most makes him apply himself, the thing without the effort to achieve which he wouldn't write at all, the very passion of his passion, the part of the business in which, for him, the flame of art burns most intensely? . . There's an idea in my work without which I wouldn't have given a straw for the whole job. . . . It stretches, this little trick of mine, from book to book, and everything else, comparatively, plays over the surface of it. The order, the form, the texture of my books will perhaps constitute for the initiated a complete representation of it. So it is naturally the thing for the critic to look for. It strikes me," Vereker adds—smil-

ing but inscrutable, "even as the thing for the critic
to find."

The thing which James hoped chiefly that his critics
would some day recognize is not that he is a great stylist,
or a learned historian of manners, or the chief of the
realists, or a master of psychological analysis. All
these things have been noted and asserted by various
more or less irreligious strollers through that cathedral-
like edifice to which we have likened his works. The
thing which he as the high priest solemnly ministering
before the high altar implored some one to observe and
to declare and to explain is that he adored beauty and
absolutely nothing else in the world. To the discovery
of beauty he dedicates his observation, his analysis, his
marvelous and all-too-little recognized imaginative energy. That is why he sends the rest of the world to the
devil, that is his romance, that is his passion, that is
why when he discusses his own creations he talks verit-
ably like a soul in bliss. The intimate relation of his
fiction to modern realities beguiles the uncritical reader
into an erroneous notion that he is a " transcriber," a
literal copyist, of life. What in his prefaces he begs
us again and again to believe is that his stories origi-
nated in mere granules and germs of reality blown by
chance breezes to the rich soil of the garden of his
imagination, where they took root, and sprang up, and
flowered; then they were transplanted with infinite art
to the garden of literature. What he offers us, as he
repeatedly suggests, is a thousandfold better than life;
it is an escape from life. It is an escape from the unde-
signed into the designed, from chaos into order, from

the undiscriminated into the finely assorted, from the
languor of the irrelevant to the intensity of the pertinent. It is not reality; he goes so far as to say quite
expressly that it is poetry. If that is true, his novels
should, in spite of Professor Pattee, " accomplish "
something; they should give us on the one hand an ideal
and on the other hand a criticism; and they do give us
both. Henry James's importance for Anglo-Saxons in
general and for Americans in particular is that he is
the first novelist writing in English to offer us on a
grand scale a purely aesthetic criticism of modern
society and modern fiction.

His special distinction among writers of prose fiction
is in the exclusiveness of his consecration to beauty—a
point which in this connection probably requires eluci-
dation. To the religious consciousness all things are
ultimately holy or unholy; to the moral consciousness
all things are ultimately good or evil; to the scientific
consciousness all things are ultimately true or not true;
to Henry James all things are ultimately beautiful or
ugly. In few men but fanatics and geniuses does any
one type of consciousness hold undivided sway, and even
among the geniuses and fanatics of the English race the
pure aesthetic type was till Ruskin's time excessively
rare. The normal English consciousness is, for purposes of judgment, a courthouse of several floors and
courts, to each of which are distributed the cases proper
to that jurisdiction. In the criticism of Matthew
Arnold, for example, there are distinct courts for the
adjudication of spiritual, ecclesiastical, moral, aesthetic,
political, social, and scientific questions; but Ruskin

handles all matters in the aesthetic chamber. In Shakespeare's criticism of life, to take the case of a creative artist, the discrimination of experience proceeds on clearly distinguishable levels of consciousness; the exquisite judgment of Sylvia—" holy, fair, and wise is she "—is a certificate of character from three distinct courts. But Henry James, on the contrary, receives and attempts to judge all the kinds of his experience on the single crowded, swarming, humming level of the aesthetic consciousness; the apartments above and below are vacant.

It is a much simpler task to indicate his position in literature with reference to the nature of his consciousness than with reference to the forms of his art. Critics attempting to " place " him have said the most bewildering things about his relationship to Richardson, Dickens, George Eliot, Trollope, George Meredith, Stevenson, Tourgénieff, Balzac, the Goncourts, Flaubert, Maupassant, Zola, and Daudet. To say that he is the disciple of this galaxy is to say everything and nothing. He knew intimately modern literature and many of its producers in England, France, Italy, and Russia, and he is related to them all as we are all related to Adam—and to the sun and the moon and the weather. He doubtless learned something of art from each of them, for he took instruction wherever he could find it—even from " Gyp," as he blushingly confesses in the preface to *The Awkward Age*. But what different gods were worshiped in this galaxy! Even Meredith, who resembles him in his psychological inquisitiveness, does not in nine-tenths of his novels remotely resemble him in form; moreover, Meredith is a moralist, a sage, a mystic, and a lyrical worshiper of Life, Nature, and other such loose divinities. James called Balzac " the master of us all," he called Tourgénieff " the beautiful genius," he sympathized intensely with Flaubert's dedication to perfection; but his total representation of life is not much more like that of any of his " masters " than George Eliot's is like Zola's.

It is a curious fact that while American criticism tends to refer him to Europe, English criticism tends to refer him to America. A pretty argument, indeed, could be constructed to prove that he might have been very much what he was, if he had not gone body and soul to Europe, but had simply roved up and down the Atlantic coast comparing the grave conscience of Boston and the open and skyey mind of Concord with the luxurious body and vesture of New York and the antique " gentility " of Richmond—comparing the harvested impressions of these scenes, and weaving into new patterns the finer threads which American tradition had put into his hands: Hawthorne's brooding moral introspection, his penetration of the shadowed quietudes of the heart, his love of still people and quiet places, his golden thread of imagery beaded with brave symbolism, the elaborated euphony of his style; Irving's bland pleasure in the rich surface of things, his delight in manorial dwellings, his sense of the glamour of history, his temperamental and stylistic mellowness and clarity, his worldly well-bred air of being " at ease in Zion "; Poe's artistic exclusiveness, his artistic intelligence, his intensity, his conscious craftsmanship, his zest for discussing the creative process and the technique of literature. As a matter of fact, Henry James does " join on " to the eastern American traditions; he gathers up all these enumerated threads; he assimilates all these forms of consciousness.   Hawthorne plays into his hands for depth and inwardness, Irving for outwardness and enrichment, and Poe for vividness and intensity.

The result of this fusion of types is a spacious and richly sophisticated type of the aesthetic consciousness of which the closest English analogue is that of Walter Pater.   James is like Pater in his aversion from the world, his dedication to art, his celibacy, his personal decorum and dignity, his high aesthetic seriousness, his Epicurean relish in receiving and reporting the multiplicity and intensity of his impressions, and in the exacting closeness of his style.   There are distinctions in plenty to be made by any one curious enough to undertake the comparison; but on the whole there is no better side light on James's " philosophy " than Pater's Conclusion to the *Studies in the Renaissance* and his *Plato and Platonism;* no better statement of his general literary ideals than Pater's essay on Style; no more interesting " parallel " to his later novels than *Marius the Epicurean* and *Imaginary Portraits.* To make the matter a little more specific let the curious inquirer compare the exposure of Pater's consciousness which is ordinarily known as his description of Mona Lisa with the exposure of James's consciousness which is ordinarily known as the description of a telegraph operator *(In the Cage).*

The reduction of all experience to the aesthetic level

James himself recognized as a hazardous adventure. At the conclusion of his searching criticism of a fellow adventurer, Gabriele D'Annunzio, he raises the question whether it can ever hope to be successful. D'Annunzio's adventure he pronounces a dismal failure—that is, of course, an aesthetic failure; for in the quest of the beauty of passion the Italian, he declares, has produced the effect of a box of monkeys, or as he periphrastically puts it, " The association rising before us more nearly than any other is that of the manners observable in the most mimetic department of any great menagerie." But, he continues, the question is whether D'Annunzio's case is " the only case of the kind conceivable. May we not suppose another with the elements differently mixed? May we not in imagination alter the proportions within or the influences without, and look with cheerfulness for a different issue. *Need* the aesthetic adventure, in a word, organised for real discovery, give us no more comforting news of success? . . . To which probably the sole answer is that no man can say."

The last sentence is modest but can not have been wholly sincere; for James must have known that his own works answer all these questions in the affirmative. His own case is an altogether different variety of the species; his " news " is infinitely more comforting than D'Annunzio's. The particular ugliness, the morbid erotic obsession, on which D'Annunzio foundered, James, like Pater, sailed serenely by. His aesthetic vision had a far wider range and a far higher level of observation than that of almost any of the Latin votaries of " art for art "—Gautier or Flaubert, for example. And yet, let us admit it frankly once for all, his representation of life offends the whole-souled critical sense intensely in some particulars and on what is fundamentally the same ground as that on which these others offend it. His representation of life is an aesthetic flat; it sins against the diversity, the thick rotundity, the integrity of life. Its exquisitely arranged scenes and situations and atmospheres are not infrequently "ugly," as he would say, with the absence of moral energy and action. In *The Awkward Age*, for example, in that society which lives for "the finer things," which perceives, and compares, and consults, and so perfectly masters its instincts, the situation fairly shouts for the presence of at least one young man conceivably capable of bursting like Lochinvar through the circle of intriguing petticoats to carry off the heroine. The atmosphere of *The Golden Bowl* is ineffable—"There had been," says the author, "beauty day after day, and there had been for the spiritual lips something of the pervasive taste of it." The atmosphere is ineffably rich, still, golden, and, in the long run, stifling; the perceptive Mr. Verver, who is in it, gives a superb image of its effect: "That's all I mean at any rate—that it's ' sort of ' soothing: as if we were sitting about on divans, with pigtails, smoking opium and seeing visions. ' Let us then be up and doing '—what is it Longfellow says? That seems sometimes to ring out; like the police breaking in—into our opium den—to give us a shake."

One may properly stress the point of his sin against the integrity of life because it is of the essence of the aesthetic case. It explains the vague but profound

resentment which some readers who do not balk at
James's difficulty, feel when they have got " inside."
Mr. Brownell, Mr. Hueffer, and Miss West all point
toward but do not, I think, quite touch the heart of the
matter when they say that James lacks " the historic
sense." A part of the historic sense he indubitably has,
and far more historical learning is implied in his work
than is explicit in it; he loves the color and form of the
past, he feels the " beauties " of history. But history
to him, even the history of his own life, is a kind of magnificent picture gallery through which he strolls, delight-
edly commenting on the styles of different schools and
periods, and pausing now and then for special expression of rapture before a masterpiece. Miss West beautifully flames with indignation at his " jocular " references to the Franco-Prussian War and at his unsympa-
thetic treatment of the French Revolution till she hits
upon the explantion that he was out of Europe while
the Franco-Prussian War raged, and that he was not
born at the time of the French Revolution, so that he
could no more speak well of it " than he could propose
for his club a person whom he had never met." The
explanation doesn't fit all the facts. He was not out of
England when in his introduction to Rupert Brooke's
letters, he expressed his satisfaction that the English
tradition " should have flowered *in a specimen so beautifully producible.*" The appreciation of Brooke is one
of the most beautifully passionate tributes ever written;
but the passion is purely aesthetic; the inveterate air
of the connoisseur viewing a new picture in the gallery
of masterpieces he can not shake off. He was not speak-

ing of events that took place before he was born when
he said of the assassination of Lincoln in his *Notes of
a Son and Brother:* " The collective sense of what had
occurred was of a sadness too noble not somehow to
inspire, and it was truly in the air that, whatever we
had as a nation failed to produce, *we could at least
gather round this perfection of classic woe.* True
enough, as we were to see, the immediate harvest of
our loss was almost too ugly to be borne—for nothing
more sharply comes back to me than the tune to which
the esthetic sense, if one glanced but from *that* high
window, recoiled in dismay from the sight of Mr. Andrew
Johnson perched on the stricken scene."

Any good American will flame with indignation when
he reads that passage; it so fails to present the subject;
it is so horribly inadequate; it so affronts what Lord
Morley would call " the high moralities " of life. With
its stricken " scene," its aesthetic rapture, its aesthetic
dismay, it insults the moral sense as a man would in-
sult it who should ask one to note the exquisite slope
of a woman's neck at the funeral of her husband. It
makes one burn to break the glass in the high aesthetic
window. It sins against the integrity of life as, to take
some distinguished examples, Renan's *Vie de Jésu* and
Pater's *Plato and Platonism* sin against it. To present
the Spartan boy as a nineteenth-century aesthete or to
present the life of Jesus as essentially " delicious " is
to miss in the quest of distinction the most vital and
obvious of distinctions. It is a blunder into which
simple, gross, whole-souled men like Fielding or Smollett
or Dickens could never have fallen. It is a crudity of

which only the most exquisite aesthete is capable; and he perching exclusively in his high aesthetic window absolutely can not avoid it. It is of the pure aesthetic consciousness, not the intellect, that Emerson should have written his terse little couplet:

> Gravely it broods apart on joy
> And truth to tell, amused by pain.

When all these discriminations against the usurpations and blindnesses of the aesthetic sense have been made it remains to be said that the infinitely seductive, the endlessly stimulating virtue of Henry James is the quintessential refinement, the intriguing complexity, the white-hot ardor of his passion for beauty. One feels the sacred flame most keenly, perhaps, in novels and tales like *The Figure in the Carpet, The Next Time, The Death of the Lion, The Lesson of the Master, Roderick Hudson,* and *The Tragic Muse,* in all of which he is interpreting the spirit of the artist or treating the conflict between the world and art. One feels it in the words of the young man in *The Tragic Muse* who abandons the prospect of a brilliant political career to become a portrait painter: " The cleanness and quietness of it, the independent effort to do something, to leave something which shall give joy to man long after the howling has died away to the last ghost of an echo— such a vision solicits me in the watches of the night with an almost irresistible force." One feels it in the words of the young diplomat in the same novel, who is infatuated with a fine piece of acting: " He floated in the felicity of it, in the general encouragement of a sense of the perfectly *done*." One feels it in the words of the novelist in *The Lesson of the Master*, who says he has missed " the great thing "—namely, " the sense which is the real life of the artist and the absence of which is his death, of having drawn from his intellectual instrument the finest music that nature had hidden in it, of having played it as it should be played."

For a born man of letters the first effect of this passion for perfection is an immense solicitude for style, that is to say, for an exact verbal and rhythmical correspondence between his conception of beauty and his representation of it. Judgment upon style, then, involves two distinct points: first, the question whether the conception is beautiful, and, secondly, the question whether the representation is exact. In the case of Henry James there should not be much dispute about the exactness and completeness of the representation; no man ever strove more remorselessly or on the whole more successfully to reproduce the shape and color and movement of his aesthetic experience. The open question is whether his conceptions were beautiful; and on this point the majority of his critics have agreed that his earlier conceptions were beautiful but that his later conceptions were not. To that, in the last analysis, one must reduce the famous discussion of his two, or three, or half-a-dozen " styles." Any one who reads the works through in chronological order can explode to his own satisfaction the notion that James in any book or year or decade deliberately changed his style. What changed was his conception of beauty, and that changed by an entirely gradual multiplication of distinctions through the enrichment of his consciousness and the intensification of his vision. To his youthful eye beauty appeared in clear light, clear color, sharp outline, solid substance; accordingly the work of his earlier period abounds in figures distinct as in an etching of the eighteenth century, grouping themselves as on a canvas of Gainsborough's, and conversing and interacting with the brilliant lucidity and directness of persons in a comedy of Congreve's. To his maturer vision beauty has less of body and more of soul; it is not so much in things as in the illimitable effluence and indefinable *aura* of things; it reveals itself less to eye and ear and hand—though these are its avenues of approach—than to some mysterious inner organ which it moves to a divine abstraction from sense, to an ecstacy of pure contemplation. Accordingly, late works like *The Sacred Fount* and *The Golden Bowl* present rather presences than persons, dim Maeterlinckian presences gliding through the shadow and shimmer of Turneresque landscapes and Maeterlinckian country-houses, and rarely saying or doing anything whatever of significance to vulgar ear or eye. The evolution of his artistic interest may be summed up in this way: he begins with an interest in the seen, the said, the enacted; and he ends by regarding all that as an obstruction in the way of his latest interest, namely, the presentation of the unseen, the unsaid, the unacted—the vast quantity of mental life in highly civilized beings which makes no outward sign, the invisible drama upon which most of his predecessors had hardly raised the curtain. The difficulty in the later works is not primarily in the sentence structure but in the point of view. The sentences in the most difficult of the novels, *The Sacred Fount*, are generally as neat, terse, and alert as the sentences in *The Europeans*, which is within the comprehension of an intelligent child. When his sentences are long and intricate they usually imprison and precisely render some intricate and rewarding beauty of a moment of consciousness luxuriously full: for example this moment of Strether's in *The Ambassadors*:

> How could he wish it to be lucid for others, for any one, that he, for the hour, saw reasons enough in the mere way the bright, clean, ordered water-side life came in at the open window?—the mere ..ay Mme. de Vionnet, opposite him over their inteusely white table-linen, their *omelette aux tomates*, their bottle of straw-colored chablis, thanked him for everything almost with the smile of a child, while her gray eyes moved in and out of their talk, back to the quarter of the warm spring air, in which early summer had already begun to throb, and then back to his face and their human questions.

Only attend till the beauty of that crowded moment reproduces itself in your consciousness, and you will not complain much of the difficult magic of its evocation.

Beyond almost all the English novelists of his time Henry James has applied his passion for beauty to the total form and composition of his stories. He cares little for the " slice of life," the loose episodic novel, the baggy autobiographical novel, so much in vogue of late, into which the author attempts to pitch the whole of contemporary life and to tell annually all that he knows and feels up to the date of publication without other

visible principle of selection. With extremely few exceptions his subjects present themselves to him either as
" pictures " to be kept rigorously within the limits of a
frame, or as " dramas " to be kept within the limits of
a stage, or as alternations of " drama " with " picture."
How he imposes upon himself the laws of painter and
playwright, how he chooses his " centre of composition,"
handles his "perspective," accumulates his " values,"
turns on the " lights "—all this he has told with extraordinary gusto in those prefaces which more illuminate the
fine art of fiction than anything else—one is tempted to
say, than everything else—on the subject. The point
for us here is that he strives to make the chosen form
and the intended effect govern with an " exquisite econ-
omy " every admitted detail. The ideal is to express
everything that belongs in the " picture," everything
that is *in* the relations of the persons of the drama, but
nothing else.

His exacting aesthetic sense determines the field no
less than the form of his fiction. A quite definite social
ideal conceived in the aesthetic consciousness is implicit
in his representation of a really *idle* class—an ideal
ultimately traceable to his own upbringing and to his
early contact with the Emersonian rather than the
Carlylean form of transcendentalism. He has a positive
distaste for our contemporary hero—" the man who
does things "; the *summum bonum* for him is not an
action but a state of being—an untroubled awareness of
beauty. Hence his manifested predilection for " highly
civilized young Americans, born to an easy fortune and
a tranquil destiny "; for artists who amateurishly

sketch and loiter through lovely Italian springs, though conscious of " social duties " that await them beyond the Alps ; for diplomats devoted to the theatre and members of Parliament who dabble in paint; for Italian princesses and princes free from the cares of state; for French counts and countesses who have nothing to keep up but the traditions of their " race "; for English lords with no occupation but the quest of a lady; for American millionaires who have left " trade " three thousand miles behind them to collect impressions, curios, and sons-in-law in Europe. Objectors may justly complain that he seems unable to conceive of a really fine lady or a really fine gentleman or a really decent marriage without a more or less huge fortune in the background or in the foreground of the picture ; and it may be added that to the sense of a truly " Emersonian " mind the clink and consideration of gold in most of his crucial instances is a harsh and profound note of vulgarity vibrating through his noble society. He is entirely sincere when he says, in speaking of Balzac, that the object of money is to enable one to forget it. Yet fine ladies, fine gentlemen, and fine society as he understands these matters are, to tell the hard truth, impossible except in the conditions created by affluence and leisure. In comparative poverty one may be good; but one can not, in the Jamesian sense, be beautiful!

Society can not in the Jamesian sense be beautiful till the pressures of untoward physical circumstances, of physical needs, and of engagements with " active life " are removed, and men and women are free to live " from within outward," subjecting themselves only to the environment and entering only the relationships dictated by the aesthetic sense. Let us not undervalue the significance of this ideal, either with reference to life or with reference to literature. It is inadequate, but it has the high merit of being finely human. It had the precious virtue of utterly delivering Henry James from the riotous and unclean hands of the " naturalists." To it he owes the splendid distinction that when half the novelists of Europe, carried off their feet by the naturalistic drift of the age, began to go a-slumming in the muck and mire of civilization, to explore man's simian relationships, to exploit *la bête humaine* and *l'homme moyen sensuel*, to prove the ineluctability of flesh and fate and instinct and environment—he, with aristocratic contempt of them and their formulas and their works, withdrew farther and farther from them, drew proudly out of the drift of the age, and set his imagination the task of presenting the fairest specimens of humanity in a choice sifted society tremendously disciplined by its own ideals but generally liberated from all other compelling forces. Precisely because he keeps mere carnality out of his picture, holds passion rigorously under stress, presents the interior of a refined consciousness—precisely for these reasons he can produce a more intense pleasure in the reader by the representation of a momentary gush of tears or a single swift embrace than most of our contemporaries can produce with chapter after chapter of storms and seductions.

The controlling principle in Henry James's imaginary world is neither religion nor morality nor physical necessity nor physical instinct. The controlling principle is a sense of style, under which vice, to adapt Burke's words, loses half its evil by losing all its grossness. In the noble society *noblesse*, and nothing else, obliges. Even in the early "international" novels we witness the transformation of Puritan morality, of which the sanction was religious, into a kind of chivalry, of which the sanctions are individual taste and class loyalty. Madame de Mauve, the lovely American married to a naughty French husband in that charming little masterpiece which bears her name, is not exhibited as preserving her "virtue" when she rejects her lover; she is exhibited as preserving her *fineness*. Her American lover acquiesces in his dismissal not from any sudden pang of conscience but from a sudden recognition that if he persists in his suit he will be doing precisely what the vulgar French world and one vulgar spectator in particular expect him to do. In the earlier novels such as *Madame de Mauve, Daisy Miller*, and *The American*, the straightness, the innocence, the firmness of the American conscience are rather played up as beauties against the European background. Yet as early as 1878 he had begun, with the delightfully vivacious and witty *Europeans*, his criticism of the intellectual dulness and emotional poverty of the New England sense of "righteousness"—a criticism wonderfully culminating in *The Ambassadors*, 1903, in which the highly perceptive Strether, sent to France to reclaim an erring son of New England, is himself converted to the European point of view.

Noblesse in the later novels inspires beauties of behavior beyond the reaches of the Puritan imagination.

It is astonishing to observe how many heroes and heroines of the later period are called upon to attest their
fineness by a firm clear-eyed mendacity. *The Wings of
a Dove,* for example, is a vast conspiracy of silence to
keep a girl who knows she is dying from knowing that
her friends know that she knows. To lie with a wry
face is a blemish on one's character. " *I* lie well, thank
God," says Mrs. Lowder, " when, as sometimes will hap-
pen, there's nothing else so good." In the same novel
poor Densher, who rather hates lying, rises to it: " The
single thing that was clear in complications was that,
whatever happened, one was to behave as a gentleman—
to which was added indeed the perhaps slightly less shining truth that complications might sometimes have their
tedium beguiled by a study of the question of how a
gentleman should behave." When he is tempted to throw
up his adventure in noble mendacity he is held to it in
this way: as soon as he steps into the Palazzo Leporelli
in Venice where the dying lady resides he sees " all the
elements of the business compose, as painters called it,
differently "—he sees himself as a figure in a Veronese
picture and he lives up to the grand style of the picture.
He actively fosters the " suppressions " which are " in
the direct interest of every one's good manners, every
one's really quite generous ideal."

The most elaborate and subtle of all James's tributes to the aesthetic ideal in conduct is *The Golden
Bowl*—a picture in eight hundred pages of the relations
existing between Maggie Verver and her husband the
Prince, between Maggie's father Adam Verver and his
second wife Charlotte, and between each one of the

quadrangle and all the rest. Before the pair of marriages took place we are made to understand that an
undefinedly intimate relation had existed between the
Prince and Charlotte, of which Maggie and her father
were unaware; and after the marriages we are made to
understand that the undefinedly intimate relation was
resumed. All four of the parties to this complex relationship are thoroughly civilized; they are persons fit
for the highest society: that is to say, they have wealth,
beauty, exquisite taste, and ability to tell a lie with a
straight face. What will be the outcome? The outcome is that without overt act, or plain speech, or displayed temper on any hand, each one by psychic tact
divines "everything," and Mr. and Mrs. Verver quietly
return to America. Why is the *liaison* dissolved with
such celestial decorum? It is dissolved, because the
"principals" in it perceive the aesthetic "impossibility" of continuing their relations in that atmosphere
of silent but lucid "awareness"; and it is dissolved
with decorum because all the persons concerned are
infinitely superior to the vulgarity of rows, ruptures,
and public proceedings. The "criticism of life" implicit in the entire novel becomes superbly explicit in
Maggie's vision of the ugliness and barbarousness of the
behavior of ordinary mortals in like circumstances:

She might fairly, as she watched them, have missed it
(hot angry jealousy) as a lost thing; have yearned for it,
for the straight vindictive view, the rights of resentment,
the rages of jealousy, the protests of passion, as for something she had been cheated of not least: a range of feelings
which for many women would have meant so much, but

which for *her* husband's wife, for her father's daughter, figured nothing nearer to experience than a wild eastern caravan, looming into view with crude colours in the sun, fierce pipes in the air, high spears against the sky, all a thrill, a natural joy to mingle with, but turning off short before it reached her and plunging into other defiles.

Does not that description of Maggie's vision throb with a fine passion of its own—throb with the excitement of James's imaginative insight into the possible amenity of human intercourse in a society aesthetically disciplined and controlled?

James's works throb with that fine passion from the beginning to the end—just as Pater's do. Criticism's favorite epithets for him hitherto have been " cold," " analytical," " scientific," " passionless," " pitiless " historian of the manners of a futile society. That view of him is doomed to disappear before the closer scrutiny which he demanded and which he deserves. He is not an historian of manners; he is a trenchant idealistic critic of life from the aesthetic point of view.

He is not pitiless except in his exposure of the " ugly," which to his sense includes all forms of evil; in that task he is remorseless whether he is exposing the ugliness of American journalism as in *The Reverberator*, or the ugliness of a thin nervous hysterical intellectualism and feminism as in *The Bostonians*, or the ugliness of murder as in *The Other House*, or the ugliness of irregular sexual relations as in *What Maisie Knew*, or the ugliness of corrupted childhood as in *The Turn of the Screw*. The deep-going uglinesses in the last three cases are presented with a superlative intenseness of artistic passion.　If the effect is not thrilling in the first case and heart-rending in the last two, it is because Anglo-Saxons are quite unaccustomed to having their deeps of terror and pity, their moral centers, touched through the aesthetic nerves.　Granting the fact, there is no reason why they should deny the presence of a passion of antipathy in a man to whose singular consciousness the objectionable inveterately takes the shape of the ugly.

What, however, is more incomprehensible is the general failure of criticism to recognize the ardor of his quite unscientific attachment to the beautiful.　His alleged deficiency in charm, it is asserted, is due to the fact that he does not sympathize with or love any of his characters.　The alleged fact is not a fact.　He sympathizes intensely with all his artists and novelists, with all his connoisseurs of life, with all his multitude of miraculously perceptive persons from the American homesick for England in the *Passionate Pilgrim* through the young woman aware of the fineness of old furniture in *The Spoils of Poynton* to Maggie and Mr. Verver in *The Golden Bowl*.　And he dotes, devoutly dotes, dotes in idolatry upon the enriched consciousness, the general awareness, and the physical loveliness of his women. He can not abide a plain heroine, even if she is to be a criminal.　Of Rose, the murderess in *The Other House*, he says the most exquisite things—" She carries the years almost as you do, and her head better than any young woman I've ever seen.　*Life is somehow becoming to her.*"　In almost every novel that he wrote he touched some woman or other with the soft breath of pure aes-

thetic adoration,—a refining and exalting emotion which
is the note of Sherringham's relation to Miriam in *The
Tragic Muse:*

Beauty was the principle of everything she did. . . .
He could but call it a felicity and an importance incalcul-
able, and but know that it connected itself with universal
values.   To see this force in operation, to sit within its
radius and feel it shift and revolve and change and never
fail, was a corrective to the depression, the humiliation, the
bewilderment of life.   It transported our troubled friend
from the vulgar hour and the ugly fact; drew him to something that had no warrant but its sweetness, no name nor
place save as the pure, the remote, the antique.

This is the " very ecstasy of love "; and for this
virtue, in the years to come, one adept after another
reading the thirty or forty volumes of James which any
one can read with ease and the fifteen or twenty richer
volumes which demand closer application—for this virtue one adept after another, till a brave company
gathers, is certain to say, " I discriminate; but I adore
him! "

X

THE HUMANISM OF GEORGE MEREDITH

THE refusal of the authorities of Westminster Abbey to allow George Meredith to sleep among England's half-canonized dead was by no means surprising. In spite of the indorsement of the Society of Authors and the Prime Minister, the future of his reputation still remains somewhat problematic. If he had died twenty-five years ago, though the work on which his fame rests had then been accomplished, it is doubtful whether the general voice would have decreed him this solemn tribute. Indeed, from his first appearance in literature down to the time of his death no writer of his power had received less recognition for his virtues or more persistent praise for his faults. George Eliot, Swinburne, Watts-Dunton, and a following of enthusiasts felt his might, and for the most part tried to persuade the world that he was a great literary artist. Others asserted with equal vehemence that he was an incoherent thinker, making his artificial, choked, and stuttering novels the vehicle for a mass of epigram. The so-called man in the street, if he chanced to overhear the discussion, promptly decided that it did not concern him, either way. If Meredith attended to the early notices of his books, he must often have sighed, as one who watches for the morning. Even so late as 1880 the *Westminster*

Review, traditionally favorable to his reputation, commented upon the recently published *Egoist*—now often considered his weightiest contribution to fiction—as follows:

> ·Mr. Meredith is, perhaps, our most artistic novelist, and, for that very reason, by no means popular with mere subscribers to Mudie's. His audience is few, but fit. . . . He is, in a word, what the world would vulgarly call too clever. . . . This is Mr. Meredith's great fault—he overdoes his cleverness. If he was more simple, he would be far more effective. *The Egotist* is full of poetry, subtle observation, and sparkling epigram.

This review, with its emphasis upon the literary artist, is typical, and, unless I am mistaken, is about the quintessence of bad criticism. For it has yet to be demonstrated that perfection of art has interfered with the success of any matter whatsoever, even among the subscribers to Mudie's. Those who value Meredith's work most wisely will not extol him for his artistry, but rather deplore his lack of it as one of the many obstacles that have stood in the way of his popularity. Furthermore, to say that he " overdoes his cleverness " is to suggest that he consciously strains for effect. If this critic had really been one of that fit audience, though few, he would rather have suggested that it was insuperably difficult for Meredith not to be clever, that it was almost impossible for him to be simple, that it was entirely regrettable that he did not receive a stiff English academic training. How might not the Oxford culture have disciplined his Celtic lawlessness and have subdued his turn for " natural magic "! Welsh and

Irish in ancestry, Meredith was educated at a Moravian school in Germany. In the plastic time of his youth, he, like Browning and Carlyle, was his own master of rhetoric. Like Carlyle, he wrote prose as if Dryden had never shown the superiority of Charles the Second's English to the flowered and conceited exuberance of the Elizabethans. Like Browning, he wrote verse as if Pope had not died to save us from the sins of the metaphysical school. If Donne, as honest Ben declared, for not keeping of accents deserved hanging, so occasionally did Meredith; and so did Meredith frequently for wanton violations of English idiom and barbarous disregard of the decencies of English style. He lacked the continence of perfect art. He was not steadily master of the means of imparting his experience to the reader and producing the effects which he desired to produce.

He was not wanting in a perception of the supreme beauty of style which appears when a clear conception is perfectly transmitted. His critical sense was sound; he knew where to send other men for light. To a correspondent who had asked him to name the writers most characteristic of the genius of France he replied: " For human philosophy, Montaigne; for the comic appreciation of society, Molière; for the observation of life and condensed expression, La Bruyère; for a most delicate irony scarcely distinguishable from tenderness, Renan; for high pitch of impassioned sentiment, Racine. Add to these your innumerable writers of Mémoirs and Pensées, in which France has never had a rival." To another correspondent he wrote with notable disparagement of English models: " *Style is rarely achieved here.* Your literary hero, lecturing on Style, may have a different opinion. The prose in Shakespeare and Congreve is perfect. They have always the right accent on their terminations. Apart from drama, Swift is a great exemplar; Bolingbroke, and in his mild tea-table way, Addison, follow. Johnson and Macaulay wielded bludgeons; they had not the strength that can be supple. Gibbon could take a long stride with the leg of a dancing master; he could not take a short one." In his essay on the " Idea of Comedy " he showed the keenest appreciation of the styles of Menander and Terence, writing with rapture of their " Elysian speech, equable and ever gracious." But two years later, in the prelude to the *Egoist,* he was capable of such fantastic sentences as this:

Who, says the notable humorist, in allusion to this book *(Book of Earth),* who can studiously travel through sheets of leaves, now capable of a stretch from the Lizard to the last few pulmonary snips and shreds of leagues dancing on their toes for cold, explorers tell us, and catching breath by good luck, like dogs on a table, on the edge of the Pole?

Judged with reference to such standards as are offered by *Henry Esmond* or *The Return of the Native,* he wanted art no less as a story-teller than as a stylist. It is true that he undertook the novelist's most difficult task. In his work the narration of events is quite secondary to the disclosure of character. His representation of men and women was designed to reveal the secret springs of conduct in speech and art. ·Sometimes, like the messenger of the Senecan tragedy, he reports the great things that are going on behind the scenes when

our English sense clamors for dramatic representation.
Sometimes with a kind of choric fury he drowns the
voices of the actors and assaults the ears of the audience with a prolonged and partly enigmatic commentary.
Sometimes he translates the conversation of hero and
heroine into a condensed telegraphic Meridithese. These
methods of telling a story are inartistic because they
do not effectively convey to the reader the mental and
emotional experience which the author has enjoyed;
because they defraud him' in the critical moment of the
legitimate and expected pleasure of hearing the *ipsissima
verba* and of seeing the decisive gesture with his own
eyes. Defenders of Meredith will say that he was bent
on our perceiving the finer meanings of act and speech,
and that he could be sure of his purpose by no other
methods. That is to confess that he lacked the skill of
the supreme literary artist, that his intention was
greater than his power, that his vehicle was inadequate
to its burden. He had himself a subtle sense of the
deeper implications of speech, but he did not possess
sovereignly that instinct which finds a single word to
tell all. When Romeo is banished from Verona, the
nurse urges Juliet to marry Paris. Then follows this
dialogue:

> *Jul.* Speak'st thou from thy heart?
> *Nurse.* And from my soul, too; else beshrew them both.
> *Jul.* Amen!
> *Nurse.* What?
> *Jul.* Well, thou hast comforted me marvellous much.
> Go in; and tell my lady I am gone,
> Having displeas'd my father, to Laurence's cell
> To make confession and to be absolv'd.

What more can one desire?   Could forty pages of commentary add anything to that one incomparable Amen?   That is what the literary artist does with conversation.   Shakespeare's plays are sown with such volume-speaking words; in Meredith's novels I do not know where you will find anything approaching it.   Too often in Meredith there is volubility where in Shakespeare silence is the orator.

If Meredith was not a supreme literary artist, is it possible that he was a first-rate literary genius; or are the two things inseparable?   It would be gratifying to find some substantial ground for the apparently extravagant claims of his friends.   One of them, Robert Louis Stevenson, has been charged with uncritically juxtaposing Meredith and Shakespeare in the enthusiasm of his admiration for *Rhoda Fleming*.   Looking through Stevenson's letters, however, I have been pleased to observe that he says very little about Meredith as a literary artist.   In Sidney Colvin's two-volume edition under the date of 1879, when *The Egoist* was published, there is a single reference to Meredith, as follows: " Chapters viii and ix of Meredith's story are very good, I think."   That is all—and he had met the author in 1878, and they had become warm friends.   But three years after that not ecstatic comment, Stevenson, in a letter to W. E. Henley, lists among those worthy of being honored with a dedication, " George Meredith, the only man of genius of my acquaintance."   " Talking of Meredith," he continues significantly, " I have just re-read for the third and fourth time *The Egoist*. When I shall have read it the sixth or seventh, I begin

tc see I shall know about it. . . . I had no idea of the
matter—human, red matter—he has contrived to *plug
and pack* (the italics are mine) into that strange,
admirable book." Finally, with a passing glance at
George Eliot, whom he could never mention with entire
decorum, he concludes: " I see more and more that
Meredith is built for immortality." A book so plugged
and packed with matter that it took four to six readings
to extract its meaning certainly did not represent
Stevenson's ideal in art. The full explanation of his
enthusiasm does not appear till 1884, again in a letter
to Henley. This time it is as plain as could be desired:
" My view of life is essentially the comic; and the
romantically comic." Then after more comment on
Meredith: " The comedy which keeps the beauty and
touches the terrors of our life (laughter and tragedy-in-
a-good-humor having kissed) that is the last word of
moved representation; embracing the greatest number
of elements of fate and character." Stevenson might
fairly call the man a genius who had opened for him
his literary gospel and had shown him a satisfactory
point of view from which to represent the moving spectacle of life.

There are numerous indications, some of doubtful
value, that the followers of Meredith are beginning to
recognize him as a spiritual master rather than a literary model. The select literary clubs which in the old
days used to study the riddle of the Sphinx in *Childe
Roland*, have discovered that Meredith's poems are less
trite, equally difficult, and therefore probably equally
profound. Some of the novels, too, have attracted those

curious persons who find their chief pleasure in perusing what their friends declare impossible. Four or five books have been devoted to the exposition of Meredith's art and ideas, not all of which are harder to read than the works which they explain. But chiefly we must reckon in the decisive tribute of the younger generation of writers who by imitation and open avowal declare their deep indebtedness to him. " At the present moment," says Mrs. Craigie, " all the most worthy English novelists, with the exception of Thomas Hardy, are distinguished disciples of George Meredith." The heterogeneous character of the alleged Meredithians— Stevenson, Du Maurier, Henley, Sara Grand, Anthony Hope, Maurice Hewlett, W. G. Locke, George Bernard Shaw, G. K. Chesterton, and many others—is sugges- tive. It means that to young authors he has not been primarily a literary model; those who have caught most of his spirit have least imitated his structure and style. It means that if Meredith is " built for immortality " he will survive not merely as an epigrammatist, or as a subtle poet, or as a psychologizing novelist, but also as a man with a fund of energizing ideas, a con- structive critic of life, if not an artist at any rate a genius, one of the spokesmen and master spirits of his time.

Herein certainly lies one of his indubitable claims to genius: that he studied and solved in some measure the basic problems of our contemporary literature half a century before it existed. Though his exposition was unequal to his insight, and his coevals missed many of his points, such of our authors as to-day face the future smiling have found him out. The basic problems of contemporary literature are, for the thoughtful and responsible writer, manifold in appearance but in essence single: How to present a view of life both wise and brave, answering to experience as well as to desire, serviceable in art or in the daily walk. Single in essence, in appearance they are manifold: How to give pleasure without corrupting the heart, and how to give wisdom without chilling it. How to bring into play the great passions of men without unchaining the beast. How to believe in Darwin and the dignity of man. How to recognize the rôle of the nerves in human action without paralyzing the nerve of action. How to admit the weakness of man without dashing his heroism. How to see his acts and respect his intentions. How to renounce his superstitions and retain his faith. How to rebuke without despising him. How to reform society without rebelling against it. How to laugh at its follies without falling into contempt. How to believe that evil is fleeing forever before good, but will never be overtaken and slain. How to look back upon a thousand defeats, and yet cling to the fighting hope. If you will go through this list of questions you will not find one that Meredith does not answer or attempt to answer. Long before Stevenson began to preach his gospel of cheerfulness and valor to a dispirited and pusillanimous world Meredith had marked the texts for his homilies. Long before Mr. Shaw broke into his Mephistophelian laughter, and long before Mr. Chesterton had discovered his loyalty to the universe, when they—if one can conceive such a thing—were quietly sleeping in their cradles, George Meredith had already bottled their thunder.

Richard Feverel, published in 1859 with *The Virginians*, and *Adam Bede*, *The Tale of Two Cities*, and *The Origin of Species*, was a repudiation and a prophecy, but was recognized as neither. The *Westminster Review*, though perceiving in it observation, humor, passion, and tenderness, declared that the " book offers no solution of any of the difficulties it lays open to us; the nineteenth century struggles through it with but faint glimpses of its goal." With interspersed hints in subsequent novels, with prefaces, and with poems Meredith sought to amend the reviewer's error, but not till 1877, when, Aristotle to his own dramatic cycle, he published the *Idea of Comedy*, did he finally make clear his message. From that time it began slowly to be evident that he had made his novels, after all, but the vehicles of an impassioned conviction. He, like so many earnest men of his troubled century, had sought a way of salvation from skepticism, melancholy, ennui, and despair; and he had found a way. Other men had other remedies. For Newman the one thing needful was to submit to authority and enter the Roman fold. Carlyle thought the best that could be done for a man was to find him a master and set him to work. For Mill the key to happiness was free logical discussion in the interests of humanity. For the men of science it was the following of truth wherever it leads. Arnold held that none of these things was of importance in comparison with the ability to recognize " the grand style," whenever it appeared. To those who have read intelligently

Meredith's *Idea of Comedy*, I do not think it will seem an anticlimax to say that he believed the one thing needful, synthesis of all needs, was to instruct men in the proper uses of the comic spirit, that they might laugh and be laughed at unto their soul's salvation. For to him the comic spirit is a fine celestial sunlight in the mind, answering to the theological Grace of God in the heart, which preserves those into whom it passes from every evil thing. It is not hostile to prayer nor to labor nor to logic nor to truth nor to grandeur, but is very friendly to them all. It keeps prayer sweet, labor cheerful, logic sane, truth serviceable, and grandeur human. But over every form of animalism, egotism, sentimentalism, cowardice, and unreason, " it will look humanely malign, and cast an oblique light on them, followed by showers of silvery laughter." For, to quote from the ode to the same beneficent spirit it is the

> Sword of Common Sense!
> Our surest gift: the sacred chain
> Of man to man.

Once grasp this Meredithian idea of comedy and suddenly you find yourself at the center of a coherent critical system. You open the works anywhere—barring perhaps some of the more cryptic poems—and you find yourself at home in an ordered well-lighted world. You perceive why the younger generation is turning toward him, and you see the relation in which he stood to most of his fellows in fiction fifty years ago. The definitions by which in the essay the comic spirit is isolated furnish a formidable critical arsenal. "The sense of the Comic is much blunted by habits of punning and of using humoristic phrase; the trick of employing Johnsonian polysyllables to treat of the infinitely little"—that by no means disposes of Dickens but it casts an "oblique light" upon him. Much more penetrating is this: "Comedy justly treated . . . throws no infamous reflection upon life." How that judges the sneering cynicism of all too frequent passages in the novels of Thackeray like the following:

Oh, Mr. Pendennis! (although this remark does not apply to such a smart fellow as you) if Nature had not made provision for each sex in the credulity of the other, which sees good qualities where none exist, good looks in donkey's ears, wit in their numskulls, and music in their bray, there would not have been near so much marrying and giving in marriage as now obtains, and is necessary for the due propagation of the noble race to which we belong.

That principle is far reaching; it condemns in a single breath the whole miasmic marsh-land of naturalism. "It is unwholesome for men and women to see themselves as they are, if they are no better than they should be"—there is the ethical, or, if one prefers, the sanitary, plank in the platform of the new idealism. "The same of an immoral may be said of realistic exhibitions of a vulgar society"—there is the repudiation of wide wastes of the dry-as-dust realistic fiction, a much-needed denial of the democratic notion that all subjects are fit for art. In some of the poems the Comic Spirit becomes almost truculent in its glee. It is clearly so in pitching upon any theatrical rebel against society; for example, in the verses called " Manfred ":

> Projected from the bilious Childe,
> This clatterjaw his foot could set
> On Alps, without a breast beguiled
> To glow in shedding rascal sweat.
> Somewhere about his grinder teeth,
> He mouthed of thoughts that grilled beneath,
> And summoned Nature to her feud,
> With bile and buskin Attitude.

Meredith arrived a little too late to play Childe Harold or Don Juan; but if he had not been protected by his guardian spirit, he might easily have taken a part in that more plaintive and dismal literature of despair represented by numerous poems of Matthew Arnold. In the crushed and crabbed verse of Meredith's jibe at Arnold's *Empedocles*, I confess to finding something very tonic, something that Arnold as critic would have himself called tonic:

> He leaped. With none to hinder,
> Of Aetna's fiery scoriæ
> In the next vomit-shower, made he
> A more peculiar cinder.
> And this great Doctor, can it be,
> He left no saner recipe
> For men at issue with despair?
> Admiring, even his poet owns,
> While noting his fine lyric tones,
> The last of him was heels in air!
>
> .   .   .   .
>
> Each life its critic deed reveals:
> And him reads reason at his heels,
> If heels in air the last of him.

But what has comedy to do with tragedy, and how do they become tragi-comedy? Well, in the luminous intoxication of the morning following the symposium, Socrates forced Agathon and Aristophanes, who alone had stayed it out with him till cockcrow, to confess not only that tragedy and comedy may be composed by the same person, but also that " the foundations of the tragic and comic arts were essentially the same." Aristodemus, who reported the conclusion of the dispute, was unfortunately asleep during the discussion. With this, for that reason, unexplained opinion of Socrates, Meredith was obviously in accord. To his view, life is neither wholly comedy nor wholly tragedy, but both at once. In order to distinguish either element one must be able to distinguish both; the comic spirit, one may almost say, is that which perceives the tragic fault. In order to represent life bravely and wisely, one must see it steadily, and see it whole. Such sight is given only to deep and grave heads. Those endowed with this vision discern that the great girders which bear up the world of man are the discipline of the passions by the mind, loyalty to reason, and faith in civilization. Whatever forces attempt to weaken these girders—the cynicism of Don Juan, the despair of Empedocles—the Comic Spirit holds them, to adopt the Caesarian euphemism, *in numero hostium*—puts them to the sword of common sense. The discernment that these great girders are essential to civilization, and the loyalty which in grave men springs with the discernment, underlie every true comedy and every true tragedy. But the struggle which most men undergo in disciplining their passions, learning to walk in the light of reason, and preserving their faith in civilization, is a strange series of ups and downs. Comedy attends to their foolish falls; tragedy to their painful failures; to represent the whole course of the struggle is to write tragi-comedy.

Tragi-comedy as the position of equipoise in life and art—that, in Meredith's time, was a notable discovery. When we attempt to measure his achievement we should not lose sight of the originality, the scope, and the difficulty of his design. He planned to produce thoughtful laughter, an aim which demanded that the characters in his novels, as well as in his audience, should possess some of the culture of the drawing-room. But he planned at the same time to move the great passions which are generally attenuated under intensive cultivation. Since the Restoration they had almost disappeared from the fiction of high life. Wordsworth had been obliged to seek out the great universal impulses in the cottages of Cumberland peasants. The Brontës studied them in mad country squires. George Eliot found them among the yeomen of Warwickshire. Even Thomas Hardy has had to resort to shepherds and dairy-maids—so fugitive is our sense of solemn splendor from the roar of cities and civilized men. But what pitiful antagonists of destiny these rural people of Mr. Hardy make. The intelligence of mortals is wholly inactive in the combat. In condemning the ways of God to man this grim artist seems obsessed by the idea that all nature is conspiring to bring a helpless humanity to degradation and shame. That is hardly to see life whole. Meredith sought his splendor in another place.

His problem was how to make tragedy and comedy meet together in the drawing-room.   Comedy was there to stay; but as for tragedy, Thackeray, for example, avoided it.   Dickens and his public really preferred melodrama and bloody murder.

To his contemporaries and predecessors Meredith appears on the whole to have owed relatively little, though his obligations were probably larger than has generally been acknowledged.   What makes him appear comparatively isolated in his time is not his exemption from contemporary forces, but his comprehensive inclusion of them within his own complex mind and temperament.   His culture is wide and deep.   His fiction gathers its virtues from poetry, history, science, and philosophy.   His purposefulness is fortified by an intimate and almost lifelong friendship with that fine austere Liberal, John Morley, and with that drily witty master of common sense, Leslie Stephen, and with that high-aspiring revered sage, Thomas Carlyle.   In *Farina*, *The Shaving of Shagput*, *The Ordeal of Richard Feverel*, *Evan Harrington*, and *The Egoist* one may possibly detect the influence of the comic spirit of Meredith's first father-in-law, Thomas Love Peacock, whose laughter leaped and flashed upon the humbugs and intellectual follies of his day with much of the Meredithian lambency and gusto.   On his graver side he shows a certain affiliation with George Eliot; but so far as the chronological indications go, he is as likely to have influenced her as she to have influenced him.   The moral high seriousness and the love of Nature, so conspicuously exhibited by both, may perhaps be ascribed in part to their common inheritance from Wordsworth. The significant chapter in the *Ordeal of Richard Feverel* entitled " Nature speaks " is strikingly parallel not merely in its spirit but also in its incidents to Wordsworth's *Peter Bell*—a poem written to illustrate the healing and redemptive impulses from a " vernal wood."

But no writer between Meredith and Shakespeare has Meredith's power of marrying tragedy and comedy, poetry and laughter. He is the single exception to the rule that no disciple can stand up under the overwhelming influence of the great Elizabethan. Shakespeare was his master. Shakespeare determined his point of view and the large feature of his artistic representation. From him he learned to choose out for the favorite theatre of his action a country-house, where, as in a court, were assembled enough actors of civilized life to be visible against the scenery. From him he learned to let poor clowns play humble parts, and if any one had to be sent out on a barren heath to send a king who even in madness was a match for the storm. From him he learned to line the back and sides of his stage with the gray and middle ages of wisdom, pedantry, sanctity, craft, and cynicism; and then to release in the foreground young Romeo and Juliet, or Perdita and Florizel, or Ferdinand and Miranda to discover the brave new world under the stinging rain of comment from prudent or disillusioned antiquity; and then, at last, whether to youth and beauty the vista of days opened smiling, or whether some dire mischance closed their fond eyes forever, to intimate that to youth belong the untrodden ways.

The " criticism of life " underlying Meredith's representations of it is in its general outlines Shakespearian,
and it is Shakespearian in the sweetness and the nobility
of its temper. Meredith, like his master, accepts the
universe with a smile; but like his master, he almost
immediately proceeds to distinguish within the human
microcosm three distinct levels of being: blood, brain,
and spirit. He is, to be sure, so far a man of his own
time that he conceives the physical, the intellectual, and
the spiritual as successive stages in the grand evolutionary process. He looks to no Hebrew chronicler to
explain how in the beginning light was divided from
darkness and man from the beasts of the field. He
ascribes these epoch-making distinctions to the inscrutable workings of Life and our mother Earth—deities
always named by him with reverence; but, unlike the
naturalistic novelists of his day, he regards these distinctions as real, substantial, and established. He does
not conceive of man as mere flesh or mere mind or mere
spirit but as, at his healthiest and completest, a fine
concord and harmony of the three. All this the reader
may find in the following lines from *The Woods of
Westermain* ":

> Each of each in sequent birth,
> Blood and brain and spirit, three
> (Say the deepest gnomes of Earth),
> Join for true felicity.
> Are they parted, then expect
> Someone sailing to be wrecked:
> Separate hunting are they sped,
> Scan the morsel coveted.

Earth that Triad is: she hides
Joy from him who that divides;
Showers it when the three are one
Glassing her in union.

For the novelists who represent man as essentially a depraved animal Meredith has little but loathing and contempt. After reading a naturalistic work by one of his French contemporaries he writes, in 1887: " O what a nocturient, cacaturient crew has issued of the lens of the Sun of the mind on the lower facts of life!—on sheer Realism, breeder at best of the dung-fly. Yet has that Realism been a corrective of the more corruptingly vaporous with its tickling hints at sensuality. It may serve ultimately in form of coprolite to fatten poor soil for better produce."

Yet Meredith declares repeatedly in his letters that " a frank acceptance of Reality is the firm basis of the Ideal." As a moralist he is anti-Puritan. He has no patience with an ascetic mortification of the flesh. Like Browning's David, he rejoices in " our manhood's prime vigour "; he accepts with a relish the legitimate physical gratifications of life—

And the meal, the rich dates yellowed over with gold dust
    divine,
And the locust-flesh steeped in the pitcher, the full draught
    of wine.

To the Rev. Augustus Jessop he writes: " Let men make good blood, I constantly cry. I hold that to be rightly materialistic—to understand and take nature as she is—is to get on the true divine highroad. That we should attain to a healthy humanity, is surely the most pleasing thing in God's sight." With allusion to Hawthorne, he says in 1865: "I strive by study of humanity to represent it: not its morbid action. I have a tendency to do that, which I repress: for, in delineating it, there is no gain. In all my, truly, very faulty works, there is this aim. Much of my strength lies in painting morbid emotion and exceptional positions; but my conscience will not let me so waste my time."

These convictions are illustrated in his novels by his representations of what we should call to-day the " eugenic " marriage, and by his unrivalled array of healthy " fair women and brave men." His heroines can walk, ride, row, and swim distances which to any one of Jane Austen's ladies would have been appalling—of which the mere prospect would probably have caused her to sink swooning into the arms of her escort. He recognizes and treats frankly enough the magnetic force of sexual attraction; but he recognizes it, by choice, in men and women who live above the level of sensuality, and in whom this mysterious force has been metamorphosed into a general energizer of the intelligence and spirit. In his exquisite poem, *Love in the Valley*, for example, the physical root of the emotion is adequately indicated, but what is offered for our delectation is its bursting through the senses into fragrant and luxuriant blossom in the mind and the imagination. The speaker, like a right Shakespearian lover, is keenly alive to the sensuous charm of the beloved being, but his higher fac--ulties exalt and transfigure the delight of the senses, and hold him rapt, reverent, and breathless with adoration.   I quote a few stanzas which may be paralleled by his description of Lucy Desborough in *The Ordeal of Richard Feverel* or by the description of Meredith's second wife in the Letters, ending thus: " When her hand rests in mine, the world seems to hold its breath, and the sun is moveless.   I take hold of Eternity."—

Under yonder beech-tree single on the green-sward,
    Couched with her arms behind her golden head,
Knees and tresses folded to slip and ripple idly,
    Lies my young love sleeping in the shade.
Had I the heart to slide an arm beneath her,
    Press her parting lips as her waist I gather slow,
Waking in amazement she could not but embrace me:
    Then would she hold me and never let me go?

   .   .   .   .   .   .

Shy as the squirrel and wayward as the swallow,
    Swift as the swallow along the river's light
Circleting the surface to meet his mirrored winglets,
    Fleeter she seems in her stay than in her flight.
Shy as the squirrel that leaps among the pine-tops,
    Wayward as the swallow overhead at set of sun,
She whom I love is hard to catch and conquer,
    Hard, but O the glory of the winning were she won.

   .   .   .   .   .   .

When her mother tends her before the laughing mirror,
    Tying up her laces, looping up her hair,
Often she thinks, were this wild thing wedded,
    More love should I have, and much less care.
When her mother tends her before the lighted mirror,
    Loosening her laces, combing down her curls,
Often she thinks, were this wild thing wedded,
    I should miss but one for many boys and girls.

   .   .   .   .   .

When at dawn she sighs, and like an infant to the window
  Turns grave eyes craving light, released from dreams,
Beautiful she looks, like a white water lily
  Bursting out of bud in haven of the streams.
When from bed she rises clothed from neck to ankle
  In her long nightgown sweet as boughs of May,
Beautiful she looks, like a tall garden lily
  Pure from the night, and splendid for the day.

The peculiar specialty of the Meredithian heroine, however, is neither health nor beauty, but brains. In behalf of women George Meredith repudiates alike Alfred Austin's old Tory ideal—the soft shy mate that sits on the nest and never stirs; the Pre-Raphaelite ideal—all lips and neck and dreaming eyes; and Thomas Hardy's romantic ideal—the fair puppet of passionate impulse. His view of the subject resembles that of John Stuart Mill in his fervid treatise on *The Subjection of Women*—a plea for the emancipation of women in their own interest and in the interest of society at large. "I can foresee great and blessed changes for the race when they have achieved independence"; he writes in a letter of 1888, "for that must come of the exercise of their minds—the necessity for which is induced by their reliance on themselves for subsistence." To his sense, many of the Victorian representations of women in art and in literature reflect but the unsubdued Turkish instincts of the male. His conscience rebels against the imposition upon fair English girls of the ideals of the harem. His intelligence is irritated, as that of most men is from time to time, by the difficulty of settling any question with a typical representative of "the sex" on rational grounds.   The subtlest sonnet sequence in English, his *Modern Love*, is a series of cries of exasperation and pain at the baffling indirectness of the dealing of woman with man:

> Their sense is with their senses all mixed in,
> Destroyed by subtleties these women are!
> More brain, O Lord, more brain! or we shall mar
> Utterly this fair garden we might win.

Clara Middleton in *The Egoist*, Diana of the Crossways, and Aminta are among his notable essays toward the establishment of a new ideal of " femininity."   With the young health of Nature in May and the beauty of the white birch tree they unite a keen critical faculty which is their mark of intellectual independence.   Emotional enough, all of them, they are not in the long run at the mercy of their emotions.   If they have been duped in their first adventure with society, they have the wit to extricate themselves from situations threatening disaster, and to reconstruct their lives in conformity with a rational ideal and, if necessary, like George Eliot in defiance of conventions—a readjustment, by the way, as remote from sensual philandering as the north pole is from the south pole.   Of Diana, Meredith says proudly, " she has no puppet pliancy."   Regarded as a character she has grievous faults.   Regarded as a piece of characterization, she is not entirely plausible.   But regarded as the imperfect human illustration of certain ideals, she is—in her valiancy and in her power of intellectual growth and spiritual rejuvenescence—one of the most interesting and inspiriting women in English fiction.

In order to " civilize " the women Meredith sees very
clearly that it is necessary at the same time to civilize
the men.   Civilization implies for him the emancipation
of human conduct from non-rational controls.   It means
establishing in secure sovereignty within each individual
man a benevolent and beneficent mind.   He has no over-
sanguine expectation of the completion of the evolutionary process.   He sees the serenity and freedom of
reason

> By more elusive savages assailed
> On each ascending stage.

He girds on the sword of the Comic Spirit and unleashes
the hounds of laughter to hunt down the " savages "
lurking and skulking in the breasts of those representatives of the race who are in outward appearance
most remote from our ancestors of the cave.   His game
includes the philosopher who bids us trust our emotional
instincts—" accept the *throb* for lord of us "; or who
bids us bow the knee to hoary and outworn conventions;
or who lays us prostrate by mumbling " the crackskull
name of Fate "; or who sets up self as God.   Meredith
had drunk deep of the intellectual radicalism of Mill
and Morley, and the spirit of it profoundly affects his
representations of men in fiction.   The qualities which,
above everything else, he glorifies in his young men are
intrepidity and will; the defects upon which his muse
looks malignly are " the untrimmed lamp and the ungirt
loin."   The virtues which he admires in men of maturity
are wisdom and generosity; the sins which he castigates
are innumerable, but most conspicuous among them are
sensuality, pride, obstinacy, and egotism.   Sir Wil-

loughby Patterne in *The Egoist* is his great and unrivalled masterpiece in the remorseless dissection of male egotism masking as sensibility and refinement. If the book were read, chewed, and "inwardly digested" by every young man contemplating courtship or marriage, we might reasonably look two or three generations hence for some wholesome clarifications and amendments in the spiritual relations of the sexes. Sir Willoughby Patterne is his most elaborate and penetrating study of a single specimen of the lordly species, but his richest and most various exhibition of critical portraits of men is in *The Ordeal of Richard Feverel*, where the light of the Comic Spirit falls brilliantly upon the sentimentality and the tragic pride, obstinacy, and egotism of Sir Austin Feverel; the deliberate sensuality and the cynicism of Adrian Harley; the gluttony and hypochondria of Hippias Feverel; the undisciplined wrath of Farmer Blaize, the dull Philistinism of Thompson père, the follies of young Richard's passion and hot-headed generosity, the dull juvenile obscenity of Ripton Thompson; and upon sundry others. Every one of these men was vitally conceived. Each one of them has his winsome and lovable aspects. Meredith seems incapable of hating or despising utterly any one of his kind. But his warm human friendliness is edged, like a surgeon's knife, for discrimination. He cuts deep but the operation is therapeutic. "By my faith in the head," he cries, quaintly imaging his reliance upon the widening of intellectual light:

> I can hear a faint crow
> Of the cock of fresh mornings, far, far, yet distinct.

What does an evolutionist like Meredith mean when he distinguishes the spiritual from the intellectual world? He has himself some difficulty in telling us, but one gathers from his various utterances that to " live in the spirit " is to live steadily above the clamor of the flesh and the crying of self-interest to the will. Intercourse with men who dwell habitually at that level has, as most of us know, an ennobling influence akin to that of great works of art, love of country, and religion. Meredith had no respect for the orthodox theology of his time, but he called himself a " practical Christian," and, to my sense, he writes, in frequent passages of his correspondence, like a man who has experienced what theologians call " the peace of God." In 1872 he writes to his son:

You know how Socrates loved Truth. Virtue and truth are one. Look for the truth in everything, and follow it, and you will then be living justly before God. Let nothing flout your sense of a Supreme Being, and be certain that your understanding wavers whenever you chance to doubt that he leads to good. We grow to good as the plant grows to light. The school has only to look through history for a scientific assurance of it. And do not lose the habit of praying to the unseen Divinity. Prayer for worldly goods is worse than fruitless, but *prayer for strength of soul is that passion of the soul which catches the gift it seeks.*

In " the first ten minutes of 1878 " he sends to John Morley a new year's greeting, pulsing still with the mystical exultation which the writer felt when he hailed the new year under the midnight skies to the sound of the new year's bells:

To come from a gaze at the stars—Orion and shaking
Sirius below him—is to catch a glance at the inscrutable
face of him that hurries us on, as on a wheel, from dust to
dust—I thought of you and how it might be with you this
year: hoped for good: saw beyond good and evil to great
stillness, another form of moving for you and me.   It seems
to me that Spirit is,—how, where, and by what means involving us, none can say.   But in this life there is no life
save in spirit.   The rest of life, and we may know it in
love,—is an aching and a rotting.

When in 1885 Meredith's wife lay dying, he wrote to
John Morley: " Happily for me, I have learnt to live
much in the spirit and see brightness on the other side
of life, otherwise this running of my poor doe with the
inextricable arrow in her flanks, would pull me down
too.   As it is, I sink at times.   I need all my strength to
stand the harsh facts of existence.   I wish it were I to
be the traveller instead."   After her death: " While
she lingered I could not hope for it to last, and now I
could crave any of the latest signs of her breathing—a
weakness of my flesh.   When the mind shall be steadier,
I shall have her calmly present—past all tears."   Two
days later: " She was the best of wives, truest among
human creatures . . . I believe in Spirit, and I have
her with me here, though at present I cannot get to calm
of thought, all the scenes of her long endurance, and the
days of peace before it rise up."

I have been attempting to show why Meredith's " criticism of life " impresses one, as, on the whole, unusually
adequate for a writer of our bewildered age.   Perhaps
the rarest note in the literature of our time is nobility
of feeling.   Meredith strikes that note on whatever level

he touches the strings of life. Like his master Shakespeare, speaking nobly of the body, nobly of the mind,
and nobly of the spirit, he sounds the chord of full
harmony for which our hearts are eager. " Between
realism and idealism," he declares, " there is no natural
conflict. This completes that." Though his craftsmanship and power of representation were inferior to his
conceptive and critical faculties, he produced a body of
work which richly remunerates the explorer. Some of
his contemporaries possessed separately in a higher
degree the intellectual or the emotional powers with
which he was gifted; but no one of them fused within
himself so many and so diverse powers. He woke early
to the necessity and the possibility of a new synthesis.
His first novel, produced far back in the middle of the
nineteenth century, seems incredibly fresh to-day, and
would seem incredibly contemporaneous if our living
writers had taught us to expect from them anything so
sound and sweet. To an American critic he wrote in
1887: " I think that all right use of life, is to pave
ways for the firmer footing of those who succeed us; as
to my works, I know them faulty, think them of worth
only when they point and aid to that end." In close
touch with distinguished leaders of Liberal thought, he
heartily partook in their sense of high responsibility to
society and in their resolution to make war without truce
upon the confederated lusts and egotisms of unredeemed
animal man. His sonnet to " J. M." is almost Miltonic
in its note of valorous consecration:

> Our faith is ours and comes not on a tide:
> And whether Earth's great offspring, by decree,

Must rot if they abjure rapacity,
Not argument but effort shall decide.
They number many heads in that hard flock:
Trim swordsmen they push forth; yet try thy steel.
Thou, fighting for poor human kind, wilt feel
The strength of Roland in thy wrist to hew
A chasm sheer into the barrier rock,
And bring the army of the faithful through.

Few, indeed, are the writers of fiction who have striven so steadily to seize and conserve for posterity the sound ideas afloat in their time. In these four lines from *A Reading of Earth* we touch upon the controlling principle of all Meredith's work:

Thou under stress of the strife,
Shalt hear for sustainment supreme,
The cry of the conscience of life:
Keep the young generations in hail,
And bequeath them no tumbled house.

XI

SHAKESPEARE, OUR CONTEMPORARY

WHEN we commemorate the death of a great man, we are accustomed to recount his virtues, and, according to the measure of our ability, to reanimate his dust. In the case of Shakespeare the dearth of biographical documents and the perverse subtlety of posterity have rendered it difficult to perform these rites of honor. Minute research recovers a christened, marrying, acting, play-writing, shareholding, litigating, will-making person of the slightest inspirational quality. Seventeenth century reference is rich in praise of the writings, but indicates little more of the man than that he was of " upright demeanor," " civil," " honest," " fluent," and of an " open and free nature." The Shakespeare whom we would honor, we know almost exclusively through his works. As Sir Walter Raleigh has finely said: " He wove upon the roaring loom of Time the garment that we see him by; and the earth at Stratford closed over the broken shuttle."

From the works, however, each age has reconstructed " Shakespeare the man " very much as, from a survey of the world, each age has reconstructed the Creator: sometimes expatiating in folios on the attributes of deity; sometimes content with asking us to adore the Great Unknowable. The young Milton meditating on the works becomes a monument of wonder and astonishment; and Goethe in his old age exclaims, " But we cannot talk about Shakespeare; everything is inadequate." In the romantic days when men worshiped Nature, a pious German editor held that the works of Shakespeare were an " integral part of nature and therefore above criticism." Since Hazlitt launched his paradox, that " no really great man ever thought himself so," perhaps the most striking and popular notion concerning the poet is that he did not know what he was about. The spirit of our day, with its new naturalistic philosophies, finds this notion in happy accord with its inclination. That he did not know what he was about is, for example, what endears to our time Romain Roland's great artist-soul, Jean Christophe. It is the mark by which we recognize the supreme figures in contemporary literature. We should like to think of Shakespeare as our own contemporary. And so our current criticism—with its new friendliness to the life of the senses, to " vital forces," to the spontaneous, the natural, the instinctive, the purposeless—pleasantly flatters itself by discovering in the works of the world's master dramatist not a thinking, deliberate human architect but an unconscious, unmoral, natural force, working effortless miracles like the apian parthenons or the intricate arras of the frost.

This current view of Shakespeare as a neutral, unmoral, unconscious creative force rests upon a superficially plausible but, as I believe, a thoroughly fallacious argument, which runs something like this: Shakespeare created a various world in the image of that in which we live. It is peopled with kings and peasants, saints and

sinners, sages and fools, men and monsters, each obedient
to the dictation of his own heart, belly, or other oracle
of his destiny. It is neither a better nor a worse place
of residence than New York or London. With impartial
hand its maker has unloosed the powers of good and evil
to work out their eternal conflict, with no more of divine
interposition than is observable upon this afflicted planet.
The virtuous are insecure in felicity; justice is frequently thwarted; the treacherous and bloody villain
works his will; and the innocent go down with the guilty
to disaster and death. To attribute to the author the
sentiment of any one of his *dramatis personæ* is, as
Juliet's nurse would say, " very weak dealing "; for the
chances are that the chosen sentiment is contradicted in
the next scene by another of the *dramatis personæ*.
" No critical test has yet been found," says Sir Sidney
Lee in the latest edition of his Life, " whereby to disen-
tangle Shakespeare's personal feelings or opinions from
those which he imputes to the creatures of his dramatic
world. It was contrary to Shakespeare's dramatic aim
to label or catalogue in drama his private sympathies
or antipathies."

This parallel between the real world and the world of
Shakespeare's imagination neglects one immensely important difference, which is overlooked only because it is
so obvious, but which, adequately apprehended, destroys
the illusion of parallelism altogether, and explodes the
theory of authorial reticence and dramatic impersonal-
ity. The difference is this: In viewing the real world
we frequently misunderstand the characters and motives
of people who are very near to us, and we frequently

miss the significance of important events which are taking place under our eyes. The grief of those we love is often inarticulate and unknown to us; passion sometimes gives no sign; hypocrisy wears its mask unpenetrated; and iniquity often goes not merely unpunished but undetected and even unsuspected to the grave. In partial or complete ignorance, even the wise and sensitive among us misplace their affection, their admiration, their compassion; and dull souls walk daily among tragic and comic friends and neighbors without a smile or a tear.

In viewing Shakespeare's imaginary world, on the other hand, we are all constrained to see and to feel poignantly the emotional and moral significance of every character and every event. We follow the course of the great passions, which for us have no underground channels, from their inception to their catastrophic close. The lid of life is off. We gaze into the heart of all the crises. The bosoms of sinners have no secrets for us; we have attended them in each step that led to their *doloroso passo*. The just and the unjust man stand for us naked in their divers qualities, as we are told they shall stand in the Day of Judgment. There is not the least ambiguity in their appeal to our emotions or our judgment. The master of the spectacle has bared to the last filament their characters, their motives, and their intentions; for Shakespeare's technique aims at delight not by the defeat but by the fulfilment of expectation. His figures are so placed, so contrasted, so lighted from within and from without—by soliloquy, aside, chorus, and direct speech and act—that our sympathies go right; go where he intended that they should go. If goodness and beauty are not always fortunate in the plot, they are invariably recognized and loved by the spectators. If the *dramatis personæ* do not receive poetic justice in the play, they always receive it in the audience!

This clarifying of the judgment and this direction of the sympathies are precisely Shakespeare's self-revelation. His intention is to be inferred, like that of any master craftsman, from his effect. To know what he thought about life, the normally constituted reader or spectator has only to consult his own emotions when they have been stirred by the presence of the master's adored and execrated creatures. But we err through a grievous lack of reflection, if we attribute Shakespeare's effect primarily to our own intelligence and discrimination; for, as I have just insisted, Shakespeare presents to us, in place of the bewildering and uncertain reality, a world artfully prepared, unveiled, intelligible, with every value already discriminated. Shakespeare holds the " mirror " up to nature, but the light which renders the reflected objects visible is not the light of the sun, but the illumination of the mirror-maker's " comprehensive soul." His characters do not wait for our praise or blame. At their very advent in the world of the imagination Iago stood in the eternal shadow of his creator's condemnation, and Desdemona walked in the light of his countenance. We, with our essentially superfluous feeling and intelligence, are asked to judge a case which has already come to judgment.

All this amounts to a declaration that Shakespeare

reveals himself through his work as a mind in which the great creative and shaping force of the imagination is constantly regulated and directed by a critical intelligence, stamping values upon the things created, and aiming steadily at a total aesthetic and moral effect which was approved by the best sense of his own time, and has endured the scrutiny of three hundred years.

Those of us who, trusting in this " argument from design," hold this view of him, and resent honoring his memory with the " naturalists " by denying him intelligence, self-knowledge, morality, and the normal human loyalties, have indeed some high modern authorities on our side. Goethe, for example, said to Eckermann, " The poet must know what effects he wishes to produce, and regulate the nature of his characters accordingly. . . . What would be the use of poets, if they only repeated the record of the historian? The poet must go further, and give us, if possible, something higher and better. All the characters of Sophocles have something of that great poet's lofty soul: and it is the same with the characters of Shakespeare. That is as it ought to be." Coleridge perhaps slightly overstated our case when he asserted that no man was ever yet a great poet without being at the same time a great philosopher. But those who stand for the recognition of the intellectual element in poetic genius, and, in spite of current poetic practice and precept, cling to the belief that the poet needs to know something and to be something, find satisfaction in Coleridge's summary description of Shakespeare's talent: " What then, shall we say? even this, that Shakespeare, no mere child of nature; no automaton of genius; no passive vehicle of inspiration . . . first studied patiently, meditated deeply, understood minutely, till knowledge, become habitual and intuitive, wedded itself to his habitual feelings."

The chief argument in favor of our view, however, is not that it is in harmony with the view of Goethe and of Coleridge, but that it is in harmony with the view of the men among whom Shakespeare lived. It is consonant with their eulogies of him, and also with their general conceptions of the poet and the poetic art. The correction of many of our modern misinterpretations is to step through and ignore the commentators of the last hundred years, and to re-read the text in the light of Elizabethan and Jacobean criticism and theory. In making this return, it is to be remembered that Shakespeare among his fellow-dramatists is, with very few exceptions, distinctly among his inferiors, not merely in respect to poetry but also in respect to morality and intelligence. If you pass from reading Shakespeare to Dekker, Marston, Middleton, Heywood, you feel yourself descending from the highlands to the foothills and the plain. If you wish to remain long in the company of the grave and capacious wits who made the glory of the Great Age, you must leave the Bankside. But you may read in turn Sidney's *Apology*, a sermon of Hooker's, an epithalamion of Spenser's, an essay of Bacon's, a chapter of the King James Bible, the literary note-book of Jonson, or the prose passage in *Henry V* discussing the king's responsibility for the souls of his soldiers—without any shocking change of elevation.

If one consults with this group of Shakespeare's peers, one learns a good many points about the temper of the age, which many recent writers have forgotten. It is perfectly clear, for example, that the Elizabethans were not ashamed of their moral intentions. From Sidney to Jonson it is agreed that the " very end of Poesie " is the delightful teaching of morality; to make men love the good and eschew the evil. And Sidney, the adored representative of his time, expresses its characteristic idealism and its high seriousness when in a famous passage he asserts the ultimate moral purpose of all learning: " This purifying of wit, this enriching of memory, enabling of judgment, and enlarging of conceit, which commonly we call learning, under what name soever it come forth, or to what end soever it be directed, the final end is to lead and draw us to as high a perfection as our degenerate souls, made worse by their clayey lodging, can be capable of." In distinction from our modern aesthetes who hold that the end of poetry is beauty, or our modern naturalists who hold that the end of literature is a scientific representation of truth, Spenser tells us that the general end of his great poem is " to fashion a gentleman or noble person in virtuous and gentle discipline." In contrast with our modern theorists who insist upon the spectatorial neutrality of the artist, " Men must know," says Lord Bacon, " that in the theatre of man's life, it is reserved only for God and angels to be lookers on." Passages such as these afford to my mind a strong presumption that if Shakespeare had any community of spirit with his peers in his own time, and it is absurd to suppose that he had not, he would have looked upon a neutral and unmoral poet with contempt.

When I hear a modern scholar call Shakespeare " the supreme child of a childlike age," I take some satisfaction in the certainty that the phrase would have perplexed Lord Bacon as much as it perplexes me. I try in vain to reconcile that conception of him with the inscription beneath his bust in Stratford, which attributes to him the judgment of Nestor, the sagacity of Socrates, and the art of Virgil. If that evidence is rejected as epigraphical compliment, I turn with confidence to that " crusty batch of nature," Ben Jonson, a man who weighed his words, notoriously chary of praise to his contemporaries, an inveterate egotist, obviously Shakespeare's rival, a confirmed and belligerent classicist, and, as such, sincerely hostile to Shakespeare's dramatic principles and practice. While Shakespeare is living, " honest Ben " jibes and jests at him, as he does at most men; but when the Stratford poet is gathered to his fathers, it is this reluctant witness who pays what is perhaps still the supreme tribute to his art; matches him with Aeschylus, Euripides, and Sophocles; puts him in comparison (as he does elsewhere Lord Bacon) with all that " insolent Greece or haughty Rome sent forth, or since did from their ashes come." It is certainly the supreme extant tribute to the personal charm of Shakespeare that this same reluctant witness should have said in another place: " I loved the man, and do honor his memory on this side idolatry as much as any." Now for our present purposes the significant point is this: Jonson, who knew both works and man, declared that

Shakespeare's mind and manners are distinctly recognizable, are indeed resplendently visible, in his works:

> . . . Look how the father's face
> Lives in his issue; even so the race
> Of Shakespeare's mind and manners brightly shines
> In his well turned and true filed lines.

If Shakespeare, whom Jonson called the " soul of the age," was after all a typical thinking Elizabethan with the Elizabethan taste for moral philosophy, we may be sure that he meditated on nature like an Elizabethan humanist. The essence of Elizabethan as of other humanisms is the understanding of man and the definition of the sphere of properly human activity. The philosophical mind of Shakespeare's age began the work of reflection by cleaving the universe along three levels. On the lowest level is the natural world, which is the plane of instinct, appetite, animality, lust, the animal passions or affections; on this level the regulation is by necessary or natural law. On the middle level is the human world, which is regulated and, in a sense, created by the will and knowledge of man; working upon the natural world; but governed by reason, the special human faculty; and illuminated more or less from the level above. On the third level is the supernatural world, which is the plane of spiritual beings, and the home of eternal ideas.

Now let us hear from Hooker, that too-infrequently-remembered " master of wit and language," what man is, and how he could demean himself in his middle state:

Whatsoever we work as man, the same we do wittingly

work and freely. . . . Two fountains there are of human action, Knowledge and Will. . . . But of one thing we must have special care, as being a matter of no small moment; and that is how the Will, properly and strictly taken, as it is of things referred unto the end that man desireth, differeth greatly from that inferior natural desire, which we call Appetite. The object of Appetite is whatsoever sensible good may be wished for; the object of Will is that good which Reason doth lead us to seek. . . . Appetite is the Will's solicitor; and the Will is Appetite's controller; what we covet according to the one by the other we often reject; neither is any other desire properly termed Will but that where Reason and Understanding, or the show of Reason, prescribeth the thing desired. . . . When hereupon we come to observe in our souls of what excellency our souls are in comparison with our bodies, and the diviner part in relation with the baser of our souls; seeing that all these concur in producing human actions, it cannot be well unless the chiefest do command and direct the rest. The soul then ought to conduct the body, and the spirit of our minds the soul.

I can but very briefly and inadequately indicate here the grounds for my belief that this beautiful passage of Hooker's summarizes very well the working philosophy which informs the dramas of Shakespeare. His plays are studded with evidence that he meditated constantly on the relation of man to the natural world below him, and to the supernatural world above him; that he had made for himself the kind of distinction that Hooker makes between the Will and the Appetite, the voluntary law of man and the involuntary law of nature; and that he looked upon Knowledge and Will as the supreme human attributes, exalting their dignity as compared with instinct, and accentuating their general importance as compared with supernatural influences.

Gray called him " Nature's darling "—" to him the mighty Mother did unveil her awful face." No one who has examined his scores of references to Nature can imagine that he worshiped his " mother " in the Wordsworthian sense—as the guide, the guardian of his heart, and soul of all his moral being. On the contrary he held up to her with somewhat unfilial candour the mirror of his own idealism, which reflected her beauty, and also every mole in her mysterious visage. As he represents her, she is an earth-born deity, a bounteous housewife, the president of the natural world, magnificently various, fertile, and vital, but secret, a dissembler, irrationally impartial, absolutely unmoral. To some of her children she gives good gifts—grace, health, strength, equability of temper; to others, wry faces, disease, stammering speech, choler. At one time or another her " darling " is driven to reflect that " Nature with a beauteous wall doth oft close in pollution "; that " Nature hath framed strange fellows in her time "; and that " there's nothing level in our cursed natures." One avowed nature-worshiper, Shakespeare presents: Edmund, the bastard son of Gloucester, who exclaims, " Thou, Nature, art my goddess "—which means that he will not acknowledge custom or civil or divine law, but will follow through adultery and murder the natural law of his own instincts. One bland believer in " natural goodness," he presents: Gonzalo, in the *Tempest*, who would establish Montaigne's ideal commonwealth in the enchanted isle, and abolish labor and government, expecting, as a result of following nature, leisure in the men and purity in the women. Is it not the Socratic insight of Shakespeare that cuts in with the laconic comment: " All idle; whores and knaves "?

From reflection upon the duplicity of Nature, it is perfectly clear, I think, that Shakespeare concluded we cannot trust her to feed these minds or bodies of ours in a " wise passivness." But as he feels Will and Knowledge strong within him, he throws out in his earlier plays many cheerful hints for " men of action." It's a mixed world, my masters, but a vigorous wrangler will wrest something sweet from the churlish Mother. The following passages perhaps come as near to optimism as anything in Shakespeare:

> There is some soul of goodness in things evil,
> Would men observingly distil it out.
> > *Henry V.*

> For naught so vile that on the earth doth live
> But to the earth some special good doth give.
> > *Romeo and Juliet.*

> Sweet are the uses of adversity,
> Which like the toad, ugly and venonmous,
> Wears yet a precious jewel in its head.
> > *As You Like It.*

Shakespeare emphasizes human responsibility not merely in opposition to the fatality of instinct but also in opposition to the fatality of stellar foreordination. Even his astonishingly intellectual villains (the intelligence of Shakespearian villains is perhaps an instance of the creator's " lofty soul " impregnating his characters) become admirable pulpiters of his humanism. Iago's exhortation to Roderigo would do credit to a bishop: " Our bodies are our gardens, to the which our wills are gardeners. . . . If the balance of our lives had not one scale of reason to poise another of sensuality, the blood and baseness of our natures would conduct us to most preposterous conclusions; but we have reason to cool our raging motions, our carnal stings, our unbitted lusts, whereof I take this that you call love to be a sect or scion."   Edmund's derision of his father's faith in celestial signs is another striking case in point: " We make guilty of our disasters the sun, the moon, and the stars; as if we were villains by necessity, fools by heavenly compulsion, knaves, thieves, and treachers by spherical predominance, drunkards, liars, and adulterers by an enforced obedience of planetary influence; and all that we are evil in by a divine thrusting on: an admirable evasion of whoremaster man, to lay his goatish disposition to the charge of a star."   In gentler mood, these are to the same effect:

> Our remedies oft in ourselves do lie
> Which we ascribe to heaven; the fated sky
> Gives us free scope, only doth backward pull
> Our slow designs, when we ourselves are dull.
>
> *All's Well.*

> Men at some times are masters of their fates:
> The fault, dear Brutus, is not in our stars
> But in ourselves that we are underlings.
>
> *Julius Caesar.*

The case for Shakespeare's humanism does not rest,

however, upon any collection of isolated passages; these but illustrate readily an impression won from his entire work of a tendency running throughout his literary career. His plays, when arranged in chronological order, indicate a progressive interest passing from the more natural and sentimental phases of feeling to the more imaginative, subtle, and intellectual; thence through a period of intense disgust with the lower instinctive level and even with the natural processes of life to a serene and benign expression of harmony in the three-fold universe.

I am unwilling to leave the subject without saying a word on his treatment of the chief topic of our novelists. At the outset of his career he does betray a curious interest, witnessed by his two narrative poems, in merely fleshly desire and in merely fleshly chastity; but, with the one exception of his youth, here indicated, he presents carnality as ridiculous, as in Falstaff; or as abhorrent, as in Tarquin. The fruit of his personal experience in that field seems distilled in the bitter sonnet beginning: " The expense of spirit in a waste of shame is lust in action."

In his earlier comedies in romantic vein, like *The Two Gentlemen* and *A Midsummer Night's Dream*, he treats love lightly, with a kind of sweet mockery, jestingly, indulgently as a toy of youth, with exquisite elvish laughter of Puck in the shrubbery at the rear: " Lord, what fools these mortals be!" It is as if he concurred more or less in the opinion of the contemporary essayist Cornwallis: " It is a pretty, soft thing—this same Love—the badge of eighteen and upwards, not to be disallowed; better spend thy time so than at dice. I am content to call this Love, though I hold Love too worthy a cement to join earth to earth."

> Love's not Time's fool, though rosy lips and cheeks
> Within his bending sickle's compass comes.

In *Romeo and Juliet*, with a burst of richer poetry, he shows the height of amorous emotion almost trans-figured by its intensity, passion's brief splendor, flashing like lightning in the summer night, and, like lightning, devoured by the jaws of darkness—" so swift bright things come to confusion." The critical function per-formed by the mirth of Puck in *Midsummer Night's Dream* is here undertaken by Friar Lawrence who holds the mirror of reason up to passion:

> These violent delights have violent ends,
> And in their triumph die, like fire and powder,
> Which, as they kiss, consume.

In the chief comedies of Shakespeare's second period every one must recognize that the author's early interest in sentimental story gives way to his growing interest in character. In *Twelfth Night* Viola and her love-sick Duke are almost eclipsed by the conspirators in the sub-plot, who are playing, it is to be observed, not romantic but classical comedy, that is to say, comedy which sports with human follies, and which shows to a pompous and self-deceived Malvolio his ridiculous visage in the mirror of common sense. In *As You Like It*, interest in roman-tic story is again overshadowed—in this case, by a many-sided philosophic commentary on life, supplied by more or less subordinate or extraneous characters, Jaques, Touchstone, and the banished duke. In *Much Ado,* finally, the traditional romantic hero and heroine, Claudio and Hero, are all but extinguished in order to allow those lambent intelligences, Beatrice and Benedict, to emerge from what is structurally the sub-plot, and to dominate the scene. In the exhibition of their intellectual fencing and in their unmasking, Shakespeare clearly betrays the shifting of his own interest from the sentimental to the rational level, from the field of the Petrarchian sonneteers to the field of classical comedy. " Do you not love me? " says Beatrice. " No more than reason," says Benedict.

An appropriate sub-title for the great tragedies of the " third period " would be, The World Lost by Passion. These plays would serve well to illustrate Bacon's saying, that " the stage is more beholden to love than the life of man "; and we know that they actually furnished matter for Burton's *Anatomy of Melancholy,* in which the " grand passion " is treated as a disease of body and mind. In them are many indications that the author's mind—whether through bitter personal experience or through delighted imaginative apprehension, does not greatly concern us—was in a state approaching revolt against the sway of the senses and the limitations and necessities imposed on man by his participation in physical nature. One recalls a faint persistent ill odor in *Hamlet* as of dead men's bones; the Prince's injunction to his rejected Ophelia: " Get thee to a nunnery; why would thou be a breeder of sinners?—We will have no more marriages "; Othello driven raving mad by the sensual insinuations of his destroyer; Lear calling on the thunder to crack nature's molds and spill the seeds of life, and wiping his hands of the smell of mortality; and Coriolanus, the hero of a tragedy notably devoid of all " sex-interest," vainly striving to free himself from the natural bond of blood and sonship, vainly protesting that he will never be " a gosling to obey instinct."

The spirit of tranquility which even the most skeptical critics observe in the latest dramas, *Cymbeline, The Winter's Tale,* and *The Tempest,* is not achieved, however, by a disgusted and ascetic secession of the mind from the natural world. The secret of tranquility is the practice of the humanistic philosophy expounded by Hooker in the *Ecclesiastical Polity,* and dramatically expressed by Shakespeare in his almost divinely beautiful " farewell to the stage." It is a philosophy which secures peace on the purely human level by a reconciliation of the soul with the body through the meditation of reason, rendered wise by knowledge, and efficient by will. I am sorry for those who do not believe that the enchanted island of *The Tempest* is man's universe, presented first in a state of insurrection, and then in a state of tranquility, when Ariel, the lawless imagination longing for liberty, and Caliban, the incarnation of the lusts and powers and instincts of our animal nature, and all the warring elements and factions—yield to the wonderworking sway and sovereignty of a benignant reason, represented by Prospero, lord of the isle.

For Prospero, the peculiarly luminous mirror of

Shakespeare's " mind and manners," the solemn pageants of the phenomenal world have lost their imposing and substantial character, have something for him of the nature of cloud-wrack and dream-stuff; and he reflects, in his sessions of solitary thought, with a certain philosophic compassion upon the emotions and pursuits of mortals who follow, hot-footed and eager, the flying feet of time. Yet he has not lost the human touch. Even toward the animal nature, provided it is obedient to discipline, he is kindly and indulgent; so that Caliban himself, after a brief revolt, returns from Trinculo and Stephano to his sterner master, saying: " O what a thrice-double ass was I to take this drunkard for a god, and worship this dull fool." Toward guilty penitents on the human level, his " nobler reason " takes the part of forgiveness against his just indignation; and toward fair and innocent human lovers his attitude is a sustained benediction; their mutual attraction he exquisitely expresses in drawing them together by a strain of Ariel's music; and upon their union he invokes all the good gifts of Juno and Ceres, earth and heaven. Before the higher powers, between whom and him the partition of the senses is growing transparent, he stands in quiet expectation of the hour when he, released from the imprisonment and servitude of time and space, shall pass through nature into the world of eternal ideas.

Thither Shakespeare swiftly followed him. When the earth rattled on his coffin lid and the churlish sexton filled his grave, if Drayton and Ben Jonson or other prophetic souls were standing by, they did not seek for their beloved master in the dust, but, turning their eyes heavenwards, watched with hearts elate, where his great spirit, creator of spirits, soared aloft to rule over the kingdoms of imagination forever. And one can fancy " honest Ben," who memorized fine verses of his contemporaries, murmuring over the body of his friend these lines of the fifty-fifth sonnet:

> Nor Mars his sword nor war's quick fire shall burn
> The living record of your memory.
> 'Gainst death and all-oblivious enmity
> Shall you pace forth; your praise shall still find room
> Even in the eyes of all posterity
> That wear this world out to the ending doom.

The proud hope of literary immortality expressed by Shakespeare and many of the Elizabethan poets our modern scholars after their fashion seek to explain away as a mere " literary convention," since it was followed by rhymsters with no legitimate title to eternal life. But what, one asks, gave rise to this " convention " and supported it? First, imitation of the ancients whose hope had been fulfilled, whose monuments had indeed been more perennial than brass, whose verses had outlasted empires. Secondly, a clear sense, at least in the supreme Elizabethan, that he was working in the spirit of all great and enduring art. He had taken his stand, as Sainte-Beuve says, " at the centre of human nature."

Though his vision of life extended to the depths beneath and to the heights above the reach and comprehension of man's mind, he dwelt habitually in that cleared and settled and spacious region of consciousness in which a man's thinking is right and his feelings are sure, in which the elementary human values are fixed, in which truth and goodness and beauty remain the same from age to age.   He was to pass through times when literature would beat vain wings in the religious inane, and through times when it would sink in the naturalistic abyss; but he knew, he must have known, that whenever men returned from these aberrations to the wide sunlit human level they would find him their contemporary, they would come upon him in the midst of it, representing still with incomparable adequacy what can be seen from that point of view.   Happy are they who diligently seek for the center of that sunlit level, and thrice blessed they that find it.

THE END

INDEX